Advance Praise for

At the Center of All Possibilities: Transforming Education for Our Children's Future

"This is a powerful text full of penetrating and persuasive analysis. What I enjoyed most is that it pulls back the curtains of power in a language that is accessible to multiple audiences. More importantly, the text weaves a politics of hope throughout. Many of the contributors, including Doug Selwyn, have been engaged in deep movement building and/or in theorizing and implementing transformative educational projects for years. A splendid achievement that will be integrated in multiple courses that I teach."

– Ricardo D. Rosa, Associate Professor of Public Policy,
University of Massachusetts-Dartmouth

"Doug Selwyn has situated children at the center of future educational possibilities, by bringing together an exemplary diversity of authors to help us reflect and transform human lives before it is too late. This array of scholars, educators, and activists will move you to consider the depths of educational possibility in children, youths, subject matters, contexts, and movements. I urge educators at all levels, policy makers, parents, community members, and students themselves to read, ponder, and act on ideas and events compellingly portrayed in *At the Center of All Possibilities*."

– William H. Schubert, Professor Emeritus of Curriculum and Instruction and University Scholar at the University of Illinois at Chicago; Fellow of the International Academy of Education; Lifetime Achievement Award recipient in Curriculum Studies from the American Educational Research Association; and Author of *Love, Justice, and Education: John Dewey and the Utopians*

"*At the Center of All Possibilities: Transforming Education for Our Children's Future* engages a diverse and powerful collection of voices to consider, from intersecting and multidimensional perspectives, the ultimate purpose of education. Core beliefs on this issue drive policy and practice – thus influencing every relationship and interaction in teaching and learning. The messages of contributors should be required reading for anyone who wishes to ensure that education supports the cultivation of humans who can construct a just, equitable world."

– Julie Gorlewski, Associate Professor and Department Chair of Learning and Instruction, State University of New York at Buffalo

"I wish that we didn't need this book, that the schools were working well for all children and preparing them for a healthy future. But they're not, and we need to make real changes in how we educate our young people. We need this book. The essays and interviews compiled in *At the Center of All Possibilities: Transforming Education for Our Children's Future* provide a very thoughtful look at how our current educational system could potentially change to better meet the needs of the children, families, and communities it is meant to serve, as well as numerous examples of educators and activists who have already begun that process. There is much useful information and inspiration to be had here, and it left me feeling encouraged about the future."

—Steve Goldenberg, teacher (now retired) of 37 years at The Little School, Redmond, Washington

"This collection offers practical and unprecedented ideas from a diverse and prestigious group of educators with equally diverse lived experiences. They are committed to helping teachers rethink their starting points, unlearn harmful practices, and commit to ongoing growth. Student belonging, advocacy, and truth is at the heart of their work. Listen to the voices for change and read the inspired words on these pages. Repeat. You will be inspired by the abundance of innovative thought and perspective taking."

—Aimee Lafontaine, English teacher, reading specialist and interventionist, Hinsdale South High School, Hinsdale, IL

At the Center of
All Possibilities

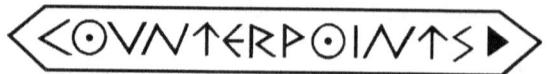

Studies in Criticality

Shirley R. Steinberg
General Editor

Vol. 532

The Counterpoints series is part of the Peter Lang Education list.
Every volume is peer reviewed and meets
the highest quality standards for content and production.

PETER LANG
New York • Bern • Berlin
Brussels • Vienna • Oxford • Warsaw

Doug Selwyn, Editor

At the Center of All Possibilities

Transforming Education for Our Children's Future

PETER LANG
New York • Bern • Berlin
Brussels • Vienna • Oxford • Warsaw

Library of Congress Cataloging-in-Publication Control Number: 2021058490

Bibliographic information published by **Die Deutsche Nationalbibliothek**.
Die Deutsche Nationalbibliothek lists this publication in the "Deutsche Nationalbibliografie"; detailed bibliographic data are available on the Internet at http://dnb.d-nb.de/.

ISSN 1058-1634 (print)
ISBN 978-1-4331-9466-5 (hardcover)
ISBN 978-1-4331-9465-8 (paperback)
ISBN 978-1-4331-9467-2 (ebook pdf)
ISBN 978-1-4331-9468-9 (epub)
DOI 10.3726/b19286

© 2022 Peter Lang Publishing, Inc., New York
80 Broad Street, 5th floor, New York, NY 10004
www.peterlang.com

All rights reserved.
Reprint or reproduction, even partially, in all forms such as microfilm, xerography, microfiche, microcard, and offset strictly prohibited.

To Mason, Alden, Adrian, and Julian

But I suppose the most revolutionary act one can engage in is to tell the truth.
                                                                    Howard Zinn

What happens when you let an unsatisfactory present go on long enough? It becomes your entire history.
                                                                 Louise Erdrich

Once we start to act, hope is everywhere. So instead of looking for hope, look for action. Then, and only then, hope will come.
                                                                Greta Thunberg

Table of Contents

Acknowledgments   xiii

Introduction   1

Section One: Schooling Within a Larger Societal Context
Chapter One: (De)-Graded by Inequality   9
    Richard Wilkinson
Chapter Two: Teaching Knowledge and Action to Promote Health
    Improvement   19
    Stephen Bezruchka

Section Two: The Purpose of Education and the Roles that Schools Play
Chapter Three: The Purpose of Education: A Brief History   29
    Doug Selwyn
Chapter Four: Beyond Education as Usual: Public Education in a Post-Covid
    World   37
    Sandra Mathison and E. Wayne Ross

Section Three: Learning from Teaching During Covid

Chapter Five: Love in the Time of Covid — 47
   Jo Cripps

Chapter Six: The Remote Suburbs — 55
   Peter Suruda

Section Four: What Our Children Need to Learn

Chapter Seven: Risk, Inquiry, and Learning — 67
   Don Fels

Chapter Eight: Social Studies, Intersectionality, and the Re Humanizing of Education: A Conversation with Jerry Price — 75

Chapter Nine: Contextualizing Student Needs Post Pandemic — 83
   Alberto "Beto" Gutierrez

Chapter Ten: Dear Educators: An Open Letter about How You Teach about Native Peoples — 91
   Jean Mendoza and Debbie Reese

Chapter Eleven: Black Lives Matter at School: A Conversation with Jesse Hagopian — 99

Chapter Twelve: Evolving Higher Education for a New Consciousness — 109
   Yves Salomon-Fernández

Section Five: Who Shall Teach Them?

Chapter Thirteen: Disposed to Democracy — 121
   Jan Maher

Chapter Fourteen: Finding Our Paths to Social Justice Education — 129
   Alyssa Arnell, Leo Hwang, and Linda McCarthy

Chapter Fifteen: Transforming the Teacher Corps: A Conversation with Wayne Au — 145

Section Six: Thinking about Freedom Schools

Chapter Sixteen: Freedom Schools — 155
   Caroline Whitcomb

Section Seven: But What about Assessment?

Chapter Seventeen: Assessing What Matters: A Conversation with Jack Schneider — 167

Section Eight: Learning Through Activism

Chapter Eighteen: School Strike for Climate: Save the World by Changing the Rules 183
Greta Thunberg

Chapter Nineteen: We Are Suing the U.S. Government: A Conversation with Aji Piper 187

Chapter Twenty: Aji Piper's Testimony before the U.S. House of Representatives Select Committee on the Climate Crisis (Excerpts) (April 4, 2019) 195

Final Thoughts (for Now) 199

Contributors 203

Acknowledgments

I want to first give thanks to those who have helped us to stay healthy, or to recover our health, who have comforted our loved ones when they (and we) were in quarantine, who have kept our stores open and our lights on, served as first responders, who have grown our food, and taken care of us in so many ways, often at personal risk. If Covid can offer us anything at all that is of value it is an awareness of who actually keeps our society running, who are truly essential to our functioning community. We honored them with our words, and with signs in our yards. Here is hoping we will honor them with a living wage, safe and adequate working conditions, health insurance and access to medical care, and the respect they deserve in all ways once the pandemic is past.

Because of the intensity of Covid, and the overwhelm that was teaching while holding family together, several of those who started out to write chapters had to bow out, and while I am sorry that their wisdom, experience and points of view are not part of the book, their willingness to engage with the questions means that they are still part of the conversation that will lead to transforming education.

And for those who were able to do everything else they have done this past year and who were somehow still able to share their thoughts in these pages, I am deeply grateful to you. I have learned from your work and am confident that others will as well. Thank you:

Richard Wilkinson, Stephen Bezruchka, Sandra Mathison, E. Wayne Ross, Jo Cripps, Peter Suruda, Don Fels, Jan Maher, Beto Gutierrez, Jerry Price, Debbie Reese, Jean Mendoza, Yves Salomon-Fernández, Jesse Hagopian, Wayne Au, Alyssa Arnell, Leo Hwang, Linda McCarthy, Jack Schneider, Aji Piper, Greta Thunberg, Caroline Whitcomb. And thank you to Lang Walsh, Rebecca Timson, and Helen Britto.

Thank you to the good folks at Peter Lang: Shirley Steinberg, series editor, Patty Mulrane, who I think may work most all of the jobs there at once, Dani Green, who has taken the editing baton mid race, Jackie Pavlovic, Naviya Palani, the production team and all others involved in making this book happen.

And finally, love and thanks to Jan Maher, who over the course of these past 40 years together has made clear that I am not the only one who is brave and foolish. Thank goodness.

Introduction

A report from the International Panel on Climate Change (IPCC) came out in August 2021 stating with absolute certainty that climate change is happening at a more rapid pace than anticipated, and that humans are at the center of that change (IPCC, 2021). The report warned that "widespread devastation and extreme weather are likely to become inevitable within the next two decades thanks to human behavior causing rising temperatures." Only rapid and drastic reductions in greenhouse gases in this decade can prevent such climate breakdown. The report found that human activity was unequivocally the cause of rapid changes to the climate, including sea level rises, melting polar ice and glaciers, heatwaves, floods, and droughts. Michael E. Mann, a lead author of the IPCC's 2001 report said, "Bottom line is that we have zero years left to avoid dangerous climate change, because it's here." And Dave Reay, the director of the Edinburgh Climate Change Institute, said world leaders "must have the findings of this report seared into their minds" at the November conference and take urgent action. "This is not just another scientific report," Reay said. "This is hell and highwater writ large."

Despite these warnings, it seems that our most significant response to climate change is to develop new vocabulary to describe our changing climate, including "a bomb cyclone," which we are experiencing at this very moment here in Massachusetts. Other new descriptors include heat domes, atmospheric rivers, tornadic waterspouts, and bombogenesis. Once in a generation storms are happening with some regularity, leaders from around the world meet together to wring their hands, and little or nothing changes.

When youth activist Greta Thunberg was approached for her reaction/response to the report she replied there is nothing new here, it's "merely confirming what we already know." When Ms. Thunberg started her school strikes in 2018, attempting to convince the Swedish Parliament to take action to save the planet, people would ask her why she was striking.

> Some people say that I should be in school instead. Some people say that I should study to become a climate scientist so that I can "solve the climate crisis." But the climate crisis has already been solved. We already have all the facts and solutions. All we have to do is to wake up and change. And why should I be studying for a future that soon will be no more when no one is doing anything whatsoever to save that future? And what is the point of learning facts in the school system when the most important facts given by the finest science of that same school system clearly means nothing to our politicians and our society. (Thunberg, 2018)

Greta Thunberg asks a fundamental question that informs this book. What is the purpose of school if what we know does not lead to action, if education does not lead to living healthier and more sustainable lives? How effective is our educational system if it leaves adults unwilling or unable to act in the face of imminent danger, be it climate change, a lethal virus (with large numbers refusing to take vaccines that would protect them and/or others), gullible enough to believe that Hillary Clinton and other liberals were running a child sex ring out of a nonexistent basement in an obscure pizza parlor, or to believe a candidate who lost an election by more than seven million votes, and lost the electoral college by a substantial margin somehow won the election. The rhetoric linking the success or failure of our schools based on test scores widely misses the mark. If the purpose of education is to help the next generation learn what they need to learn to maintain and improve their lives and the lives of those in their community, then our educational system is failing miserably, and has been failing for many years.

Which leads to the over-arching questions that are at the heart of this book. How do we educate our young people so that they know what they need to know and learn what they need to learn so that they are able to live healthy and sustainable lives, and to pass on a healthy and thriving society (and planet) to their children and grandchildren? What do we value most, that we hope they will carry with them and how do we help them to learn it? What role might schools play in this process and how do we transform our current system into one that truly meets the needs of all of our children? And how do we gather the will, the urgency to act that will begin to turn this massive ship around? Large, fundamental changes are needed, and they won't happen quickly, which is all the more reason for us to get started now.

The presence of the Covid-19 pandemic has highlighted the disparities of our society, and the failures of our institutions, including our educational system. We learned that some families, communities, and towns were and are relatively well equipped to deal with the dangers and challenges brought by the pandemic while a higher percentage of communities of color and communities living in poverty experienced death and/or serious illness, economic devastation, struggles to maintain housing and food security, and educational challenges as schooling went remote. None of this was a surprise to anyone paying attention; Covid has simply made it more difficult to ignore or hide the disparities in our increasingly unequal society. A character in Louise Erdrich's novel *The Plague of Doves* observes that "What happens when you let an unsatisfactory present go on long enough? It becomes your entire history." We are very much in danger of having our increasing inequality become our entire history moving forward unless we act, unless we refuse to let this increasingly unsatisfactory present go on. The question is what, if anything are we willing to do about it, and what is (are) the most effective path(s) of action?

There is no agreement as to the answers to those questions, and I've seen very little active interest in considering them seriously, given the level and immediacy of the crises the schools are facing. Current educators, families and communities are too busy trying to survive to consider the fundamental changes those questions point to, and those in power, who run and profit from the system as it is, are in no hurry to bring drastic change that might threaten their positions of privilege. Thus, the push to get back to "normal," to how things were before the pandemic sent us into quarantine.

But that's not good enough. It will not move us closer to an equitable, just, sustainable society, and won't help us to meet the true crises we are facing on virtually every level of our lives. We have to do better, and education has a critical role to play in bringing the fundamental change we need. That's the subject of this book.

I sent a call out to educators, some of whom I knew and some I did not, asking for their thoughts on what our young people need to learn and how we might help them to get what they need. I sent several sub questions along with my request, urging them to respond to whatever question(s) called to them, and to write about it. My questions covered a wide range, from wondering at the values of our society and the role that education plays in teaching them, to the purpose of education, to the kinds of content our students should be learning, to questions about who should be teaching and what do they (the educators) need to know, to wondering how we might assess whether our children are getting what they need. There was no requirement that the educators who responded to my invitation agree with me or with each other, and no intention to pull it together into a neat package at the end.

What I hope readers will get from our work is an appreciation for how complicated and complex the challenge is, how essential it is that we work towards fundamental change, transforming how we educate our children, and that there are many, many factors to consider. There are no simple solutions, no one-size-fits-all programs or approaches that will serve all of our children. There is much overlap in the educational situations across the thousands of communities in our country, but each is also unique. I trust that some chapters will speak more loudly and clearly to some readers while others may respond more to different voices and issues. It is unrealistic that anyone, or any community will take on everything presented here, but it is realistic, and crucial that we start the work of transforming our communities and educational systems now.

I also hope that readers get from the many different issues, points of view, and concerns expressed in this book that if we are to truly serve all of our children, we do best to invite our communities into the planning process. Many of the writers in these pages speak to issues I would not have known to consider, or how best to consider them, and I have learned a great deal from listening to their voices. We are smarter together and it is essential that we involve as broad a spectrum as we can to help us think through how best to transform education so that our children have what they need to transform the world.

REFERENCES

Erdrich, L. (2008). *The plague of doves*. New York: Harper Perennial.

IPCC. (2021, August 9). *Climate change widespread, rapid, and intensifying. Intergovernmental Panel on Climate Change*. Retrieved from https://www.ipcc.ch/2021/08/09/ar6-wg1-20210809-pr/

Thunberg, G. (2018). *School strike for climate – Save the world by changing the rules*. Retrieved from https://www.ted.com/talks/greta_thunberg_school_strike_for_climate_save_the_world_by_changing_the_rules/transcript?language=en

SECTION ONE

SCHOOLING WITHIN A LARGER SOCIETAL CONTEXT

I worked with a group of approximately 30 teachers, administrators, family members, health officials and others in our town over the summer of 2020 attempting to plan for the opening of the 2020–2021 school year. Covid was raging and we had to make choices about whether to have in-person schooling, a hybrid model that had children in schools some of the week and learning remotely the rest of the week, or to conduct school entirely remotely, at least to start. The state of Massachusetts pushed all districts to consider those three options and to develop a plan for each that would offer all students a high-quality education, that would keep children and adults in buildings safe, and that could be put in place to start the school year.

As we considered each option, several things became very clear. First, there might be no institution as inextricably bound to the community than are schools. That meant that any decision we made would reverberate through the community, with consequences for families, for businesses, for virtually every aspect of town life. It also meant that what was happening in the community would have significant consequences for what was happening in the schools. Second, it was clear that what we already knew, that there was (and is) significant inequality across our community, was even more prevalent and more consequential than we had realized, and that this inequality was something we had to respond to and consider in our planning. Third, our schools were already severely underfunded and under-resourced before Covid, with buildings badly in need of upgrading, and the district badly in need of resources, supplies, and qualified, skilled, and adequately compensated faculty and staff. The arrival of Covid made things even worse, stretching resources beyond the breaking point, which made realistic planning all but impossible because there was no way to really do what needed to be done. Fourth, there would be no time to offer adequate professional development or preparation time for faculty and staff, who were going to have to carry out a full educational program in an entirely new (to them) modality, and that the state's timeline and approval of our choice (in person, hybrid, or remote) would leave almost no time to plan or adjust before the school year started. And fifth, it was clear that the federal and state governments were prioritizing political and economic interests over educational or health-related concerns. There was immense pressure on schools and the individuals within our community to make the best of a situation governed by people who did not know us, who did not care about us as much as they cared about politics and economics and the way it all played in the media and to their financial backers.

When I was researching my previous book, All Children Are All Our Children (2019) my focus was on the health and wellbeing of our children and my guiding question was, what would schools look like and be like if they were our highest priority. My research led me back to the work of Richard Wilkinson and Kate Pickett, British researchers who had written an extraordinary book, *The Spirit Level*, documenting the overwhelming impact that inequality has on the health and wellbeing of a population. They found that "for each of eleven different health and social problems: physical health, mental health, drug abuse, education, imprisonment, obesity, social mobility, trust and community life, violence, teenage pregnancies, and child well-being, outcomes are significantly worse in more unequal rich countries." (The Equality Trust, n.d.) Wilkinson and Pickett showed this to be true no matter what the country and showed the same results to be true across the fifty U.S. states. Those states that have the most inequality have the poorest health statistics across the board, and that includes educational results. These findings require that we re-assess the so-called standardized test measures that at this time are used to evaluate individuals, schools, and districts and to recognize that much of what happens in schools are the consequence of the overall state of our particular state or country. David Berliner (2009) estimates that approximately 60 % of what happens in schools is due to out of school factors, and Wilkinson and Pickett's work helps us to understand the social determinants that strongly impact our lives. It is irresponsible and wrong to simply blame students or teachers or schools; there are factors out of their control, out of their family's control that play a major role in their results at school.

The chapters in this section, by Richard Wilkinson and Stephen Bezruchka focus on placing schools in the larger societal context when we think about the overall health and wellbeing of our children, and on how we approach transforming education. Richard Wilkinson targets the myth of meritocracy, that those who get better grades or scores on tests are simply smarter than other kids, a persistent myth that ignores what he and other researchers have found about the impact of inequality and other factors on our lives. We can't transform schools if we don't also address the gross and increasing inequality that exists across our country. Dr. Bezruchka echoes the findings of Drs. Wilkinson and Pickett and writes of the many ways he has gone about educating his students and the public about the role that inequality plays in our failing societal health and in our schools.

REFERENCES

Berliner, D. C. (2009, March 9). *Poverty and potential: Out-of-school factors and school success.* National Education Policy Center. Retrieved from https://nepc.colorado.edu/publication/poverty-and-potential

Selwyn, D. (2019). *All children are all our children.* Peter Lang.

The Equality Trust. (n.d.). *The spirit level.* Retrieved from https://equalitytrust.org.uk/resources/the-spirit-level

Wilkinson, R., & Pickett, K. (2009*). The spirit level: Why greater equality makes societies stronger.* Bloomsbury.

CHAPTER ONE

(De)-Graded by Inequality

RICHARD WILKINSON

Too often we talk as if our ideal education system would be one that enables children to "realize their potential." But that is a weasel expression which contains the hidden assertion that some children are naturally endowed at birth with more "potential" than others. Rather than being about providing the best education, extending abilities and helping children's development, "potential" is used – at least in conservative circles – as a cover for systems of social grading that actually limit children's development. In practice, potential means something close to intelligence or IQ, and the main interest in IQ research has always been primarily to distinguish between children with more and less of it. Prejudice becomes disguised as science.

FAILED JUSTIFICATIONS FOR INEQUALITY

The idea that children are innately endowed with different amounts of *whatever it takes* (assumed to be a kind of all-embracing one-dimensional ability) is a necessary prop for the belief that we live in a meritocracy where ability is the key to success, and success is measured by the steps up the social ladder. If we believe that people's social position is a reflection of how much ability they are endowed with, then it is hard to avoid thinking that an essential function of schools is to sort kids out according to their different endowments – the wheat from the chaff: helping kids "realize their potential."

Social hierarchies have always needed their rationalizing myths. History is full of attempts to justify inequality, class and caste differences. Plato suggested that people's position in the social hierarchy depended on whether their souls contained gold, silver, or brass. Hindu ideology encourages people to believe that their caste reflects how they behaved in a previous life, so that from the Brahmins at the top to the untouchable Dalits at the bottom, everyone is where they deserve to be. Kings believed – and liked everyone else to believe – that they had a divine, God-given, right to rule. The discovery of evolution inevitably gave rise to ideologies based on a belief in the genetic superiority and inferiority of different classes, and so to eugenic ideas that it was important to breed from the superior rather than the inferior classes. And yet still today, the perception that the social class hierarchy is a meritocracy resulting from genetic differences in IQ is uncomfortably similar. But in reality, these are nothing more than empty and disreputable ideological attempts to justify systems of privilege, dominance, subordination, and inequality.

That is not to say that people do not have differences in ability: we have endless and wonderful differences. But the idea that there is a single gene for intelligence – that you either have or haven't got – is a failed research program (Nisbett et al., 2012; Ho, 2013; Richardson, 2017).

We now know that there are hundreds, perhaps thousands, of genes affecting different aspects of ability – how musical you are, whether you learn foreign languages more easily, how you take to mathematics, your literary aptitude, your social awareness, your artistic talents, your spatial awareness, whether you are a good gymnast or footballer, and many, many, more. But their effects are small. Much more important is your education and training. You can have all the genes in the world for mathematics, but what determines whether you are a competent mathematician or as unprepared as people in societies without written number systems (with words only for one, two, three and many), is whether or not you have been taught math. And the same goes for almost any other ability. We also know how the environment amplifies underlying differences in our various abilities. We like doing what we feel good at, so if, for instance, you are good at football, you practice more, you then get chosen for the school team and get special training, with the result that what was perhaps a very small inbuilt advantage ends up meaning you are very much better at football than the kids who were initially bad at it and always tried to avoid it. Brain scans show that the brain actually changes as you learn things. Whether you learn a musical instrument, or a foreign language, become a ballet dancer or learn "the knowledge" of London streets as London taxi drivers have to, all develop different areas of the brain (Wilkinson & Pickett, 2020). We are not born with any of these skills or knowledge. They are instead part of our common human culture developed by people over the generations on whose shoulders we stand.

WHY ARE OUTCOMES BETTER AT THE TOP THAN THE BOTTOM?

People at the bottom of the social hierarchy are not only seen as endowed with too little talent, but they are also seen as suffering from all sorts of other weaknesses. No one can deny that, as things are, the educational performance of school children is less good at each step down the social hierarchy. The same is true of poor health and lower life expectancy – and many other problems including obesity, teenage births, mental illness, violence, imprisonment and more. Again and again, the worst outcomes are at the bottom of society. The question is what causes this pattern?

The most popular explanation is that people with these problems, along with those who are vulnerable to them, move down in society and the resilient and talented move up. This is part of the belief in meritocracy: social mobility works to move those with the most talent upwards and those with least downwards.

But we now know much more about how inequality works than we did, and the picture turns out to be rather different from what we thought. While there is probably a little truth in these views, they miss what is much the most important part of the picture. Let us start with the *effects* of inequality. If you look at the scale of income differences in a society – that is at the gap between rich and poor – you find that societies with greater inequality have more of almost all of these problems with social gradients. Averaged across their populations as a whole, societies with bigger income gaps have worse health, more violence, more people in prison, lower math and literacy scores among young people, higher obesity rates, lower social mobility – and so on (Wilkinson & Pickett, 2009). For example, if we compare just the rich developed market democracies, we find that the USA is not only amongst the most unequal, but it has – averaged across the whole population – almost the lowest life expectancy, the highest homicide rates, the highest obesity rates, poor educational performance of school children, low rates of social mobility, and the highest rates of incarceration. In contrast, the Scandinavian countries, which all have much smaller income differences, have low rates of these problems. And the differences in how societies perform are large: imprisonment, homicide and teenage birth rates may be as much as ten times as high in more unequal societies, compared to the more equal ones. Differences in infant mortality rates and rates of mental illness are smaller, but both are still twice as high in the more unequal countries.

It isn't just international comparisons that show this pattern. The picture is very similar if we look at the 50 states of the USA: again, the problems are worse in the more unequal states. Indeed, for health and homicide, where comparable data is most plentiful, studies all over the world have found this pattern (Wilkinson & Pickett, 2017).

Confronted with this evidence, some would like to believe that instead of greater inequality making these problems worse, that the relationship might be the other way round – that the high frequency of these problems creates the higher inequality. But that is disproved by studies which show that changes in inequality came well before the changes in health (Zheng, 2012). It is also disproved by the fact that problems like high infant mortality, obesity, or homicide rates, are unlikely to have much impact on levels of income inequality. In addition, research has uncovered some of the causal pathways through which inequality, acting as a social stressor, increases these problems (Wilkinson & Pickett, 2020).

What then does this pattern of problems becoming more common in more unequal societies, tell us? First, it doesn't fit the idea that the reason why problems are more common lower down the social ladder is because social mobility sorts out the vulnerable from the resilient. Although a sorting process could change each person's position in a society, it wouldn't make a problem more common among the population as a whole. For example, if you sorted people by hair color to make a ranking from dark hair at the top to light at the bottom, you would have done nothing to change the number of people with light or dark hair in a society. In contrast, inequality not only makes social gradients steeper, but – as we have seen – it also increases the overall frequency of these problems across whole societies. This strongly suggests that their frequency *responds* to the burden of inequality in a society – that many, or most, of the problems with social gradients are in some way a response to the power of social status differences, to the scale of relative deprivation and inferior social status itself.

Lastly, because there is actually less social mobility in more unequal societies, social mobility can't explain why social gradients turn out to be even steeper in those societies.

INEQUALITY MAKES PEOPLE FEEL INFERIOR

In short, we must conclude that it is lower social status – the burden of social inferiority – that makes people more vulnerable to ill health, poorer education and so on. In rich countries that's not so much because of the direct effects of low living standards themselves; instead, what does much of the damage is how your standards compare with other people's, where you come in the hierarchy running from the most superior to the most inferior. Human beings are highly sensitive to social status, to position in the social hierarchy. We react strongly to being put down and disrespected. Indeed, the reason why homicides are so much more common in more unequal societies is that bigger material differences make status seem even more important, so people are even more likely to react violently to feeling devalued. After all, the most common triggers to violence are disrespect, loss of face and humiliation (Wilkinson, 2004; Gilligan, 1996).

People often think that poverty simply means material hardship and the difficulty of making do with too little. They fail to recognise how much feelings of inferiority and of being devalued can hurt. Interviews with poor people in Norway, the UK, South Korea, China, India, Pakistan, and Uganda, showed this very clearly. Poor people in these high- and low-income countries live in very different material conditions. But despite these differences, the *subjective* experience of poverty is extraordinarily similar (Walker et al., 2013). Whether the "poor" live in an apartment with central heating and at least some of the latest technology as in Norway, or in a one room shack without sanitation or running water as in India or Pakistan, they not only felt they were failures, but also that they were seen as failures, and so tried to hide their poverty. They lived with a deep sense of shame, felt devalued, and said they despised themselves for being poor. The paper reporting this research says "Even children could not escape this shaming for, with the possible exception of Pakistan, school was an engine of social grading, a place of humiliation for those without the possessions that guaranteed social acceptance."

This research shows, once again, that how material resources affect people most powerfully is through social comparisons and their implications for social status – superiority and inferiority. We hate being made to appear inferior to others. The same conclusions also came from studies of how satisfied people are with their income: how satisfied you are is strongly influenced by how your income compares with other people's.

Lastly, there is a large body of evidence from psychological experiments showing that just knowing that you belong to a stigmatized group – regarded as inferior – harms performance on a wide range of tests. For example, Indian children from high and low castes were given pen and paper tests and did them in two conditions, one in which they did not know each other's caste and a second in which they all knew who was high and who was low caste (Hoff & Pandey, 2004). When caste was unknown, there was almost no difference in the performance of high and low caste children, but as soon as they did know, a huge gap opened up – the low caste children then did much less well. Experiments like this are called "stereotype threat" experiments and similar results have been shown with differences in class, ethnicity, and gender. In some of these, people were not even reminded that they belonged to a stigmatized group; for example, when black and white Americans students were told a test was a test of intellectual ability the black students performed much less well than when they were told the same test was not a test of ability (Steele & Aronson, 1995). The belief that their IQ was being tested invoked the prejudiced slur about the ability of African Americans.

Experiments have shown that girls are vulnerable to these stereotypical prejudices – for instance that they are less good at math. An experiment in Italy in which some girls were given a short talk about flowers while others were told about ten famous mathematicians, only one of whom was a woman, found that the second group of girls did less well in a math test (Muzzatti & Agnoli, 2007). The more people are subjected to social stereotypes of inferiority, the more their performance and ability suffers.

People often think that social hierarchies and inequality are inevitable in human societies, but that is false. Throughout at least 90 % of our existence as "anatomically modern" human beings, with brains as large as they are now, we lived as hunters and gatherers in highly egalitarian bands, based on food sharing and reciprocal giving of other items (Sahlins, 2003). Unlike animals, it was not the strongest who ate first, nor were there dominant males who monopolized access to females (Boehm, 2012).

This tells us that inequality represents a return to what was a *pre*-human – essentially animal – form of social organization. Its re-emergence started with the development of the very early cities, only some 5,000 years or so ago. When early agriculture allowed a surplus to be extracted from the local population, it enabled the development of an exploitative ruling class (Scott, 2017).

WHAT DOES THIS MEAN FOR EDUCATION?

The large-scale inequality that exists in modern societies costs us dear, not only in terms of the lives of those devalued by it, but also through the wider costs to society. As more unequal societies have less social mobility, more mental illness and drug problems, lower math and literacy scores, and are less creative and innovative (as measured by patents per head of population), they waste much of their talent (Wilkinson & Pickett, 2009, 2020).

The social class differences in educational performance and in other problems with social gradients, turn out to be much more a *result* of your class or status than a determinant of it. To believe that we live in a meritocracy in which innate ability determines social class, is to mistake the main direction of causality. We know that poverty, lack of opportunities and stimulation, harms brain development, just as education, training and practice develop your abilities. Your circumstances affect the development of your abilities very profoundly. So much so that, when measures of IQ have been made across entire populations during long periods, they have been found to increase dramatically over time, despite population genetics remaining the same (Flynn, 1987, 2006; Pietschnig & Voracek 2015).

What we are up against is the upper-class tendency to believe that their social position reflects their superior inborn ability and intelligence. And similarly, to regard those living in poorer circumstances as innately inferior. This tendency to attribute positive characteristics to one's own group, the in-group, and negative characteristics to the outgroup, is a familiar theme in social psychology. It contributes to racial, class and gender prejudice, but can be diminished if people learn to be on their guard against their prejudices.

Nevertheless, education systems are too often still based on the idea that children have different fixed potentials, that some are born bright and others not – so that some are regarded as "no hopers." It's like people in the 19th century who, when only the upper classes were literate, imagined that reading and writing were beyond the ability of the lower classes and it was not worth trying to teach them. I have met adults who were so phobic about their educational experience, of being seen as a no hoper, that they tried to avoid walking past their school: they felt it had taught them only that they were stupid. Unskilled manual workers sometimes believe that the reason they don't have a better paid job is because school – as they experienced it – made them feel they lacked any other abilities.

In these circumstances it is no wonder that a substantial minority of children drop out of high school, nor is it surprising that a higher proportion to do so live in the more unequal states of the U.S.A. In addition, international math and literacy tests also show that inequalities in children's scores are bigger, and average performance is worse, in countries with bigger income differences between rich and poor (Dorling, 2017). Similarly, a study of infant cognitive development showed that it is slower in more unequal countries (Bird et al., 2019). These are all signs of the predictable way bigger differences in income and wealth increase the power that class and status have over us.

Children's educational performance is of course powerfully influenced by home background and reducing inequalities of income and wealth is primarily a political, rather than a school, problem. But the experience of school as a system of grading, and for many of degrading, has to end. A powerful indication of how the external issues of inequality pollute relationships in schools is the fact that bullying among school children – a clear demonstration of the struggle for rank as the key to self-worth – is as much as ten times as common in more unequal societies (Elgar et al., 2009). We need to create schools which are havens of equality, consciously egalitarian environments in which children recognize social injustices and all are equally valued. This should be enshrined in an Equality Charter for every school, a charter which commits the school to:

1. Ensure that every child and *all* members of staff, feel valued members of the school community. Every pupil and every member of the school community should, from time to time, have experience of participation in

egalitarian meetings involving a cross section of the school community, including pupils, teaching, administrative staff, cleaners and janitors.
2. Train teachers to understand and be on their guard against the often-hidden effects not only of overall inequality, but also of ethnic, class and gender differences.
3. Promote cooperative rather than competitive learning and working among pupils and teachers.
4. Check that these policies ensure the wellbeing of all students by doing frequent surveys, including some confidential face-to-face interviews and focus groups, so that problems such as bullying, depression, self-harm and anxiety are addressed and not overlooked.
5. Make schools places in which there are so many different activities and learning opportunities that every student feels they are good at something. The surveys (4. above) should discuss with children what they feel good at and efforts should be made to find activities for those who have not yet found where their abilities lie.

REFERENCES

Bird, P. K., et al. (2019). Income inequality and social gradients in children's height: A comparison of cohort studies from five high-income countries. *BMJ Paediatrics open*, 3(1).

Boehm, C. (2012). *Moral origins: The evolution of virtue, altruism, and shame.* Basic Books.

Dorling, D. (2017). *The equality effect: Improving life for everyone.* New Internationalist.

Elgar, F. J. et al. (2009). Income inequality and school bullying: Multilevel study of adolescents in 37 countries. *Journal of Adolescent Health*, 45(4): 351–359.

Flynn, J. (1987). Massive IQ gains in 14 nations: What IQ tests really measure. *Psychological Bulletin*, 101, 171–191.

Flynn, J. (2006). *Beyond the Flynn effect: Solution to all outstanding problems – Except enhancing wisdom* [cited 2006, December 15]; Available from: http://www.thepsychometricscentre.co.uk/publications/BeyondTheFlynnEffect.asp.

Gilligan, J. (1996). *Violence: Our deadly epidemic and its causes.* G.P. Putnam.

Ho, M.-W. (2013). No genes for intelligence in the fluid genome. *Advances in Child Development and Behavior*, 45, 67–92.

Hoff, K., & Pandey, P. (2004). *Belief systems and durable inequalities: An experimental investigation of Indian caste.* Policy Research Working Paper. World Bank.

Muzzatti, B., & Agnoli, F. (2007). Gender and mathematics: Attitudes and stereotype threat susceptibility in Italian children. *Developmental Psychology*, 43(3), 747.

Nisbett, R.E., et al. (2012). Intelligence: New findings and theoretical developments. *American Psychologist*, 67(2), 130.

Pietschnig, J., & Voracek, M. (2015). One century of global IQ gains: A formal meta-analysis of the Flynn effect (1909–2013). *Perspectives on Psychological Science*, 10(3), 282–306.

Richardson, K. (2017). *Genes, brains, and human potential: the science and ideology of intelligence.* Columbia University Press.

Sahlins, M. (2003). *Stone age economics.* Routledge.

Scott, J. C. (2017). *Against the grain: A deep history of the earliest states.* Yale University Press.

Steele, C. M., & Aronson, J. (1995). Stereotype threat and the intellectual test performance of African Americans. *Journal of Personality and Social Psychology, 69*(5), 797.

Walker, R., et al. (2013). Poverty in global perspective: Is shame a common denominator? *Journal of Social Policy, 42*(02), 215–233.

Wilkinson, R. (2004). Why is violence more common where inequality is greater? *Annals of the New York Academy of Sciences, 1036,* 1–12.

Wilkinson, R. G., & Pickett, K. E. (2017). The enemy between us: The psychological and social costs of inequality. *European Journal of Social Psychology, 47*(1), 11–24.

Wilkinson, R., & Pickett, K. (2009). *The Spirit level: Why equality is better for everyone.* Bloomsbury.

Wilkinson, R., & Pickett, K. (2020). *The Inner level: How more equal societies reduce stress, restore sanity and improve everyone's wellbeing.* Penguin Random House.

Zheng, H. (2012). Do people die from income inequality of a decade ago? *Social Science & Medicine, 75*(1), 36–45.

FOR FURTHER STUDY

Flynn, J. R. (2007). *What is intelligence? Beyond the Flynn effect.* Cambridge University Press.

Reay, D. (2018, Oct. 2). Miseducation: Inequality, education and the working classes. *International Studies in Sociology of Education, 27*(4), 453–456.

Richardson, K. (2017). *Genes, brains, and human potential: The science and ideology of intelligence.* Columbia University Press.

Wilkinson, R., & Pickett, K. (2009). *The spirit level. Why equality is better for everyone.* Bloomsbury.

Wilkinson, R., & Pickett, K. (2020). *The inner level: How more equal societies reduce stress, restore sanity and improve everyone's well-being.* Penguin.

CHAPTER TWO

Teaching Knowledge and Action to Promote Health Improvement

STEPHEN BEZRUCHKA MD, MPH

INTRODUCTION

As a nation we have worse health outcomes than 40 to 50 other countries, both rich and poor, challenging the belief that this is the greatest country on earth. The ultimate reasons for our not achieving the health of so many other countries lie within societal structures we have set up, live by, and cherish. The COVID-19 pandemic has vividly exposed those factors, which have at their base our historic pandering to the powerful. However, the virus may also allow us to address those structures if widespread awareness can be created. I have been teaching key concepts around societal inequality and health for the last 25 years, for groups ranging from primary schools to retirement communities. I'm convinced that the change agents we need will be today's youth who, once they grasp these concepts, will work to make America the relatively healthy nation it once was. Hopefully this chapter will provide teachers with details about our poor health status that will lead to their students being aware of a crucial problem in the U.S. and offer some ideas about how to help them to gain that awareness.

BACKGROUND ON POOR US HEALTH STATUS

How well we compare with other countries is the appropriate way to evaluate health among nations. If health were an Olympic event measured by death rates, the US would not make the top 35 nations by any commonly used mortality indicator. When ranked by measures such as life expectancy, infant or child mortality, and maternal or adult mortality, the United States ranks below all the other rich nations and a number of poorer ones such as Slovenia, Costa Rica, and Sri Lanka. American mortality has increased in the last few years for some indicators, and the COVID-19 pandemic has even further depressed U.S standing, which now ranks behind more than 50 nations in mortality indicators.

If the U.S. could eliminate deaths from our two biggest killers, heart disease and cancer, only then would we approach being one of the world's longest-lived nations. We have more deaths in childhood, adolescence, adulthood, and from maternal causes than other comparable countries. These startling figures indicate the severity of our health gap, but most Americans are unaware of how poorly we fare compared to so many other nations. There is in fact no indicator of health and well-being for which we stand among the top ten countries much less lead the world.

The National Academy of Science, Engineering and Medicine's 2021 report: *High and Rising Mortality Rates Among Working-Age Adults* presents the latest results from the most reputable source of health information available. Our health, compared to other nations, has continued to deteriorate. Instead, our claims to being "number one" in the world apply to leading in incarceration rates, opioid deaths, and health care spending. Something does not compute.

EXPLANATIONS FOR POOR U.S. HEALTH

The range of reasons for the poor U.S. health status compared to other nations include high rates of poverty, lack of universal health care, racism, the paucity of social spending directed towards early life, rising income inequality, and individual health-related behaviors. We have high rates of child poverty, single-parent households, divorce, violence, opioid use, and incarceration as well as poor educational attainment, all of which affect our health. American societal values such as individual freedom and self-reliance embodied in a meritocracy suggest that the government's role in health-promotion should be limited, yet nothing could be further from the truth. At its core, our poor health results from the political choices we make.

Contemporary media rarely go beyond blaming adverse personal behaviors, such as smoking or drug use, as the cause of our pathetic health. Like some other claims, that theory doesn't hold up in the face of evidence: the world's longest-lived country, Japan, has more than twice the rates of male cigarette smoking as the U.S. Ample evidence is now available showing that personal behaviors are less important in producing good health than is commonly believed.

One element of the confusing discussion around health is that too often we conflate the terms health and health care. We speak of accessing health, paying for health, and insuring health, when we are accessing healthcare, paying for healthcare, and insuring healthcare. While having access to health care is an important social good, much like healthful personal behaviors, it is less important in producing health than structural factors such as reduced economic inequality and support for early life.

Another important and poorly understood determinant of health is the experience of early life. What is called the "life course" approach recognizes the importance of the first few years after conception in producing later health. Roughly half of our health as adults is programmed in the first thousand days of life so in the first 2 or 3 years after birth, time for parents to provide intensive attention to the child is vitally important. Public policy can mandate that time, and it is widely seen as so essential that only two countries in the world do not have a federal policy to grant a working pregnant woman paid time off after she has her baby. One is Papua New Guinea and the other is the U.S. This opportunity to assure better outcomes for young children is mostly squandered in the U.S., reducing the prospect of improved adult health.

HOW CAN WE GET HEALTHY?

Our federal government produces documents outlining health goals for the next decade in its Healthy People series beginning with Healthy People 2000. The latest sets the targets for 2030. None of these documents refer to other countries. It is like our Olympic teams not setting goals to outcompete other nations. Without a global comparison becoming healthier lacks a gauge of what is possible. We never reach the internal goals for the preceding decade before setting out more ambitious ones for the next.

Necessary steps to improve our health were laid out in The National Academy of Science, Engineering and Medicine's 2013 monograph *US Health in International Perspective: Shorter Lives, Poorer Health*. This book laid out three improvements required to reverse our poor standing. First, achieve national health goals as are stated in the Healthy People decennial series such as reduce obesity, substance abuse, suicide, and adolescent sexual intercourse. The second was to inform the public about the health crisis, and the third to consider what other countries do that could be of use here.

POPULATION HEALTH TEACHING AND LEARNING STRATEGIES

It is essential that the general public understands the reality of our failing health as a country, including the social and economic (i.e., political) factors that lead to improved, or reduced population health. Very few courses at the university level mention the relatively poor health status of Americans, and even fewer go into details as to causes or highlight successful policies in other countries. I have tried many different approaches to communicating this information and will share a few of those approaches.

Since 2000 I have developed and taught graduate and undergraduate courses in population health at the School of Public Health at the University of Washington. The courses focus on the country as the unit of analysis, exploring how different countries achieve their health outcomes. I've been impressed with how very few of the students taking these courses were aware of the shameful state of U.S. health, reinforcing my concerns about the need to increase understanding of this problem among the general public.

I used the standard lecture format for the first few years, highlighting U.S. health status together with the determinants of health, the role of medical care, and health outcomes for a selected range of countries including Japan, Western Europe, Canada, India, China, the former Soviet Union, Latin America and Africa. In subsequent years I've added an outreach activity, during which students carry out a community action to inform and motivate others. The students choose from a number of activities during which they bring specific population health issues out of the classroom to inform others. Examples: students can submit a letter to the editor of a newspaper detailing a relevant issue from the course; conduct interviews with two outsiders about the course ideas; write a brief essay for a publication in plain language explaining poor U.S. health status; give a lecture to a group; and develop a public service announcement or website. They also undertake activities such as tabling at an event, producing and distributing a fact sheet, or developing a "talking points" script and communicating it in person with five strangers. The key idea of all these activities is to seed course content outside of the classroom. I've discovered that if such exercises are in the course (and required as part of the grade), students do not object to them – and many become actively enthusiastic about the activities.

I expanded these community outreach efforts to having students screen a segment of the PBS series, "Unnatural Causes: Is Inequality Making Us Sick," for an audience they organize, then conduct a discussion afterward on the concepts presented. "The Raising of America," another PBS series highlighting early life, is another possible screening. Some from the undergraduate course went back to their high schools and presented course concepts there. Another option has been playing a board game called "The Last Straw" that illustrates the social determinants of health with a group.

Each year I require students to watch the movie "Where to Invade Next," which shows how many Western European nations provide more social services than in the U.S. They also carry out a "population health web ramble," namely an exploration of factual Internet sites ranking countries by various health indicators. This allows students to discover course concepts from other sources than those used in the classroom.

A colleague developed an environmental justice exercise using real-life scenarios for the class to decide where to dump toxic waste based on different communities in the Puget Sound region. The class is divided into groups representing different neighborhoods. They then discuss where the waste should go. One of the groups with limited English proficiency remains silent in the discussions. Since they don't voice any concerns, the others typically decide the waste should go there.

After discovering how little students knew about both US governance because of the decline of civics instruction as well as the importance of international politics for health, I added a class entitled: Global Political Economic History. In an attempt to broaden students' understanding of health, I also added discussions on the topics of non-mortality measures of health, biological mechanisms through which early life and inequality work, mental illness, and a theory of global health (reflecting on the impact of different forms of colonialism on present health). We also discuss methods of influencing public policy.

In 2014 the undergraduate course moved to an Active Learning Classroom, in which students sit in groups at tables and work through exercises together to discover the material, minimizing the lecture format. An early activity called a country "card sort" of various health indicators required that students find out for themselves the abysmally low ranking of the U.S. in health measures, rather than my presenting the material. After drawing maps to locate their countries and estimating health outcomes without using outside help, they meet and review the correct sorts and values and communicate them to the rest of the class.

In the latest face-to-face course in a larger classroom 15 tables were divided into parts of the North American continent, representing various "Americas:" Examples are the left coast, the deep south and Appalachia. This helped students recognize how culture, policies and policy outcomes varied by region, making consensus for progressive change difficult. Presidential election results reflect this splintering of ideologies within the U.S. that is at best unlikely to change much even with new governments. I have added preparing an advocacy policy brief that tackles a federal policy process that could stop declining US health.

For several years before the COVID-19 pandemic I had taught an online course for distance learning Master of Public Health (MPH) students. Having worked through that process simplified the transition to virtual learning when the pandemic ended face-to-face instruction, and all my courses were offered online. The community outreach exercise changed from requiring a physical encounter with subjects to its being conducted online through social media. As an unexpected outcome of that requisite change, the students reached far more people than would typically come to a physical meeting. Online learning, I've found, has some important benefits compared to face-to-face classrooms. For example, short periods in breakout rooms of five to six students allows greater participation among some learners who otherwise might feel inhibited to speak. Once face-to-face classes return, a hybrid model using some of the beneficial aspects of synchronous online learning could enhance the physical classroom process.

Feedback from students as to their learning progress is important, and I have developed various forms of soliciting their reactions. One approach requires students to submit 3x5 cards after each class with answers to prompts. In the online learning environment, a weekly student evaluation helps me improve the course.

EDUCATIONAL EFFORTS BEFORE COLLEGE

My colleagues and I have presented material on population health to students from grade six on through high school. I worked with Andra Devoght, a physical therapist, who developed a month-long curriculum for sixth-graders and piloted it in a Seattle school. Andra used active learning approaches such as the "agree or disagree" method: a statement was made that required students to take one point of view or the other by moving to the side of the classroom representing their choice. Students were then asked why they picked that side; as they voiced their ideas, some might cross from one side to the other. A sample question might be: "Eating healthy, staying fit, and avoiding tobacco is all you need to be healthy." Another might be "If you are sick and see the doctor you will get well." Another is: "America is the healthiest country in the world." There are myriad other questions that could be asked to bring out students' critical thinking processes.

Another method Andra used was to display a building on a felt board, beginning with a foundation, then adding walls, floors or levels, then roof. Elements that could be part of the building to promote health might include food, water, safety, housing, good jobs, governance, friendship, community, education, parenting, and societal values. Modeling a "house of health" provided a useful metaphor that broadened the students' understanding of health.

Many of the same concepts can work in high school as well. As students learn to graph, we use an exercise that asks them to produce a bar chart of life expectancies of the top 25 countries, using UN data. Some students will do what is asked, showing only 25 countries, but others will add more bars until the United States shows up!

I've learned about using readers' theater for high school instruction. In the "Health Olympics Race," students choose countries and wear provided t-shirts with that country's flag. A student announcer describes the race. Japan crosses the finish line first, and almost 6 years later the US completes the competition. Another uses a sports analogy to discuss two professional baseball teams, one of which pays each player the same salary, and another that pays the players who hit more home runs much more. Students discuss which team they would want to play for, and which team would score better. Some are surprised to learn about studies that show that more equally paid teams actually perform better.

OTHER OPPORTUNITIES

At the opposite end of the age spectrum, I've developed a course for retired folk to cover the same material. Such students are older and have experienced more life events to guide understandings of health in this country, making for lively discussions. I discovered that courses located in more affluent areas were less popular than those in more modest communities. Perhaps being economically privileged makes one less interested in discovering what that means for society. As one gains experience teaching population health, many other opportunities arise.

EVALUATION OF EFFORTS

Formal course evaluations have demonstrated ratings among the highest at the University of Washington's public health school. However, I've found that reflecting on course content and changing one's beliefs about health may take considerable time. I've heard from students, years after taking my courses about how exposure to the material has influenced their lives and careers.

While COVID-19 has drawn some attention to excess deaths in the US, the efforts of the 2013 report on our shorter lives and poorer health have not led to either wide dissemination of this information or to substantive action. From my perspective, public health in this country has never grasped its mission as making the health of the public the best it can be, namely achieving that of the healthiest nations. It is time for organized public health to sound the call for action. Teaching such material to diverse audiences is a first step.

CONCLUSION

Before the COVID-19 pandemic, it was much harder for the public to grasp the relatively poor health status of Americans. The differential effects of the pandemic on Americans of various ethnicities and social classes provides an opportunity to enhance understanding and promote political action to make America healthy again. Key concepts can be seeded in elementary schools and carried on in diverse communities by youth, who will be the changemakers of the future. Although our health to date has continued to decline, the end of that decline is in sight as we prepare the younger generation to change the world we produced. COVID-19 has provided this golden opportunity. Hopefully the examples of how I have educated students over the past decades might prove useful for others who have the privilege of being teachers.

FOR FURTHER STUDY

Bezruchka, S. (2019). Epidemiological approaches to population health. Staying alive: Critical perspectives on health, illness, and health care. In T. Bryant, D. Raphael and M. H. Rioux (pp. 4–37). CSPI. This chapter for a college textbook contains further details for the material presented here. It can be accessed at http://depts.washington.edu/eqhlth/pages/resources.html

Devoght, A. (2005). *Population health teachers manual* (unpublished).

Mogford, E., Gould, L., & Devoght, A. (2011). Teaching critical health literacy in the US as a means to action on the social determinants of health. *Health Promotion International*, *26*(1), 4–13.

SECTION TWO

THE PURPOSE OF EDUCATION AND THE ROLES THAT SCHOOLS PLAY

The purpose of education has been contested for as long as we have had schools. There has rarely been agreement about what should be taught, how it should be taught, who should be taught, who should be teaching, and who should pay for it, and governments at all levels (federal, state, and local) perpetually struggle over those questions. There is additional question about the role that schools play when the social safety net fails, as is now the case. Schools have increasingly served as de facto social service agencies, food and nutrition centers, health care agencies, child-care sites, and sometimes as adult education/job training agencies when those resources are not otherwise available in communities.

The articles in this section offer some perspective on what schools are doing, and how that fits within the longer and larger context of their history. I offer a brief history of schools, placing the debates about purpose within the push-pull of our ideals of democracy and the demands of the corporate capitalistic economic system that dominates our economy and politics at the moment. Schools are asked to serve both and can't realistically meet what is expected of them.

Sandra Mathison and E. Wayne Ross write of the roles that schools have taken on in meeting the needs of the community beyond simply educating children, and how it is necessary for us to be honest and clear eyed about what that means in terms of how our society is functioning, or not functioning in meeting the needs of our population, and how that informs our thinking about transforming our schools.

CHAPTER THREE

The Purpose of Education

A Brief History

DOUG SELWYN

THE PURPOSE OF EDUCATION

Each year I taught in teacher education I asked the new group of teacher candidates three connected questions: Why do we have school, what should happen at school, and who should decide what is taught at school? The students would look at each other in some confusion; these are not questions most had considered before. Their first responses were what you might expect. We go to school because it's what you do, because it's what we've always done, or that we need to go to school so we can learn what we need to learn so we can be successful adults. And we study what they tell us to study. There are requirements. It had not occurred to many of them to ask why there are those requirements, or who made those decisions, or to ask if there is something that could be more useful to them and to their future students. It's what you do. When we began to dive into the third, most fundamental question of the three, about the purpose of education in terms of who it serves and for what ends it always proved to be the most disquieting, door opening, and crucial aspect of their introduction to teacher education. We make a mistake when we take the purpose of schools for granted and assume they exist for the benefit of the children. It is way more complicated than that.

Caught Between Democracy and Corporate Capital. For many people the United States symbolizes the power and virtue of both capitalism and democracy, and the two are often intertwined when politicians talk of what makes the country great. Here's an excerpt from a speech by President George W. Bush in 2001:

> Our Founders considered themselves heirs to principles that were timeless and truths that were self-evident. When Jefferson sat down to write, he was trying, he said, to place before mankind "the common sense of the subject." The common sense of the subject was that we should be free. And though great evils would linger, the world would never be the same after July 4, 1776.
>
> A wonderful country was born, and a revolutionary idea sent forth to all mankind: Freedom, not by the good graces of government but as the birthright of every individual; equality, not as a theory of philosophers but by the design of our Creator; natural rights, not for the few, not even for a fortunate many but for all people, in all places, in all times. (President George W. Bush, 2001)

These self-evident truths of Jefferson and the other founders, that all men are created equal, has been held up to the world as evidence that America is truly an exceptional country, a "shining city on a hill," as President Reagan phrased it. And, as we know, those aspirational words were written by a man who owned hundreds of other human beings (as did many of our so-called Founders), at a time when women and children had no rights, or legal standing. Native Americans had no rights either and were being driven from their lands and/or murdered, and there were tens of thousands of enslaved Africans, owned by those "equal men." It was clear that the American ideal, which came to be called the American Dream, was intended for and reserved only for white men of some means living on American soil.

Frederick Douglass brought this point to an audience he had been invited to address on July 4, 1852, in a speech now titled *What to a Slave is the Fourth of July?* Here is a small part of that speech.

> What, to the American slave, is your 4th of July? I answer; a day that reveals to him, more than all other days in the year, the gross injustice and cruelty to which he is the constant victim. To him, your celebration is a sham; your boasted liberty, an unholy license; your national greatness, swelling vanity; your sounds of rejoicing are empty and heartless; your denunciation of tyrants, brass fronted impudence; your shouts of liberty and equality, hollow mockery; your prayers and hymns, your sermons and thanksgivings, with all your religious parade and solemnity, are, to Him, mere bombast, fraud, deception, impiety, and hypocrisy-a thin veil to cover up crimes which would disgrace a nation of savages. There is not a nation on the earth guilty of practices more shocking and bloody than are the people of the United States, at this very hour. (Frederick Douglass, 1852)

Despite hundreds of years of evidence to the contrary, America still presents itself to itself and the world as a beacon of freedom and possibility. It is a myth that reaches down to the lowest levels of our economic ladder, promising that anyone can grow up to be successful, no matter how humble their origins. It is, to repeat, a myth that has no basis in the real world. There is less mobility in America, from poor to middle class much less to the wealthy class, than in virtually any developed country on earth (Kraus & Tan, 2015). Despite the promise of democracy, where the government exists to serve the people who retain the ultimate power, the realities of corporate capitalism, the economic system that serves as the foundation of the nation's economy undermine and nullify any possibility of equality. These two fundamental systems on which American society rests, democracy and corporate capitalism are in fact perpetually at odds, the goals and tenets of the one contradicting the goals and tenets of the other. At times through our history there has been some movement towards more democracy. The Civil Rights movement, the women's movement, the gay rights movement and the labor movement all brought changes that improved the lives of the people by both winning more rights, by opening the door to fuller participation, and by protecting the public from the excesses of exploitation by corporations in pursuit of profits.

At other times, such as what we are experiencing today, the ruthless behaviors of corporate capitalists and their political allies, intersecting with increasing attacks by white supremacists on people of color and on our democracy have assaulted our people, our institutions, our environment, and our basic morality in pursuit of short-term profits, and in the determination of those in power to maintain that power and position. As a consequence, many perceive there to be even less democracy than there had been. The top 1% of our population has nearly 30% of the wealth of the entire country (Beers, 2020), which leaves them wielding enormous power and influence, while the 99% have little wealth, power, or influence over major factors in their lives. This contradiction has led to millions living in poverty, living with little hope of experiencing the life promised by the fine words penned by Jefferson centuries ago.

It is both unavoidable and often overlooked that the public school system has played a significant role in maintaining the myth that presents the U.S. as a democracy, and while there have been minor swings between a more liberal, child centered orientation and a more corporate, competitive model, the overall impact of public education has been to maintain the position and wealth of those in power.

A BRIEF HISTORY OF SCHOOLS

Schools have answered to (and continue to answer to) multiple masters and have often worked at cross purposes in those conflicting roles over the years. They have served individual students and communities by providing a relatively safe place for children to come together with caring adults to learn basic skills, to gain knowledge and awareness of the wider world, and to have access to possibilities broader than they might have found on their own. The early schools were gathering places for communities, often serving as the location for town meetings, social events, religious services, and governmental functions as well as the place where children came to learn some basic reading, writing, and arithmetic. Schools have helped new immigrants to learn how to "become Americans," have served as social service agencies supporting families by providing food, clothing, basic medical care and connections to resources in the community. And they have opened some doors to potential employment, the arts, athletics, and relationships with the commons, providing a place for members from different communities to come together. Schools have been the place where we have learned the basic skills that society has decided we need to contribute to the common good, and it's the place where some of us have connected with an adult, a mentor who inspired a passion for a field, a topic, a question that launched us into our next years, or who provided a safe place to come for mentoring, guidance, and support. Serving the students and helping them gain the knowledge, skills, and confidence they will need to move into their roles as responsible and engaged adults is part of the promise of and requirements of democracy.

At the same time public schools have served to socialize young people towards unquestioning patriotism, towards automatic obedience to adults, towards studying what they are told to study and ignoring their own interests, passions, and concerns. They have championed the idea that the United States has served as a beacon of democracy and freedom while minimizing the full spectrum of costs and consequences that America's pursuit of wealth and power has brought to people here and around the world. Schools, both K-12 and at the college/university level, have taught students that their role was to fit in to society, to help maintain the status quo, which has served a very few at the expense of the rest, particularly those from underrepresented populations. They have decided not only who could become educated but who would not be allowed through the schoolhouse doors and determined what kind of education those in classrooms would receive. Researchers such as Jean Anyon (1980) made clear that those going to school in wealthy communities were being educated to rule, while those attending schools in the poorest neighborhoods were more often trained for service and other low wage jobs. They may all be public schools, but they have been anything but equal. Public schools, through their miseducation about the country's history, through segregation and resegregation, inequality of resources and options, and through their insistence on largely divorcing their curriculum from the issues and concerns going on in the larger society in favor of year-long test preparation have helped to maintain the economic, social, and political inequality that dominates our system today.

While the public schools are not solely responsible for this inequality, they have surely played a significant role in its existence, maintenance, and growth.

It is unlikely there will be fundamental change until enough of the population understands how we have come to this point in our history, and gains the skills, knowledge, and attitude necessary to effect change. This is a role that schools can and hopefully will play in our future. It has happened before.

An Excess of Democracy. When schools were more student-centered during the late 1960s and 1970s, and there were intentional efforts to connect what students were learning in the classroom to what was happening around them, students were taking their studies of democracy and movements for justice to the streets with demonstrations against the Vietnam War, and for Civil Rights, gay rights, and women's rights. The Trilateral Commission, a group of politicians, business leaders and other powerful people formed in 1973 by David Rockefeller "to foster cooperation between North America, Western Europe and Japan" issued a report entitled "The Crisis of Democracy." The report cautioned against what they termed "an excess of democracy." It said that "The effective operation of a democratic political system usually requires some measure of apathy and noninvolvement on the part of some individuals and groups" (Chomsky, 1981).

Samuel Huntington, one of the authors of the report, expressed his concern that this excess of democracy was bad for the country because it made the country look bad on the world stage. Huntington lamented the increasing actions and influence of the common people. He said, "Truman had been able to govern the country with the cooperation of a relatively small number of Wall Street lawyers and bankers," but activism made this much more difficult by the mid-1960s. The population was much less governable because they were less willing to be submissive. Huntington notes that previously passive or unorganized groups in the population, such as "blacks, Indians, Chicanos, white ethnic groups, students and women – all of whom became organized and mobilized in new ways to achieve what they considered to be their appropriate share of the action and of the rewards" were a threat to the smooth functioning of our democracy, which depended on "some measure of apathy and noninvolvement on the part of some individuals and groups" (Chomsky, 1981).

James Baldwin made clear the challenges that an educated population posed for those in power in his 1963 talk to teachers:

> The paradox of education is precisely this – that as one begins to become conscious one begins to examine the society in which he is being educated. The purpose of education, finally, is to create in a person the ability to look at the world for himself, to make his own decisions.... To ask questions of the universe, and then learn to live with those questions, is the way he achieves his own identity. But no society is really anxious to have that kind of person around. What societies really, ideally, want is a citizenry which will simply obey the rules of society. If a society succeeds in this, that society is about to perish. The obligation of anyone who thinks of himself as responsible is to examine society and try to

change it and to fight it – at no matter what risk. This is the only hope society has. This is the only way societies change. (Baldwin, 1963)

What we want for our children, to be critical thinkers and passionate learners who care about others and who stand up for justice is someone that "no society is really anxious to have (...) around." That's it, in a nutshell. People who think for themselves, who can see through the smoke screens that politicians, governments, corporations, media outlets and history textbooks produce, to see the "men behind the curtain" are much more difficult to control, to program, and are more likely to challenge the injustice that serves those in power at the expense of those most distant from power. We may want it for our own children, but the thought of everyone's children thinking for themselves and acting in their own interests, and in the interests of communities that are not ours, seems to be perceived as a danger, a threat. It might produce "an excess of democracy."

Having too much democracy in a democracy is a curious paradox, and one that really gets to the heart of the questions in this book as we consider what role education should play in our next decades. When the democracy stops being democratic, when the society based on serving the common good stops serving that common good, what does "right action" look like? Are schools doing their jobs when they educate people to notice the injustices and feel moved to act, using the skills and knowledge they gained from public education? The authors of the Trilateral Commission did not think so, and scolded institutions such as schools, churches and synagogues for failing to keep their populations passive. Their concerns led to the pendulum swinging back the other way, beginning towards the end of the 1970s, picking up steam with the arrival of Ronald Reagan in 1980, the release of A Nation at Risk in 1983, a report critical of the nation's schools, and particularly once Congress passed No Child Left Behind (NCLB) in 2002. NCLB brought about high stakes standardized testing and attached punishments and penalties for poor performance on standardized tests that can trace their lineage to the eugenics movement of the early 20th century.

We are a long way from a child-centered education that encourages students to think critically about their education and their world and to act on their critical thinking. Students today are being bullied into passivity, into doing what they are told without asking questions, and to keep their questions and concerns to themselves. They are being trained to fit into a corporate capitalistic structure that wants workers who are educated and skilled enough to accomplish their assigned tasks, but not so educated or motivated to do more than that.

Given the increasing influence that standardized tests have come to have in public education, more and more decisions about how schools should operate and how they should be assessed are coming from the federal government and from state departments of education while fewer and fewer decisions are being made by the educators who know their children, including their teachers, administrators, and families. We are losing local control, we are losing funding, we are losing the ability to adequately serve the most vulnerable populations, and as a consequence we are getting less healthy and whole as a people, and as a democracy. As the pendulum continues to swing towards the domination by the interests of corporate capital it becomes more and more clear that schools can't follow those demands and also attend to the needs and well-being of their students. With the rise and surfacing of white supremacists within our government, our military and police forces, and in media it becomes unavoidable to notice the intersection of corporate capitalism and white supremacy.

The arrival of the Covid 19 pandemic in March 2020 has forced public education into reset mode. It obviously can't continue with business as usual, and many if not most school districts across the country started the 2020 school year remotely, placing the safety and well-being of students, educators, and their families as their top priority. As I write this in May of 2021, most states have re-opened to in person schooling in time to administer their standardized tests before the end of the school year. There is money to be made by testing companies, and fear that, if the tests are cancelled for a second year it may help people to realize that those high stakes tests are not all that necessary after all.

The question is, once vaccinations and CDC protocols allow schools to reopen, what should be happening there? It is crucial that we engage in a critical examination of the role that education has played throughout our history, and then move into focusing on what public education could bring to an effort to establish a more just and equitable society. It is time to reconsider, to re organize our educational system so that it truly serves all of the students with the goal of helping them to become healthy, confident, and able to act on their own behalf and on behalf of their communities and the planet.

Note: Parts of this chapter appeared in *All Children Are All Our Children* (2019).

REFERENCES

Anyon. J. (1980). *Ghetto schooling: A political economy of urban educational reform.* Teachers College Press.

Baldwin, J. (1963). *A talk to teachers.* Retrieved from http://richgibson.com/*talktoteachers.htm*.

Beers, T. (2020). *Top 1% Of U.S. households hold 15 times more wealth than bottom 50% combined.* Forbes. Retrieved from https://www.forbes.com/sites/tommybeer/2020/10/08/top-1-of-us-households-hold-15-times-more-wealth-than-bottom-50-combined/?sh=5cb7d9c35179.

Bush, G. W. (2001, July 4). *Remarks by the President in Independence Hall Celebration, Independence Historic National Park, Philadelphia, Pennsylvania.* Retrieved from https://georgewbush-whitehouse.archives.gov/news/releases/2001/07/text/20010704-2.html

Chomsky, N. (1981). *The Carter administration: Myth and reality.* Radical Priorities (excerpt). Retrieved from https://chomsky.info/priorities01/

Douglass, F. (1852). *What to the Slave is the Fourth of July?* Freeman Institute. Retrieved from http://www.freemaninstitute.com/douglass/htm

CHAPTER FOUR

Beyond Education as Usual

Public Education in a Post-Covid World

SANDRA MATHISON AND E. WAYNE ROSS

> Barn's burnt down – now I can see the moon.
>
> – Mizuta Masahide

Now that the barn is gone it is an opportunity to pause, gaze at the moon and to resist rebuilding the barn. The pandemic has given us a new vision of what schools are and perhaps can be and we should resist a "return to normal," resist the deep felt need to get back to the way things were before Covid-19 tore the barn down. We write this chapter invoking the spirit of John Holt who in 1971 said:

> I do not believe that any movement for educational reform that addresses itself exclusively or even primarily to the problems or needs of children can progress very far. In short, in a society that is absurd, unworkable, wasteful, destructive, secretive, coercive, monopolistic, and generally antihuman, we could never have good education, no matter what kind of schools the powers that be permit, because it is not the educators or the schools but the whole society and the quality of life in it that really educate …. More and more it seems to me, and this is a reversal of what I felt not long ago, that it makes very little sense to talk about education for social change, as if education was or could be a kind of getting ready. The best and perhaps only education for social change is action to bring about that change … There cannot be little worlds fit for children in a world not fit for anyone else. (Cited in Miller, 2002, p. 90)

School reform and social change are inextricably connected and as Holt suggests, school reform that creates "little worlds fit for children" will not create a world fit for everyone. In this chapter we will discuss the inextricability of schools and society as illustrated by the school closures and disruptions that have occurred during the pandemic. We describe the clearer understanding of the multiple functions schools play in society, functions that are obvious when there is no one to perform them and nowhere for them to be performed. We provide a utopian vision of what schools, schooling, and more importantly education could be, a vision that steps into rather than rejecting the complex role schools play. And a vision, we hope, that is true to Holt's rejection of schooling as preparation for social change and promotes a vision of schooling (and education) as part of a lived experience that is social change.

Covid-19 is a mirror, and the flaws in many institutions, including schools, are being reflected back to us. Schools and education have been disrupted by war and disease, but this pandemic may be one of the most significant disruptions in education we will ever see. It has revealed much about schooling and education. The central role of education, and especially public education, in the economic, social and political life is more obvious than ever. And although schooling and education are commonplace experiences, the pandemic has given the general public a new and more fulsome understanding of the roles schools play.

The pandemic has shone a bright harsh light on many current vulnerabilities and exacerbated already unacceptable inequities. While no one would have wished for this societal trauma, we might consider what we can learn about the centrality and essential role public education plays by thinking big to envision change in these unprecedented times. History tells us there will be more events like Covid-19 that will potentially disrupt public education, including the effects of climate change increasingly displacing schooling because of wildfires, hurricanes, and flooding. Imagining education in a context of change and disruption better prepares us to serve the public interest in an uncertain future.

At the end of January 2020 Chinese schools were closed, and by the end of March virtually the rest of the world had followed suit. Ninety-one percent of the world's school age students were without school.[1] While many countries began opening schools, at least to some students in September, still many remained closed and there has been a see saw of openings and closures across the globe. This instability in the availability of schools has revealed what many already know, but often resist – schools perform many functions beyond what might be considered their core academic purpose. The resounding rhetoric is that schools are asked to do too much, asked to do things not in their purview, asked to do things that they do not have the resources to do. This is a rhetoric that keeps schools from change, that denies a reality about what schools do, in fact, do, even if not always well.

---

1   See UNESCO's website for current and historical data on school closures during Covid. https://en.unesco.org/covid19/educationresponse

In particular, schools provide food, childcare, safety, and are a major part of the political economy. We focus especially on the role of schools in addressing food insecurity and the need for childcare. We encourage rethinking what schools can be and decenter schooling as we know it in favor of education.

FOOD INSECURITY

As schools closed, it was most immediately obvious which services were no longer available, especially to vulnerable students and their families. The impact of food insecurity, which is to some extent alleviated in schools through breakfast and lunch programs as well as food banks for families, was immediate. In Canada, one in three children are projected to be food insecure and in the U.S. the rate has doubled since the pandemic to 28%.

Clearly, schools are a nutritional safety net, especially for low-income children. After the school closures, school districts made valiant efforts to feed children by creating centrally located food and meal delivery sites, grab and go locations, grocery gift cards, and home food deliveries. Through what is often a patchwork of funding and programs, during "ordinary" times many children's nutritional needs are met. There are calls and plans for expanding and solidifying schools' role in feeding children, but these solutions merely rebuild the barn and create a little world to meet the needs of children.

We wouldn't argue against the importance schools can play in promoting food security and indeed they are a community-based place that connects food distribution to specific geographical area. Indeed, food security requires that food be available near where people live. And, alleviating food insecurity must mitigate "holiday hunger" by disconnecting the provision of food from the school calendar. The current situation does not create food stability, also a key element of food security. Perhaps even more radical would-be schools providing nutritionally sound free meals to ALL students, and not require the demonstration of need thus jettisoning the deficit mind set around food insecurity. Children deserve proper nutrition regardless of demographic characteristics.[2]

Schools can continue to address food by feeding children, possibly including gardening and local food production as well. But this is a larger problem requiring conceptions of schools not as they are now working and requires attending to a broader social framework to alleviate hunger. Breakfast and lunch programs are a first order solution that does little to address underlying causes of food insecurity. There are many causes of food insecurity but in western industrialized nations

---

2 The Finnish free school meals are a prototype, providing free meals to all students since 1943. In Finland, food education is a holistic pedagogic tool extending beyond school lunches.

poverty and racism are the primary causes, which must be addressed to create a world fit for everyone, not just children but families and communities. Basic guaranteed incomes, child benefits, affordable housing, and equity in food costs and availability are parts of the puzzle for alleviating poverty that leads to food insecurity. In other words, food insecurity must be conceptualized as a social problem not an individual one.

CHILDCARE

To live and work, parents and caregivers must have childcare. Schools provide safe and low cost childcare for many families, a fact that has been painfully demonstrated during school closures. This idea is resisted in large part because it is presumed to diminish the role of teachers, to in some way de-professionalize them by suggesting they are babysitters. In fact, teachers are, or ought to be, childcare experts. Childcare needs to be understood differently… caring for society's children is an immensely important task that is core to communities and the public interest.[3]

Pandemic induced school closures reveal the extent to which school serves this role first for those considered to be essential workers, like health care workers, and then for working women, especially low income, minority, immigrant, and single mothers. The conflation of essential work done by these same women punctuates the childcare function of schools. Schools have therefore provided a resource that allows women to work. The greater likelihood of women losing their jobs meant they were able to care for their children, but this in turn creates a cycle where their ability to look for work is diminished when jobs do come available. Even when women were able to work from home, the unequal distribution of household and childcare responsibilities means women are especially vulnerable when childcare is unavailable. During the pandemic, women have been more likely to quit their jobs, reduce their work commitment, juggle work hours to accommodate childcare, or take leaves from work (Heggeness, 2020).

The care schools provide for children and families is not isolated from other social, cultural and economic factors and should be recast as a social responsibility. What is revealed by the absence of childcare ordinarily provided by schools are deep seated gender inequities in employment, remuneration for work, and health and wellbeing. Schools (as well as workplaces) could be a physical place to provide stable affordable/free childcare that is not inadvertent because children

---

3   Two dominant models of childcare are the educational model, based on the idea that public education serves a purpose for all and especially in alleviating inequities, and the work-care reconciliation model, which focuses on gender equity, especially enabling women to work.

are legally obligated to be there, but intentional because it is socially responsible to provide care for all children. This includes day care, before and after school care, early childhood education, and universal kindergarten all of which are ongoing and year round in keeping with the needs of caregivers, especially women. As with food security, the provision of childcare cannot be done within the confines of the school year as it is now conceived, but rather must be seen as a year-round, ongoing responsibility that schools play a significant part in fulfilling.

THINK EDUCATION RATHER THAN SCHOOLING

While schools closed for some (sometimes most) of the time during the pandemic, education never stopped. There has been much focus on the pivot to distance learning or hybrid models, which emphasizes both the heroism of teachers in doing so as well as the challenges for teachers, students and families without ready or any access to computers or Internet connections. Drawn in clearer relief was the fact that educational employers do not fully provide the infrastructure for teaching and learning and that teachers ordinarily subsidize underfunded schools, and they did so to an even greater extent during the pandemic, providing their own computers, cameras, Internet connections, and so on. Also remarkable was the shift to learning outdoors, either simply being in nature, but often using the outdoors in innovative pedagogical ways. What is remarkable in this pivot was the swiftness with which it happened, fundamentally challenging the notion that school reform is difficult or even impossible.

But education wasn't confined to online schooling. In an instant, many people, especially parents and siblings, became educators thus illustrating the potential breadth of those who can provide educational opportunities with children. What the pandemic revealed is that learning happens whether there is a teacher present or not, and that learning is not a building-centric experience. Parents and children realized learning continues with or without schools, with or without teachers.

Much of the learning during the pandemic is informal learning, learning that emphasizes engagement, conversation, choice, working at one's own pace, on topics that are personally engaging. Learning with these characteristics stands in contrast to hegemonic conceptions of learning that emerge from schooling as it has been shaped by hierarchical power relations, pre-determined and measurable ends (learning objectives, test scores, outcomes), and learners as consumers rather than producers of knowledge.

This suggests we might refocus our attention on learning, and especially an understanding that learning happens in many contexts, with many different kinds of people, and might be most profound when learners (children) have a say in what they are learning. Schools are adult-centric, hierarchical environments that foster adultism, usually in the name of creating "little worlds fit for children." Such relationships value adult perspectives at the expense of young people's interests, experiences and capabilities. Current "cops out of schools" efforts are a clear example of this when adults presume police officers make youth feel safe when in fact youth, especially racialized youth, say they feel scared and intimidated. Age segregation in schools is another manifestation of adults determining who can congregate with whom and why and when in the school. It is time to turn to a different kind of schooling, one that centers children, gives them agency, and promotes the idea of a community of learners. In *Emile*, Rousseau (1921) wrote: "Childhood has ways of seeing, thinking, and feeling, peculiar to itself, nothing can be more foolish than to substitute our ways for them." (p. 22) We see examples of the rejection of adultism in free schools, folk schools, forest schools, anarchist schools, and Montessori and Emilio Reggio schools. These examples can help orient us toward learning rather than teaching and have profound implications for the ways in which we think about the nature of education.[4] And such schools take their role in caring for and feeding everyone, children and adults alike, seriously.

CONCLUSION

Schools will be with us after the pandemic, and when in person attendance begins it is an opportunity to not get back to business as usual but to gaze at the moon without rushing to obscure it. Taking from what we know about learning, these schools must attend to the wellbeing of students in ways that acknowledge their personal autonomy, and in addition to traditional academics must provide wrap around services like childcare, food, health, and other social services. And in so doing, reject the catching up lost ground[5] metaphor that can only create bad pedagogy, like over-testing and mind-numbing remediation, and increased stress. Schools should become community hubs where complex and multi-faceted needs

---

4 Some anarchists argue from an anti-pedagogical position asserting that teaching is impossible – we can learn, we can help others learn but we cannot "teach."

5 See, for example, Linda Darling Hammonds recommendations for "Accelerating learning as we build back better" https://www.forbes.com/sites/lindadarlinghammond/2021/04/05/accelerating-learning-as-we-build-back-better/?sh=240e21fe6722 and Joel Westheimer's essay "Three essential lessons Covid-19 has taught us about education" https://ottawacitizen.com/opinion/westheimer-year-one-covid-19-laid-bare-the-inequalities-in-education?fbclid=IwAR312eO1fdbAxwlFSX9zr69gSZZt09m5pnSLSJvXVMCSF_6R6crzUZgUK90 . Both illustrate how schools must be different: more about relationships, more about student wellbeing, and deep engagement with content.

are met, where children and adults work together. They must operate year-round, incorporate many different kinds of professionals and workers in addition to teachers, and become places of authentic experience that in John Holt's view are fit for everyone.

REFERENCES

Heggeness, M. L. (2020). Estimating the immediate impact of the COVID-19 shock on parental attachment to the labor market and the double bind of mothers. *Review of Economics of the Household, 18*, 1053–1078. https://link.springer.com/article/10.1007/s11150-020-09514-x#Tab1

Miller, R. (2002). *Free schools, free people: Education and democracy after the 1960s.* State University of New York Press.

Rousseau, J-J. (1921). *Emile, or education.* Translated by B. Foxley. E. P. Dutton.

SECTION THREE

LEARNING FROM TEACHING DURING COVID

We have learned an immense amount over the past year of teaching remotely during Covid, and some of what we learned will inform teaching post Covid. While we have focused most on the struggles of children and families during the pandemic it has also been an overwhelming year for educators, many of whom found it nearly impossible to keep their families afloat while maintaining their remote classrooms. Several who had committed to writing for this book had to bow out, apologetically, as they did not have the time or focus to write a chapter and were clear that their first priorities were their students and families. We know that, in the best of times teachers are working long, long hours beyond the school day, and one lesson I hope we take from this past year is that a functional system that meets the needs of the students cannot be maintained on the backs of overworked, under-resourced, and under-paid teachers, who are constantly rescuing our current system by working extra hours, buying supplies from their own thread bare pockets, feeding children who are without, and doing whatever else needs doing to support their students.

What follows are stories from two teachers from the greater Seattle area, where the first identified deaths from Covid in the U.S. occurred. Jo Cripps and Peter Suruda share their reflections on what the year was like and what they will take into their next years of teaching. Not surprisingly, it begins with knowing and caring for their students.

CHAPTER FIVE

Love in the Time of Covid

JO CRIPPS

— For Our Students: Near, Far, and Both

— Jo Cripps

ONLY CONNECT

One year ago, it was Donald J. Trump, not a virus, who appeared to be the single greatest threat to America's well-being. Then Covid stormed in, and on March 11, 2020, our governor sent the students, and the teachers, and the classroom hamsters packing. Those first days at home felt like snow days, and many of us enjoyed our respite while assuming we'd back in action just as soon as the Lysol dried on our desktops. But within a week the governor made it clear that our situation was no snow day. We would close for an undetermined amount of time.

Seattle Schools scrambled. District specialists threw together one-size-fits-all lessons, heavy on the social-emotional. With negligible pushback our union signed off, and as we went "live," our wisest administrators advised us, "Be radically welcoming and light on curriculum."

Covid Spring was all about trauma and triage, and those last weeks of the cruelest month – weeks we had traditionally squandered on state testing – morphed into a frontier of teachers as travel guides, coaxing students onto uncharted and frequently unwelcoming platforms. They were tough days, but here's the thing. I have never felt a deeper connection with my students than I felt last spring, when we were all castaways, all innocent, all real-life team-mates in the strange new world of – what else? – MS Teams. However.

We hadn't been basking long in the warmth of intergenerational camaraderie when reality came calling: my U.S. History students were not exactly crushing the 2nd semester curriculum. They ignored meaty readings on the Palmer raids. They failed to show up at a Scopes Trial re-enactment; in fact, the only action in the chat that day was a baffling parade of Bitmojis unrelated to evolution. I was distraught.

Then it hit me. Covid was teaching lessons we teachers never imagined. How to cope with paralyzing loneliness. Where to find work – babysitting, running errands, mowing lawns – when your mom lost her job. How to make the daily sacrifices required to keep your elders from getting sick. And after a panic-induced meltdown, how to pull it together.

Those were the life-or-death lessons the kids were learning, and only after that existential homework was done could they address schoolwork. Tackle Schoology. Crack Kiddum. Even perhaps solve the mysteries of hot spots. A few students mastered the platforms. Most didn't. But whatever students were doing or not doing, one thing was clear. My beautiful US History curriculum needed a makeover. Now.

We changed tack. Facing Covid head-on, each student became a practicing historian, a primary source producer. Bearing witness to a defining moment in history, students photographed and sketched and sculpted and wrote. They followed the syllabus laid out by Professor Covid, and like so much real, important work, this was difficult and painful.

"My teacher and mom are making me do this," one student wrote in an April journal entry. As Covid bore down, so did she – describing playgrounds full of ghosts and a rent strike tearing her neighbors apart. By June, she had published her Covid Diary. "Legit, this is keeping me from losing it," she wrote, and she spoke for all the kids who were mining inner resources, struggling to access the deep courage they would need to survive.

Across the country, competent teachers joined the students' struggle. We loved kids into learning. We asked kids what they needed and kept asking until the kids finally believed we truly wanted to know – and they trusted us enough to answer. Then we showed up at their houses and apartments and trailers and shelters with books and groceries and gift cards.

And school became what it should be: Love Central.

Slow forward. The vaccine is finally here, and the end of remote learning seems reachable if not close. But what comes next?

THE FUTURE

If you can read and write, you own the 21st century. (Stephen King)

That great American pedagogue says it all. Let there be literacy. In all its forms. Going forward, our kids need to read the world; that is how they will write the future. Students need to decode and deconstruct and decipher – they need to detect the truth and the lies – in everything from cave paintings to One America News Network. And unless kids learn from that other great American pedagogue Ernest Hemingway and start wielding their bullshit detectors like John Brown's spear, we might as well all roll over and let the One Percent devour us. That's the worst-case scenario. This is the best: Kids acquire the necessary knowledge, and skills, to build the future they need and deserve.

They won't do it alone. Their teachers – allies, coaches, friends – must guide them through the process of becoming literate. Key to the social, emotional, moral, and academic literacy students will need to acquire, *political literacy* stands center-stage, a foundational skill essential to world-building.

Democracy starts in the democratic classroom, and it dies without political literacy. Students need to acquire a working vocabulary so that we can all understand each other. Students need to define *for themselves* the terms we all throw around like frisbees. Take *justice*, for instance. Students must examine and reject the white supremacist model that is steadily destroying us. Students must construct their own model, a structure that will uplift all of them, in all their glorious diversity.

How will students define their terms and construct a common language? Studying injustice is one approach and related to that is the study of resistance to injustice. Connecting with activists is invaluable not only for learning what justice is – but how to grow it.

I hope future schools will borrow from classic models. The Highlander School. The Black Panther Community School. The Sandinista schools on horseback. Zapotecan classes where tests are collective, Nahuatl is the language of scholarship, and failure is an empty concept. Any school where the system is serving the student – and not vice versa – is one we can learn from. All great schools share a common denominator: they were established by activists motivated by love for their people.

Keeping that in mind, we can ally with our own local activists. In Seattle, schools partner with Black Lives Matter, *El Centro de la Raza*, the Urban Native Education Alliance, the Holocaust Center for Humanity, and the Densho Project, to name a few. Individual teachers also ally with activists to create classroom kitchens where kids dream, create, test, refine – and feast.

It's hard to imagine such places ever being under-enrolled. All families know what their kids need, and often frustrated parents of underserved kids are the very best at finding the schools they need *if they are there*. If they aren't, then we teachers – guardians, caretakers, and public intellectuals – need to put them in place, and as we do so, we need to proceed from the premise that education, like literacy, takes many forms. On the run. In the field. At sea. On stage. Education is what happens *wherever kids are*. And this is irrefutable: kids are all over the place.

So, all over the place, the future depends on education that depends on going well beyond the 3 R's. Education for the future centers on some of those *other* R's. Resistance. Rebuilding. Revolution.

And then there's reclamation. Teachers must reclaim their profession. Their unions must walk away from corporate "partnerships" that offer "free" hardware – in exchange for 50 million K-12 hostages. Those branded kids might as well have Microsoft tattooed on their foreheads.

From its beginnings, the public education model has been no secret. Schools train workers. That was the mission in the 19th century, it's still the mission, and it is the enemy of a just society. It's also here to stay and slay unless teachers act. Like any able-bodied monster, the student-as-future-cog model will not die until teachers kill it. No one else in the education-industrial complex seems ready or willing to do the job. It's delusional to imagine that our current political and corporate bosses have any intention of changing a system that works so perfectly for them and their ilk.

So, it's up to us, and – in our favor – there's plenty we can do. In Seattle, for example, we can start by pressuring our elected School Board members to force the district to sever ties with Pearson and Macmillan and all the other "education" publishers and "experts" who sell the fraudulent grading systems that honor and perpetuate white privilege. We need to throw out any grading system that fails to tell the whole story of a kid's progress – as viewed by that kid and their teacher.

It's also imperative that we scrap standardized tests. Aside from doing an excellent job of measuring how capably a student takes a standardized test, their only function is to serve as white supremacy's bouncers: they make sure the white kids get into the club and everyone else goes home. Or worse.

And while we're taking out the trash, let's get rid of commercial reading curricula. They undermine the goal of literacy – which is freedom – by promoting texts, teaching methods, and assessments that celebrate and uphold white supremacy. Rather than treating for-profit reading programs like VIPs at the party, we ought to show them the door.

Doing so will free up time and money to give kids what they need. Every kid, for example, should major in citizenship, and we don't need Cambridge to teach it or the SBA to measure it. We measure students' citizenship by the actions students take. If they're on the front lines marching, if they're online posting, if they're arguing with the old order, then they are learning, and any so-called expert who claims otherwise needs to be schooled: our kids, during Covid, have proven their strength and creativity and compassion in ways few adults ever have.

What do all our citizen-students need? Praxis. Theory and practice. To tackle theory, kids need Civics, Street Law, and Media Literacy classes. They need literature classes that run like book clubs, where kids are laughing and crying through *Stamped* and *Ghost* and other books that let them know, as Jason Reynolds puts it, "You have a friend." For practice, kids need internships with local activist groups. They need big brothers and sisters from the Juvenile Justice Center. They need field trips to Puyallup restorative sweats and the Muckleshoot Tribe's technology classes. They need incarcerated folks to help teach them about prison. And they need the unhoused to help them understand, and end, homelessness.

Last spring saw too many students betrayed and abandoned by their schools. While attendance data are spotty to put it mildly, it's nonetheless clear that some 3 million enrolled K-12 students in the United States did not sign on to remote classes. They did not hand in a digital assignment. They fell away from the virtual learning opportunities we hustled like fake Rolexes. And then they got blamed! Currently it is common – and it is also wrong and absurd and hateful – to call our kids failures.

The failing is ours. Our most vulnerable students were driven away by a late-stage, last-gasp capitalist system that depends on elitism for its survival. The elite have no intention of sharing wealth and power, and for all their tragic flaws, stupidity is not among them. Corporate fascists see what's going on in the streets of America. They see the gathering storm, the groundswell movement, the people demanding change, and they will not have it. Not on their corporate watch!

The more people demand change, the harder the elite bear down on public schools, because schools – at least the democratic ones – make trouble for the powerful. Democratic schools nurture students who speak up, stand up, and fight back. The powerful respond by digging in and doubling down. They press on, cranking out the desired worker bees – and using the undesired to fuel the school-to-prison pipeline. This corrupt tactic has worked for generations. Indeed, what better method exists to maintain disparity and elevate the rich than to rig the education system?

Greed is the heart of the problem. Fortunately, another heart – a more robust and powerful one – is the solution, and teachers have the numbers, and the collective will, to perform a transplant! Backed by our union, we can undermine greed and force districts to get serious about redistribution of the resources that all kids need. These include access to technology and tutoring, food security, health care, dependable transportation, and mentors, advocates, and teachers who look like them. Without these basic necessities, our students will barely make it to the building, let alone focus and attend to class work. But if we offer substantive, ongoing support – if we really do reclaim schools for our students – they will come, and they will stay. And they might find a class that looks something like this middle school history course. Naturally the specifics vary, but the basic ingredients can work in all kinds of recipes for all kinds of educational kitchens!

8TH GRADE WORLD HISTORY

Goal: Today I Make Some Necessary Change
Opening:

- Land and Stolen Labor Acknowledgments, to remind us of our responsibilities
- The Do Now writing warm-up, to get brains and pencils moving.
- The Mood Meter (the college-level version, with 240 possibilities), to enable students to communicate how they're feeling and therefore how others might want to engage with them.
- The Class Meeting, to clear the air.

Activities & Topics:
Note: Activities are tasks tied to the day's (or week's, or term's) Topics.

Topics are nominated and agreed-upon by students. Dissenting students may be investigating individually chosen courses of study.

Activities and topics change up frequently, but all are related to some aspect of our Big 3, the Questions that guide our course. The Big 3 must engage and ultimately activate students, and activation is key: critical thinking that fails to compel critical action is useless in a post-Covid world.

While students generally brainstorm their own questions, experience shows that some types of questions seem to grab and hold kids' attention best, so we often stick with variants of these all-stars:

1. Why are some countries rich, and some poor?
2. What makes a society just or unjust?
3. How does change happen?

Activities are always changing, but in general they will fall into these categories:

- Mapping
- Research
- Data interpretation and analysis
- Discussion

- Action Planning
- Presentation/Performance/Individual Action
- Class Action
- Debrief/Evaluation/Future Focus

Topics are generated by students and often fall into one or more of these genres:

- Events
- Places
- Change makers
- Movements
- Time periods
- Problems and Crises

LAB

Students think, talk, and act.

There's nothing groundbreaking here, nothing particularly "innovative." But hopefully there is enough to arm our young. Hopefully they will leave the classroom and head into the larger world, and, as poet Wallace Steven exhorts, they will "piece the world together … "

Stevens cautions, "Not with your hands," and how right he is. Hands are clumsy and weak. But if we teachers do our job, the young will grow agile and strong. They will bring their kindled spirits to the task at hand, and they will nail it. Love Central will open its welcoming arms, and the future, for all, will burn bright.

CHAPTER SIX

The Remote Suburbs

PETER SURUDA

The quickest way to reform any system is to traumatize it. The trauma of the Covid era has changed schools irrevocably. Remote education during the pandemic put my students and me in a dizzying and painful age of adaptation. As we reopen our schools, we need to preserve our best adaptations in two areas: what we teach and how we reform. We also need to address issues made obvious by the events of the last few years.

I teach at Juanita, a comprehensive suburban high school outside Seattle. It's big – 1,600 or so students, with everything you might expect, a wide variety of academic programs, athletics, a vibrant PTSA, and growing diversity. I've been there 15 years.

Our community, Kirkland, was the earliest epicenter of the Coronavirus outbreak in the US. Cases were spiking at the Life Care facility next door to our school and at Evergreen Hospital on the other side. Those cases that were going to one day, like a miracle, disappear? That was us. On March 11, 2020, the governor shut down all schools in Washington. After a hasty pep talk, I was home, figuring out new interfaces and boiling down my curriculum to its essential bits. My colleagues and I swapped advice and we were off and running. Change radically and quickly, we were told.

I put together the most user-friendly material I had, short essays and stories, and wrote some questions. Everything came back by e-mail. A third of my students disappeared and the rest became my correspondents.

Half-way through the spring I assigned a compare-and-contrast essay. The students would compare their routines before and after the shutdown. They'd look at what was in front of them and write about it authentically.

Most of the students blew past the word limit. They had much to report. Families got sick with Covid. Parents lost their jobs. Students began working at grocery stores. The honor student cheerleader and the stoner skater both reexamined their lives. A sophomore migrated to her lenient mom's house so she could see her boyfriend. Softball players and baseball players were devastated when their seasons ended before they began. I asked students to expand on their best writing moments. They usually did. I had stumbled upon one of the defining attributes of successful remote learning.

SOCIAL EMOTIONAL LEARNING WAS CRUCIAL IN OUR SECONDARY SETTING

Elementary teachers devote lots of time to social emotional learning. Kids have rug time. Teachers conduct class meetings, where conflicts are worked out publicly and emotional health is modeled and praised. Traditionally, high school teachers assume students are ready to learn. A Calculus teacher rarely starts class with a meaningful check-in. Lessons about the subjunctive voice begin whether Chloe is prepared to grasp them or not. During remote learning, teachers and students did not see one another. We had to work hard to figure out if the people behind the icons had the bandwidth to learn. Over the course of our online year, we developed a system of check-ins that helped us know who was sick and who was well, who had a 3-year-old sister melting down, and who was at or beyond the breaking point. Invisible students were referred to counselors who were often able to contact families. They offered the families help and relayed crucial information back to the teachers.

The students educated us well. We learned which families were in crisis. Now that we were asking more, the students told us more.

Several students welcomed the remote learning; they were happy to be away from in person classes. Mason took up photography and was out shooting when he ran into me on my favorite walking trail one afternoon. At a reasonable distance, he summed up remote learning. "I feel like I'm learning as much and I'm working about as hard. I'm just not sitting through all the bullshit. Pardon my French." Our 3-hour day didn't waste much time. Students were free to do what they had to do or what they wanted to do. With his new hobby, Mason was probably an exception; many students leveled up in video games, spent months on their phones, or worked.

Holly was relieved that she didn't have to endure the guys who dominated every class discussion. For the first time, she could work on her essays and only on her essays. She was finally learning without flinching. We teachers knew we were trying to hear every voice. Holly reminded us that we had not hit that standard. The students who spent every spirit assembly staring at their phones didn't have to sit parked in the bleachers while the staff stood by the exits.

When we returned remotely in the fall of 2020, our school had a longer, better structured school day. The students soon began rebuilding community.

In a traditional high school year, a series of events roll by with a haphazard inertia. There's a homecoming football game and a dance. Seasonal decorations hit the walls. Assemblies punctuate the year, running the gamut from the frivolous homecoming assembly to the pious Veterans commemoration. Elections are held in the spring and the seniors have their moments as the year grinds to June. Almost all of these are patterned after last year's events. This continuity contributes to a sameness that ranges between comforting and insipid.

Remote schooling made most of this unworkable. It did not take long for our students to answer the more pressing needs of the community. Our remote learning week contains a homeroom period. When different student organizations offered content, our administration said yes, and the students were the teachers. Our African-American Student Advocacy Program taught during Black History Month. Their presentation on Black Lives Matter sprang from their own experiences and offered opportunities for engagement never seen in our MLK assemblies. The student ACLU club followed this with a lesson on qualified immunity and policing. The Period Club tackled the stigma of menstruation and ran a products drive. Voters were registered in homeroom. The Global Health students once again outdid the state curriculum, teaching a unit on Sexual Health and reproductive choices.

THE STUDENTS DETERMINED AND DELIVERED CURRICULUM

Before the lockdown, political tensions often bubbled up in our classrooms. During a unit on the Holocaust, we were learning about the Nuremburg Laws and the scapegoating of Jews in 1930s Germany. Maria blurted out that that was exactly what was going on with Mexican immigrants and Jack in the MAGA hat was instantly on his feet. I was now a referee trying to keep everyone safe. We never finished that dialog. Keeping everyone safe was often more important than keeping everyone talking.

After lockdown, the nation grappled with the murders of African Americans by police. Black Lives Matter marches made it to the suburbs. My students marched in their neighborhoods. In early June, armed militia members brandished weapons in downtown Kirkland. Students wrote about the murders of George Floyd, of Breonna Taylor, of Armaud Arbery. Caitlyn wrote about the twenty-dollar bill George Floyd was alleged to have passed. Andrew Jackson kept killing, she said, because his face lived on our money and his ideas lived in our history.

The presidential election season which divided the nation did not miss our students. In our check-ins the students often reported that the political volume was too loud, and the election season was far too long. We tried to make school the calmest hours of their days. In the aftermath of the January 6th insurrection, all teachers spent days listening to the students and reassuring them as well as we could. One sophomore summed up his anxiety over conspiracy theories. "Adults can't handle the internet." He had a point.

For years I taught a unit on logical fallacies to our juniors. The unit was usually well received; students enjoyed learning the Latin names and they could easily find obvious examples to present to their peers. Social media was the easiest place to find an Ad Hoc argument or an Ad Hominem attack.

Getting the students to acknowledge fallacies in their own thinking was always the tougher part of this unit. A few precocious students would finally admit their own missteps and, at least for a moment, we remembered not to always trust our own thoughts.

CRITICAL THINKING NEEDS TO BE TAUGHT AND REINFORCED AT EVERY GRADE LEVEL

For several years I had been teaching English to the neediest students. My bosses and I agreed that this did the most good. My classes were heavy on boys, heavy on English language learners, and heavy on students with IEPs. Even though they kept me on my toes, they were delightful. As I worked more with this population, our school moved into a co-teaching model. I was paired with a Special Ed teacher, and we learned to work as a team. By the 2019–2020 school year, I had been working with Jen for several years. We planned together and tweaked lessons. We met every morning and debriefed every afternoon. Jen is whip-smart, compassionate, and hard-working. We made a good team. The students flourished.

During the summer of 2020, I was offered an intern teacher. I accepted, hoping the pandemic would lift. Collin would be working with Jen and me for the fall. When the pandemic continued unabated, we set about constructing our digital partnership.

Having a teaching team saved our remote school year. We met each morning on our TEAMS platform, video chatting and planning away. Collin experimented with the teaching technology. We were accountable to each other, and we had to talk out all our collective decisions. Throw in Collin's supervisor from the university program, and there was a solid team of adults trying to get our students through this unprecedented year. Any one of us could suffer a computer malfunction or a particularly tough day and the others took up the slack. In the digital classroom, we traded tasks. One of us took attendance. One of us monitored the student chat. One of us delivered direct instruction. We read incoming assignments in turns.

All my colleagues in English formed tight teams. While most could not double up in classes, everyone planned together as never before. Each grade band (9th, 10th, 11th, 12th) came up with common curriculum, common presentations, and common assessments. Our administration trusted us to innovate.

ANY TEACHING CONFIGURATION THAT PUT MORE ADULTS IN THE CLASSROOM RESULTED IN HEALTHIER LEARNERS AND MORE LEARNING

Juanita plans to place support personnel in classrooms and to continue team teaching long after we normalize instruction.

During our remote teaching, our curriculum and teaching methods shifted with dizzying speed. When schools first restarted remotely in the Spring of 2020, schools acted as if the students would continue earning letter grades for their transcripts. When too many students began failing, my district, like every district around us, radically altered our grading policies. Any student who showed any engagement earned an A.

In the fall, we returned to A through F grades. We spent our pre-teaching prep days paring down curriculum. We would focus on the most crucial learning standards in each course. We would only give points for demonstrated learning, not for attendance, participation, or turning in a signed copy of the class rules. As we looked at every adjustment before us, we resolved to strike a balance of compassion and the right amount of rigor.

In our system, a high school student has a seven-class schedule. By mid-October, the students let us know we got the whole workload balance wrong. When grades began plummeting and parents tipped us off to students crying or falling asleep at their laptops, we adjusted again. A graded assignment every week from every class was far too much work. We again shifted our approach. In online meeting after online meeting, the entire faculty reexamined our approach to assessment and homework.

Our utterly reasonable adjustments seem remarkable when contrasted with the usual reform in any school. Schools are rarely reformed from the bottom up. During my time teaching, I've been reformed upon by presidents, by state education officials, and by committees somewhere up my district food chain. Curriculum publishers land a deal with a district or a new book on pedagogy takes hold. The next August, I'm being pitched a new approach at a staff meeting. Teachers are asked to turn to their table neighbors and brainstorm how we will implement that year's innovation. We give it a good look. If the reform is sound, it leaves a positive residue on our classroom practice in May. When the reform isn't sound, we all figure it out and move on.

During remote learning, we pivoted nimbly to the needs of families, to national catastrophes, and to the performance of the students.

SCHOOLS WILL REFORM RAPIDLY AND WISELY WHEN GIVEN AUTONOMY

In Washington, students take a battery of state assessments, usually in the spring. I have proctored these for most of my teaching career. The tests have evolved from booklets and bubble sheets to on-line tests, all of them designed to measure student progress in learning state standards. No matter what the delivery method, the tests begin with an elaborate materials check ("Raise your hand if your name is incorrect/if you do not see the state testing browser on your laptop/if you need a piece of scratch paper") and a scripted pep talk. I read off the intentions of the test, a list of consequences for non-compliance ("Yes, it's a graduation requirement"), and an admonishment to do well. I am prohibited from helping students or looking at the materials. Then the classroom becomes silent and we get it done.

Several months later, scores arrive from the testing companies. Educators up and down the chain of command grind the data. The next fall, teachers spend meeting time looking at the data. We generally learn what we knew; our relatively affluent students do better than the state average. English Language Learners, poor students, and students of color don't do as well as the white students. All educators know this already. Working to produce equitable outcomes is our biggest challenge.

In both of our remote years, the state cancelled their tests. I cannot imagine the students would have taken them seriously without the teachers standing in the room. The data never arrived this fall. The data will not arrive next fall. No teacher, parent, student, or administrator is going to miss it.

ELIMINATING STANDARDIZED TESTS HAD NO EFFECT ON STUDENT LEARNING OR WELL-BEING

The past two school years have traumatized schools. This trauma revealed existing needs. The underserved and unengaged students were obvious; a few spoke up and many drifted away. Educators worked hard to pull them back and to re-engage them. As we did, we realized just how many students could not thrive in a remote setting, just how many students were living beyond the edge of engagement.

This trauma created new needs as well. Many families were poorer. Students took jobs and school mattered much less. The pandemic and the quarantine, political turmoil, and our pivot to online school took a toll on all of us. Families across the economic spectrum fractured. Some students disengaged and some became diminished versions of themselves. Many students have spent the years muddling through in a depression. There's much healing to be done.

As we reopen schools, we have to acknowledge this trauma and act accordingly. Students will need more reconnection and safety. Educators will dedicate more time to checking in, to offering appropriate resources, to giving authentic voice to the many. At the same time, we will have to determine just what skills the students need to move beyond school into productive, responsible citizenship. With bold vision, compassion, and superhuman effort, the students will go on to shape a better world.

FOR FURTHER STUDY

Sheltered Instructional Observation Protocol (https://www.cal.org/siop/).
The SIOP Model* is a research-based and validated model of sheltered instruction that has been widely and successfully used across the U.S. for over 15 years Professional development in the SIOP Model helps teachers plan and deliver lessons that allow English learners to acquire academic knowledge as they develop English language proficiency.
Hammond, Z. (2014). *Culturally responsive teaching and the brain: Promoting authentic engagement and rigor among culturally and linguistically diverse students.* Corwin Press.
Social justice teaching: The Holocaust Center for Humanity in Seattle. Holocaust Center for Humanity – Home (holocaustcenterseattle.org)
The American Civil Liberties Union, Washington State. https://www.aclu-wa.org/teachers-students.

SECTION FOUR

WHAT OUR CHILDREN NEED TO LEARN

School has looked like school for a very long time. Classroom photos from a hundred years ago look uncomfortably familiar, and the curriculum and structure of the school day would be familiar as well. The structure of K-12 and secondary education is built around the so-called Carnegie Unit, developed by Andrew Carnegie in 1906 in order to establish a pension system for educators. The unit was developed as a measure of the amount of time a student has studied a subject. To qualify for participation in the Carnegie pension system, higher education institutions were required to adopt a set of basic standards around courses of instruction, facilities, staffing, and admissions criteria. The Carnegie Unit, also known as the credit hour, became the basic unit of measurement both for determining students' readiness for college and their progress through an acceptable program of study. Over time, the Carnegie Unit became the building block of modern American education, serving as the foundation for everything from daily school schedules to graduation requirements, faculty workloads, and eligibility for federal financial aid (Silva, White, & Toch, n.d.).

To repeat, the Carnegie unit that has formed the fundamental building block of the American educational system was essentially a bookkeeping strategy for developing a pension system for teachers. Carnegie was an "industrialist," a capitalist with a capital "C," not an educator, and the focus on seat time rather than on what subject matter students needed to learn, or the quality of that learning rather than the number of hours sitting in class has left open many questions about what the content of our educational system should be. Many of the decisions made about what students need to study, and for how long were made decades ago, and there is increasing questioning of whether those decisions still apply in today's world, much less the future.

The recent efforts by states (particularly southern states) to pretend that slavery did not happen (or to minimize its impact), to eliminate any analysis of the impact that slavery and racism have had on our history, and to minimize or eliminate an honest study of the genocide and relocation that was carried out by "settlers" against indigenous people who were guilty only of living where the European invaders wanted to live makes depressingly clear that decisions about content are as much (or more) political, economic, and ideological as they are educational, and that's a problem. It is hard to imagine how hiding painful (but accurate) aspects of our history serves a society that continues to wrestle with white supremacy, racism, and inequality.

The particulars are unique to our time, but the contested nature of curriculum has been with us throughout our entire history. There are many questions wrapped up in the debate about the curriculum and content our schools should offer, questions such as these: What do we value most and how can we help our students understand those values? What do our children need to learn, and on what basis do we make that decision? Who should be making that decision? What do our students care most about, what is of most interest to them, and should that matter in how we educate them? Should everyone learn the same curriculum no matter where they live? What skills and dispositions will help our children to deal with the overwhelming volume of information they encounter, to recognize the information they can trust and to see through the smoke and mirrors of the bogus claims that appear on their screens. How do we best prepare students to be ready to deal with an unpredictable, unknowable future?

The chapters that follow offer thoughts on aspects of what our young people should be learning and how we might help them to do that. There is a focus on skills, on content, on the intersectional nature of the world and the ways we teach/learn about it, and some clear focus on specific content. The authors in this section point to the incredible range and complexity of the questions about what our children need to learn, and how we need to adddress those questions rather than mindlessly continuing the curriculum that was handed to us. They obviously cannot take on every aspect of content and curriculum in the limited space of these few chapters, but hopefully they will inspire readers to reconsider what is most essential about our work as educators, what it is that will best serve our learners, and how we can transform our classrooms so that we are placing the most time and attention on what matters most, and what holds most meaning for our young people.

REFERENCE

Silva, E., White, T., & Toch, T. (n.d.). The Carnegie unit: A century-old standard in a changing education landscape. Carnegie Foundation for the Advancement of Teaching. Retrieved from: https://www.luminafoundation.org/files/resources/carnegie-unit-report.pdf

CHAPTER SEVEN

Risk, Inquiry, and Learning

DON FELS

In 2019 I traveled to Central Asia to conduct research and teach the art of research to undergraduates in Tashkent, Uzbekistan. Being and working there was a fabulous experience, even though my efforts to introduce research to the students were an abysmal failure. Uzbekistan is just now coming out from the shadow of Joseph Stalin, who died in 1953. The heavy lid that he and the Russian government clamped over inquiry was left firmly in place by the Uzbek government when the country became independent in 1991. Asking questions was extremely dangerous for generations.

Intentionally, the previously public censorship became internalized; citizens were discouraged from openly or even secretly being curious. Not surprisingly, though they are no longer being actively censored, my young students acted as though they were. They told me that research is only for important scientists in their laboratories. When I pointed out to them that they all do some research all the time, looking on the web for things to do, buy, people to meet or things to think about, they just laughed.

Unfortunately, their refusal to consider doing research is far from funny or inconsequential. It presents a huge deficit for the young country and was essentially the reason I was brought there to teach. At the same time my students were trying to figure out why I or their university thought they should learn how to carry out research, a large new building was taking shape directly across the road from their school.

The new building is to house the new Ministry of Pre-school Education. The country's president, recognizing that there are enormous and important gaps in the education system of Uzbekistan, has declared the entire curriculum in need of revising. Wisely, in my opinion, he has begun his re-forming efforts with pre-school, reckoning that if children and their teachers can get off on the right foot, the rest will follow. Thinking about the two buildings across from one another has me thinking about the relationship of early education to university teaching and learning. I was told the country's leadership, unhappy with the amount of original research being done in the country, decided to try and change that.

As it happens, I spent many years teaching at both ends of the age spectrum (and several years teaching the intervening grades as well). Though I eventually settled into teaching graduate and post-grad students, I admit that I preferred working with much younger students, which I did for a couple of decades. There are plenty of reasons for this, but primarily I enjoyed the chance to interact with the openly curious and help them find ways to extend their joy of inquiry.

I would like to explore here why I think the penchant to question the world underlies or should underlie all true education, why it very often does not, and how in the future we might help encourage it in that direction. I will do so by looking at early childhood education, knowing that right across the street is higher education. And down the block, so to speak, is the rest of life. We know from the pandemic that preparation for the unknown cannot be accomplished by memorizing the answers to what has already happened.

The word "intelligence" derives from a compound Latin word that from its origins meant to choose between. Very much still today, if students are to exercise their native intelligence, they must be adept at choice-making. To make choices means being open to risk, or even openly courting it. Faced with a choice, one is forced to leave one possibility behind while embracing the other. What if such a course of action leads to a dead-end, embarrassment, or even failure?

One doesn't get more intelligent or learn to exercise one's intelligence by being reticent to try. And yet, I would argue that most of what passes as education not only doesn't encourage choice-making, or question-asking, but actively discourages it.

The essential problem with education at most all levels is that the teacher is positioned as a police person. S/he is there to direct traffic and impose sanctions when rules are broken. There is an expected outcome, answer, path, as defined in the rulebook/curriculum. There is a correct answer, which of course implies there are a great many incorrect ones.

If the teacher is there to enforce order, and if order implies pre-determined answers and responses, then clearly it would be exhausting, disturbing, and crazy-making to spend hours in a classroom full of little or even big persons each making independent choices, choices that might be the right ones for them, while less right for others.

But if we might see education as helping children to become as intelligent as possible and helping them learn how to make the choices that seem most interesting and efficacious for themselves, the teacher becomes facilitator, not enforcer. Instead of upholding a rigid set of rules, the teacher becomes an activator of a number of possibilities. I realize that to many this will seem anathema. It implies that the classroom be a free-for-all, a kind of race where everyone is running in every conceivable direction.

Yet some of the directions that children might choose to explore are knowable upfront. If I am aware that 5yr-olds are particularly interested in how animals make their homes, it would not be out of place for me to be ready to help young minds find out about that part of the universe. There might be many ways in which kids become curious about such a matter. They might find a nest, they might watch a litter of kittens being cared for by a mother cat, they might see pictures in a book, or a cartoon on TV. Or they might be convinced they are an animal and naturally wonder what their home would be like.

Since most teachers didn't have the opportunity to learn at school as I've sketched out here, it is unreasonable to expect that they would automatically embrace such an approach to conducting a classroom. It is too scary and too open to what they might imagine would look like failure. What about the parents, the other teachers, the principal? I am not writing this lightly. I do understand how threatening this would appear to the teacher. Because I am temperamentally inclined to being very curious about the world, and equally shall we say disinclined to following rules, I didn't worry about these things. But I can see the dilemma for those who do.

Yet, though it might be uncomfortable at first and might be very difficult to embrace such a seemingly non-sensical approach to teaching, the rewards are enormous, for students and teachers. I would argue, that unless education shifts profoundly in this direction, teachers cannot properly prepare their students for the uncertain times ahead.

If students are primarily prepared to root out certain answers and responses, as if they were pigs digging for truffles, they will be lost and deeply disappointed when none are to be found. If on the other hand students are taught how to look for what might be effective ways to make choices and discoveries, the malleability that is built into that way of thinking will serve them throughout their lives.

Mental agility can and should be learned at school. This is a rudimentary skillset, not unlike learning to ride a two-wheeler. Every kid knows from looking at the bike that there is no way it will stay upright, let alone carry them along. Yet she also knows from watching other kids happily whiz by on their bicycles, that riding one must be simple and fun once the process is understood.

One of the inherent screw-ups in the practice of education in most schools most of the time is that the teachers aren't modeling the behavior that might enthrall and motivate the students they teach. I know from my own education and watching my son go through school, that the teachers who got the most from me were the ones who seemed the most different and unknowable at first. They startled, stimulated, and excited me. I wasn't at all sure what to expect, even after months together. They kept me on my toes and paying close attention. I couldn't wait to be with them.

Entering the pre-school classroom for the first time, the children, and even some of their parents, were literally shocked to see me there. They expected, and had every right to expect, a woman. In those days, most of the children in my classes saw far less of their fathers than mothers. Being with children was not what most fathers did except perhaps on the weekends. I was usually one of very few, or the only male, wherever I taught.

One of the attributes I brought to the class was that I existed outside of the child's experience and expectations. I mention my "advantage" in this regard only because I believe it is a key component of every teacher's job to surprise their students, to keep them guessing, wondering and figuring things out.

In my classroom, we had "circle time" every day. We used the time sitting together on the floor to discuss ideas that kids had questions about, to look at books together, to talk about something of interest that someone wanted to share. And from time to time, I brought in a cloth bag with an object or two inside, collected from my wanderings in the city, the country, the Goodwill, or my studio. I would open the bag, take out the object(s) which would be placed on the floor in the middle of the circle.

My question was always the same: what do you think this is? The object would be passed around for the kids to touch and examine up close. They always had answers, almost never did they "correctly" identify the thing immediately (unsurprisingly, since I picked things that I hoped would be puzzling to them).

I never told them they were incorrect but did help the discussion head in a productive direction. I would ask many questions – why did she think it was a (...), what suggested that? Bit by bit, the group would try out several hypotheses. I encouraged them to say if and why they thought an answer may not have been the best possible one. With experience they became wonderfully fluid and creative about guessing and narrowing their inquiries. If the object had a protuberance in the corner, how come? Why was it green? Was it a part of a machine, if so, what do you suppose the machine did?

The kids loved the guessing game and surprisingly they often actually figured out what the object might have been used for. They also conjured up their own plausible stories of what the thing was, calling it by a name that suggested its use. I went along with this as long as the use assigned by them bore logical consistency, which we tested together as I asked more questions. We had a shelf where we put these objects in the class, and from then on everyone remembered their names and "purpose." My interest in doing this, besides the fun it provided the kids, was to help them learn to think critically, to sharpen their ability to make sense of the unknown.

If you can't make guesses about the universe, and try out those guesses, how in the world will you develop knowledge about how things work or are put together? If everything you know is pre-sorted, pre-described, and pre-digested, how do you develop the means for doing that classifying yourself?

Young kids have the capacity to test out theories and ideas but are not always given the opportunity. Nor do adults always take seriously their conjectures. My rule of thumb was to ask why, perhaps even more than the young kids themselves. Essentially, I was helping them examine the logic behind their ideas. I wasn't interested in the "validity" of their ideas, but in the consistency of their thought process. Young children have had limited experiences in the world, so it makes sense that assumptions based on their experience can be short-sighted. But they can certainly learn to think critically, and that thinking can and should stretch out beyond their immediate world.

Children's imaginations are rich and wonderful. When they would imagine some function for one of the things I brought in, we would follow those ideas as far as we could. If they held together, the other kids and I were happy to go along with the given explanation. I would be careful to say," well that could be." Sometimes another child would "correct" me and explain why the offered explanation couldn't be, pointing up the logical inconsistencies. I would congratulate the interlocutor for pointing out problems with our conclusions. I would say something like, "I should have thought of that." I wanted them to understand that just because something can be imagined, it is not necessarily true.

When in our circle time an idea or question came up that was new to kids, I tried not to provide the answer myself. I would suggest that likely the school library could be of help. I would then send a couple of kids off to the library. The librarian was a very willing participant in this sport. She would help them find books that might hold a key to finding the answer, and they would return to the class with the books. I'd look at them after class and pick one or two to share with the kids the following day.

Most of these children were not yet readers. But I was trying to help them believe that books held knowledge, and that by consulting them they could find out stuff. I wanted them to know that looking in books was a fine way to do research. I would pick some parts of the books to read aloud to them, reminding them of the information we were seeking. Then I'd ask if the book had provided us with the information that we sought. If not, we'd discuss how else we could find what we were looking for. Maybe another trip to the library, and/or an invitation to an adult one of the kids knew who might be able to join us at circle time with more information.

When I was trying to teach the undergraduates in Tashkent about doing research, I pointed out to them that in America grade-schoolers do research projects and continue to do them throughout their schooling. Because I was trying to make the point that research is a "normal" school activity, I didn't tell them that unfortunately most of the research projects students do in school are not very useful to them. This is because usually the kids aren't free to research subjects of their own particular interest but must choose subjects from a list provided.

The process of doing research is often misunderstood to mean finding and parroting information that is "certified" by others. Real research is the act of examining something about which the researcher (in this case the child) knows very little, but about which s/he might want to know more. The act of searching and synthesizing what's found is what's important. Critical thinking comes into the process in several ways – figuring out where to look, learning how to evaluate and prioritize what's found, and then how to report the results. Choices must be made all along the way.

The teaching profession badly needs people who badly want to teach. To attract those who might be the right people to inspire the young, the profession needs to be attractive to them. If teaching is accomplished in a way that excites the curiosity of the children and invites them in as I have very briefly outlined above, it leaves the teacher energized and grateful for the interactions with the kids and the wisdom they bring. It's very exciting work to see children grow emotionally and intellectually blossom, to see them open-up to possibilities they knew precious little about. I never grew tired of watching it happen. I felt privileged to be able to facilitate the acquisition of knowledge and experience.

Teaching children, perhaps because it has always been there, has failed miserably to project itself as the life-transforming activity it can and should be. Transformative for the students, for the teachers, and the greater society. It offers the possibility to create work environments as laboratories of human development, where everything is on view, and feasible.

I viewed my teaching with young children as on-going problem solving. What did the children need, and how could I help them get there? This meant I stepped back as much as possible and observed their interactions. Much of what transpires in early childhood education is social development, young beings learning how they might benefit from being with other young people. I watched and tried to think about how I could perhaps help a glitch occur with less frequency, how I could help strengthen the resolve of a child to try something new.

We all possess strengths and areas in which we are less strong. I needed to observe to understand as much as I could about the children's strengths. In the laboratory that was our classroom, I might suggest a child try a particular activity to see how it went, and then depending on the amount of engagement and success, recommend another. This trial and error on both of our parts gave us a chance to feel safe and explore together. It was predicated on my paying close attention, not as a cop or a judge, but as an investigative reporter.

To my mind the teaching of children in American schools is terribly hindered by self-fulfilling prophecies. Often, people who are not particularly excited about discovering the world are put in charge of both teaching teachers and teaching children. They expect the children to behave and to pass curricular rubrics. They might be pleased that the children develop curiosities and special knowledge but are unprepared to consistently help bring those discoveries about within the classroom.

Children often encounter things of interest by accident, but in a successful classroom, it is no accident that those discoveries are being made. Without discovery, children cannot appropriately test the boundaries of their world, and without that testing, they cannot fully develop their inherent intelligence. Personally, this failure becomes a lifelong tragedy for the children, and a great burden for the society in which they will long exist as adults.

CHAPTER EIGHT

Social Studies, Intersectionality, and the Re Humanizing of Education

A Conversation with Jerry Price

Doug: Everything happens in some context, in some place, with a history, or several intersecting histories, with political and economic consequences, the stuff of social studies. As the social studies coordinator for Washington State, it would be great to have your perspective as you are trying to help educators in Washington be more effective in serving all our students with an education that better prepares them to deal with the present and future.

Perhaps we can ground our conversation on four areas you've mentioned before. The first is culturally responsive teaching and the folly of anti-Critical Race Theory activism; the second is civic action and empowering students to engage in wrestling with policy solutions to solve community problems. The third is civics as a transdisciplinary practice; and the fourth is what inquiry-based learning looks like in the context of culturally responsive humanizing practices.

Let's start with that first point of view. Critical Race Theory, is clearly generating a lot of heat around certain parts of the country, with some states trying to actually prevent teachers using CRT or firing them if they do. This reminds me of that movie *The Princess Bride*, where one of the characters keeps saying, I don't think that term means what you think it means. When we are thinking about Critical Race Theory what are we talking about?

Jerry: One of the things we seem to be doing is conflating Critical Race Theory and culturally responsive teaching practices, or any critique of historical wrongdoing. Culturally responsive teaching practices, and Ethnic Studies as a subset of CRTP are not Critical Race Theory, which is a specific lens in the legal education community for analyzing systems put in place to uphold white supremacy, such as redlining.

One of the things that we're talking about within the context of ethnic studies I think applies across social studies. We have to first bring in the identity of the students that we have in front of us, and really honor that. I want to emphasize that I am not an expert in ethnic studies, and I make no claim to be, but I think that many of the main tenets of ethnic studies are aligned with high quality social studies instruction.

The first entry point to connecting students to the complexities of the larger world is through their identity, who they are and how where they come from has helped to shape that. The second entry point is civic action. Once we understand who we are and the water we're swimming in, how do we identify things that we have agreement on where we can take collective action for the common good? I have heard concerns locally and nationally that if you give students a voice, they're all going to become activists and leave the classroom and take to the streets. There's this idea that somehow giving access to the tools to create civic engagement and action is going to radicalize students. But that's not the intent at all. I taught in a very conservative community, a "red state community" for more than two decades. We taught civics all year as part of social studies, including civic action. When we engaged in civic action as part of our social studies courses, kids identified problems in our community, and they weren't red problems or blue problems, not democratic or republican problems; they were problems that impacted students and their community. Students were concerned about the lack of a traffic light where they had to cross a highway to get to and from school, and the nutritional value of the food served at school. Kids had domestic abuse issues or homeless issues or drug abuse issues that are prevalent throughout our society they wanted addressed. These concerns are not specific to urban or rural or suburban settings. The kids recognize each as problems that they could engage in addressing. No matter what the issue, they had to ask the same fundamental questions: What tools do I need? Who are the people in power I need to talk to in order to engage in this change? What can I do on my own? What information do I have, what information do I need?

So you have these ideas of identity and being able to express themselves and to see themselves reflected in the classroom, and then taking action on problems and issues of concern to them.

The third entry point is history. How does learning about history from more than one perspective, not just a traditional Eurocentric perspective, but from other, traditionally underrepresented stories or narratives change our knowledge of the world? How does that help students have a clearer picture of our collective history? How does that help us create a more just and equitable society?

The thing I didn't do well when I was in the classroom was to engage all of these questions of identity, civic action, and history using the lens of power. In my current position I have had the privilege of learning so much about this from Dr. Vera Velez at Western Washington University and Brooke Brown, a world class educator in Tacoma. Initially, perhaps, I may have talked about who in government or society has the power, the control over situations and our lives and where does that control come from? That critique of power is not unusual in a traditional social studies classroom. What Vero and Brooke emphasized to me is that it's not just the idea of looking back at the harms that have occurred because of the power structures in place over time, but also looking at regenerative and restorative power, turning our focus forward and talking about how we can re humanize education. How can we bring joy into the classroom? You have to have power in order to do that. How do we focus on the future and on improving opportunities for all of our students? And maybe that has to do with rethinking how we do education, maybe that has to do with how we decide what curriculum is or is not used, or once again, going back to the idea of community-based education, or education informed by the community. If I'm living in Yakima, my community may have a large migrant labor community. What are the things that are important for those families? What do they feel that their children need to know and be able to do? If I'm in central Seattle and I've got a significant Japanese American or Vietnamese population, what are my local resources? How are my kids seen and recognized in the classroom? Different communities, with different contexts, have different wants and needs for their children.

Doug: This brings us back to what do our young people need to know, what do we need to help them learn if they are going to live in a world that is sustainable and supportive of all of us? My assumption is that too many teachers do not know enough to bring this educational experience to our children. The teacher corps is still overwhelmingly white, many from suburbs, and many were taught in ways that kept them from asking the questions they needed to ask, or from even knowing there were questions to ask about the history they were taught, and that was in their textbooks. If those who are teaching don't know the history, don't understand how to honor the cultures and experiences, the identities of their students, how can they serve them? And how can we help the teachers, current and future, to learn?

Jerry: Something that's hopeful is some great work being done around standards. There is an elevation of critical thinking skills and a de-emphasis on pages of disconnected content. It used to be the focus was, teach this specific content, and then also teach your kids how to cite, to use APA, or whatever. And now, we've gone so much more towards an inquiry model, where we say, okay, how do you recognize when somebody is lying to you or not? How do I engage in a conversation about a controversial topic where I can support my reasoning with evidence?

Based on what I have learned, I think ethnic studies helps students develop these inquiry skills. What are the stories that aren't being told, or that we're not aware of? What are the narratives that we need to hear? There's been a lot of debate across the state about this and concerns that the standards have been whitewashed. The last revision of standards removed a lot of prescriptive content, a long list of specific facts to teach. Those were replaced with inquiry questions teachers could ask students to research, to dig deeper. The problem with that is that when you are prescriptive, you can suggest specific content and teachers who may not know those topics at least are prompted to look it up or figure out what it means. But we were running into the problem in that it created a canon where even though they were suggested content, they were often turned into items on a checklist of what to teach, to the exclusion of deeper, richer exploration and inquiry.

Doug: What guides those kinds of conversations or what grounds them, because those conversations and decisions are crucial. And I'm thinking that many of the people who are having to make those decisions were educated within a system that didn't necessarily value ethnic studies or teaching in a way that honored and included all students. How do we learn to do better?

Jerry: It's going to be generational, and I think that's part of that tension. There are a lot of us who want this to happen now, think that it should have happened 20 years ago, 50 years ago, 100 years ago. We are thinking about how we promote the most effective and welcoming ways of engaging in these questions. What do we need to do differently, to be more supportive of an anti-racist, culturally responsive delivery of content? And part of that is those little conversations that we're having that are transdisciplinary, where we say, how can we help students encounter the content in a more integrated, connected way? That also means coordinating with pre-service education, so then it becomes a much bigger question of how do we engage with higher ed, and how does higher ed influence K 12? It goes to graduation requirements. One of the things I have heard suggested is, could we have more of a social sciences credit requirement so we can get our geography back in, so we can get our human geography or our creative writing, or poetry courses. Right now, your choices of what you can take are very limited by categories you need for graduation.

I feel like we're on a slow path towards some re humanization of teaching and learning. I am really proud of our work in Washington, especially with folding in tribal, indigenous knowledge. That has done wonders for the thinking around courses like biology, and courses like social studies, where we're bringing in sovereignty and the idea of what that means and wrestling with ideas around genocide. I think we're really wrestling with how to incorporate ethnic studies without creating 100 new standards because we already have too many. How do we do this dance? We have a lot of work being done to create opportunities for a more accurate and inclusive story to be told. We are building Holocaust and genocide education, ethnic studies, and African American studies, which is a kind of ethnic studies. These are all legs of a culturally responsive "stool," and then I see civic action, that's sort of the table top on which these legs support, so how do we do this?

I think intentionality is an important part of the work. My mantra has been forever, when everything is important, nothing is important. So how do we stop ourselves from creating that listserv where you have 5,000 sources, and nobody knows which one is the one they really should look out to get the nuggets? What's the starting point? I think that's really what we're wrestling with. And if I'm an educator, and I have 9 months and a scope and sequence and I am told to do education the way we've been doing education – go an inch deep and a mile wide, instead of a mile deep and a couple feet wide – how can I possibly succeed?

Doug: That's part of what I was saying earlier. We might need to start with the question, what is it our kids really need to learn and how can we organize to help them learn it? I mean, assuming that one of the functions of society is educating our young, what is it they need if they're going to live in a way that works for the planet that works for their community that works for themselves? What do they need to know? And then asking, in what ways does what is happening currently in schools support that, and in what ways does it undermine it?

Jerry: I'm seeing a lot of success in problem-based learning. With support, students identify a problem they care about and that they engage with, and the teacher helps them to learn and then apply that skill set, regardless of what your content is, to solve the problem. In Washington we have a gift in that districts are supposed to partner with their local tribe to teach about the history, culture, and lifeways of that tribe. This creates incredible opportunity for problem-based learning, such as food sovereignty, or understanding the meaning of "usual and custom" in the treaties.

Doug: It's also a way of teaching or a context that enables you to teach those skills in a way that the kids are listening, because they need to know because they want to know, they want to be able to do X. Helping kids have a reason to want to learn those skills and inquiry processes in a context that matters to them.

Jerry: That's what drives me so crazy about the civics conversation is when people are like, you just need to know the three branches of government. Sure, but for most students their city council member has far more effect on their daily life than the president of the United States does, so let's teach them where those structures exist, within their own community, instead of focusing exclusively on the federal system. If I, as a student, create an initiative to propose the school day start an hour later so that I am not falling asleep in my first period class, what is the actual process, besides writing an email to my principal, which will likely go nowhere? What is the process for actually taking community action to solve a problem? And how do I get the data?

Doug: Civic action, I'm just going back to your four points. So culturally responsive teaching, starting with who the kids are, where they come from, how they find out about where they come from, through whose lenses they have learned to see, and what they care about. Civic action, we've talked about. Civics as a transdisciplinary offering. I'm haunted by the people who keep banging on the door to open civics up to the way it was and thinking, how much of a tool of the status quo civics education can be. Let's describe the three branches of government. Well, where does Mitch McConnell and his pledge to do everything he can to make democratic presidents fail, fit into that? Where does dark money fit in? How does government really work? I remember seeing Howard Zinn give a talk about how all three branches represent the same class, the moneyed class. They're all on the same side. They're not checking or balancing anything. If you want to actually get something done, what really brings change?

Jerry: I think students have a lot of influence when they engage in civic action. For example, we just had an initiative in Washington, which has been on the table for a couple of years about menstrual products in schools. There were a lot of questions. Who's going to manage the products? How much is it going to cost? But when 15-and-16-year-old kids, mostly girls, showed up to testify, the members of the legislature heard them. The students were confident and unflinching. It was transformative. And legislators seeing a human face, a young human face around the policy question that they were wrestling with helped them to see human beings who were suffering because they didn't have access to something that they should have had available to them.

Doug: And maybe some of those folks had daughters. How do we help people who have not been brought up this way as educators to start making that transformation? Because if we're going to move forward, there is a transition that's required. And you're clearly working on that in the state. So how are you thinking about it? What are you learning about that process?

Jerry: I think we're struggling. We are trying to figure out how to honor the labor of the people who are working on it and everything else. I think exposure is so much of the battle. Districts who have done their own work are implementing, or thinking about implementing, ethnic studies because now they recognize it, and they see the value and they see the connection, they see that it's not scary. I'm working on a civics project now, because I wanted to provide more examples for communities that may not, or students who may not recognize all of the potential places for civic action in their community. We started talking about how there are a lot of barriers and challenges that marginalized communities are encountering, whether that's because a student's parent is incarcerated or because there is a refugee with a language barrier. We've started a project and we're just finishing up our first animation, it's five minutes long, basically a former student telling their story of what it was like to be homeless as a student, and we hired an animator to animate it. We won't be able to do a lot of that because it is expensive, but we were able to map out the sort of transdisciplinary opportunities for civic action, places where we see that students may not recognize that they have power to solve a problem. We looked at English language learners, we looked at special education and access to resources, we looked at tribal sovereignty and native education, we looked at environmental sustainability, and what's going on there. So we created these sort of spokes of stories that we wanted to tell. And then we just started going out to the community and asking for who wanted to tell their story and I was expecting it to be a struggle. And people are coming out of the woodwork. They just want to talk about the difficulties they're encountering.

We have Iraqi parents talking about how they were professors in Iraq and are now working menial labor jobs in the United States and their kids are severely developmentally delayed and they have a language barrier. What does it look like to try to go to school? We have a story from a collaborator of a kid who was in a refugee camp who got a head injury and is developmentally delayed who continues to persevere even though he's been subjected to discipline because he didn't understand rules that were never explained clearly. We're just starting to pile up these stories. And one of the things that we're wrestling with is this started out as a service, a civic action project, but some of these stories aren't age appropriate for kids. Number one, there is too much trauma, without a lot of scaffolding, but also, there's a lot of stress here that teachers probably are not aware of that are in their classrooms every day. So how can we reframe? We have some of these that are in these buckets for student civic action projects. Maybe there are kids in my community that can't get services they need because they don't speak English well, or maybe there's a homeless issue that I'm not aware of, that I can help engage our community in solving. But then there are ones that are really, it gets to your idea that teachers are often unaware of what's happening in their classrooms. You know, some teachers are gifted in developing those relationships, or maybe there is a go-to teacher in the school for kids who are trans or are homeless, or whatever the case may be. But, you know, a teacher may say, that's not my job. My job is to teach chemistry. My job is to teach geometry. So how do we start engaging? How do we understand the stories that our kids want to tell, need to tell, or sometimes don't want to tell?

Doug: And it's not enough to just know or care about chemistry; we are teaching children. Which raises the question again, who should be teaching? How do we change the hoops, the hurdles that too often keep out people who are great with kids, who are strong learners and communicators and maybe poor test takers, or who have been turned off by the hyper focus on testing and rigid, uncreative lessons? That question is a crucial one, rethinking policies that keep potentially great teachers from teaching?

Jerry: There are concerns from some that white teachers should not be teaching ethnic studies, because it's not their story to tell us, not their narrative. And that butts up against the reality that the teaching corps where I live is mostly white and is not changing any time soon. So rather than saying teachers can't teach it, how do we provide scaffolds and supports to make sure that those teachers understand how to access those stories appropriately and respectfully and without caveats, and that's been a real struggle. It's really important, so now it's like, okay, we're going to have this, how do we provide high quality, professional development and make sure that we're not doing harm to kids?

I think this is work that needs to be done in community. I'm deeply committed to the work, but probably, push comes to shove a 50-year-old white guy is probably not the person who should be making these decisions alone. We've been working, together, on getting there. These conversations are complicated. And, you know, I say that from a point of privilege, I can't imagine trying to be, for example, Hispanic teacher, Hispanic family, trying to engage in this conversation with, with the power structures of a district or an ESD, or a state office. I am committed to doing better.

CHAPTER NINE

Contextualizing Student Needs Post Pandemic

ALBERTO "BETO" GUTIERREZ

In the spirit of, "What do students need post COVID-19?" I am proposing that social studies teachers, if not already, consider delivering the content in a scientific fashion. Proposing the incorporation of scientific methods into the social studies is inspired by the cyclical arguments often centered around science versus religion, that further divided the nation during the COVID-19 pandemic.

All elements of this proposal were initially developed while teaching intro to reading and writing, in preparation for GED courses to adult inmates at California Health Care Facility (CHCF), a Level 1 and 2 (lowest level) state prison. Though I developed the curriculum upon realizing that some of the students were previously exposed to the course content and struggled with learning, my anticipation of religious fanaticism by institutionalized inmates was also a factor in establishing healthy parameters for class discussions. Their struggle with learning varied, from physical head trauma to a dysfunctional relationship with schools, and everything in between.

Even though a low-level prison classroom inspired the curriculum, prior to teaching at CHCF I had already entertained this idea, after years of teaching in secondary public schools and higher education where many students also struggled with the learning process and making a distinction between a fact versus opinion.

The curriculum, in the form of handouts, was so effective inside CHCF that I have since modified and used it in secondary public schools. For this reason,

I strongly believe that it's very applicable to post-pandemic curriculum since we are dealing with something very comparable, science versus religion. Prison, CHCF, was the first institution in which I dealt with a high concentration of students who use their deity to explain the world. Similarly, during the pandemic Donald Trump's God-fearing anti-science loyalists rallied to denounce the pandemic, the economic shutdown, and vaccines alike. While the Trump loyalists are approximately 30 % of society, I speculate that an additional 30 % of society struggled to embrace the pandemic for other reasons, including libertarianism and anti-ivory tower sentiment that is deeply rooted in blue collar culture centered around fate. For Trump loyalists, their anti-science beliefs strongly intersect with blue-collar loyalty, which creates tension with the ivory tower.

Due to the limitations of space for this chapter I cannot share the specifics of my entire curriculum but will introduce the following three central pillars: Context vs Content; Distinctions vs Differences; and Quantifying.

CONTEXT VS CONTENT

While all educators are familiar with content, I introduce *context* as a teaching and learning tool. The objective behind using context as a tool is deeply rooted in the current resistance towards science. To address the anti-science dogma inside the classroom, context can be used to scientifically study the social sciences, particularly history. The online Merriam-Webster dictionary defines *context* as,

> (…) the environment or setting in which something (whether words or events) exists. When we say that something is contextualized, we mean that it is placed in an appropriate setting, one in which it may be properly considered.

Building on Merriam-Webster's definition, to establish context, particularly in the social sciences, requires that the teacher understand and accept history in its totality. This can be extremely challenging when we factor people's pride in traditional narratives. In addition, placing a unit of analysis in an "appropriate setting" requires that teachers understand the short and long-term effects of history. If a teacher does not know the short and long-term effects of history, a willingness to know is vital. Essentially, students and educators alike can use context as a scientific tool for analyzing and understanding the past and present.

Without context, a discussion can lead to a cyclical, never ending, apples versus oranges argument. These cyclical never-ending arguments generally occur in one of the following three scenarios: attempting to disguise a valid point as an absolute fact; imposing today's social values into a previous historical time period; speaking of the present devoid of history.

Upon being hired at CHCF, I contemplated my approach to the classroom. While I had almost 20 years of classroom experience, teaching adult inmates was not one. In my preparation, understanding the context of my new assignment was central to my strategy. On day one, before the students arrived, I wrote the following two sentences on the board:

> Because I struggle with reading, does not mean that I struggle with thinking.
> Because I speak with an accent, does not mean that I think with an accent.

Within the first 10 or 15 minutes of my introduction, an 84-year-old man stated, "You won't be having any trouble here, those sentences you wrote have our attention." Everyone else listened attentively. I explained to the students that frontloading my curriculum during the first 2 weeks of class would assist with processing the GED material as well as their ability to comprehend new material and current events. A couple of weeks into the semester, several students expressed gratitude for the frontloaded content, openly sharing that it improved their communication with family and friends. Understanding context was key.

Whether the educator plans to cover a foot-deep and a mile-long or a mile-deep and a foot-long worth of content, it is imperative they understand the relationship between the content and context of their students. It is equally as imperative that students understand the content and context in relation to their life. The purpose of understanding the students' context is to maximize their learning experience. Over the years I have met a lot of educators with great intentions but not knowing how to be intentional, they treat each class the same, ignoring the context of their audience. However, it is also possible to know the context and not know how to be intentional about delivering the content. Understanding the context of the students is a huge step towards teaching with intention and maximizing the potential of each willing participant. I include the notion of willing participant because not every student shares the same intention inside the classroom; too many are content with a passing grade free of the challenge, and it is up to the educator to evoke the students' interest; context may play a role in why some students are willing to skate by.

In understanding their context, a student can begin to explore life altering distinctions such as, "being dumb" vs. "being bored," "not liking to read" vs. "reading the wrong books," "speaking with an accent" vs "thinking with an accent," and "completing high school diploma requirements" vs "earning a high school education".

DISTINCTIONS VS. DIFFERENCES

The resistance towards the COVID-19 pandemic and vaccine alike is part of an ongoing ideological battle between the right and left, whiteness and people of color, blue collar and white collar culture, the elite and its employees and consumers.

Because the term *different* is the more commonly used of these two words, I also introduce *distinct/distinctions* as a teaching tool to differentiate events and ideas. Online Merriam-Webster Dictionary defines distinct as;

1. "distinguishable to the naked eye or mind as being discrete or not the same: separate; distinct cultural group; teaching as distinct from research. 2.) readily and unmistakably apprehended; a distinct possibility of snow; a distinct British accent; the distinct odor of sulfur."

Unlike the word different, which according to Merriam-Webster, can be "partly" different, with distinct there can be no comparisons because of the uniqueness, not the same. For example, a prison guard and a teacher each play a very distinct role inside a prison; the guard is there to preserve status quo and the teacher should be there to teach students to question status quo in a critically and reflection fashion.

In the case of the pandemic, the flu is distinct from the COVID-19 virus and should be discussed as such. First, the annual common flu does not lead to a pandemic. This should be enough to nuance these two viruses within distinct categories. Second, even if the COVID-19 mortality rate is low, the exponential growth, transmutability and unknown effects to the human organs, is in itself distinct from the annual flu. The annual flu, in general, is not known to produce "long-haulers" – people who "experience lingering health problems even when they have recovered from the acute phase of the illness" (Merriam Webster Dictionary).

Within public schools, there is a major distinction between professionals and intellectuals. Professionals are driven by the pension and benefits while intellectuals are driven by the dialectical pursuit of a higher truth. Within the current public-school setting, those who are inclined to pursue a higher truth will either suffer in silence, do the transaction anti-intellectual culture of most public schools, or be pushed out by administrators and some colleagues alike.

While teaching in public school, especially inside the state youth prison, I met plenty of teachers who compromised the search of a higher truth in exchange for the salary and benefits. For the guards, state prisons are the highest paid state job for someone with a high school diploma and an Associate of Art's degree makes it very easy to promote. I jokingly argued that if the Department of Motor and

Vehicles (DMV) paid more than CDCR, prison jobs would be hard to fill. Making this distinction is key; overwhelmingly most prison employees do not care about institutional or criminal justice and are drawn to the prison jobs for the economic opportunity. Making this distinction is imperative given the tension between incarceration and rehabilitation.

The following can be used in a classroom for students to practice distinctions.

1. father vs dad
2. poverty vs ghetto
3. opinion vs fact
4. listening vs hearing
5. rights vs responsibilities
6. high school education vs high school diploma
7. being a student vs doing student things
8. being a teacher vs doing teacher things
9. growing old vs growing up
10. saying something vs having something to say

The main objective about teaching distinctions is to create a critical self-awareness and clarity about the students' life and world at large. I first began to dabble with teaching distinctions when a student referred to an outdoor clothesline as "ghetto." I then asked the student, "If someone cannot afford a dryer, and relies on a clothesline, does that make them ghetto?" Rather than answer the question, the student proceeded to say, this is America, not Mexico, people should not be hanging their clothes outside. Years after this discussion, while teaching distinctions inside a California state youth prison, I asked about poverty vs ghetto. One young man shared, "poverty is when people are financially poor and ghetto is when people are financially poor and there is a lot of violence."

In my experience, too often students think that "ghetto" and "poverty" are synonymous. In our anti-intellectual culture, blurring the line or interchanging words or concepts is not uncommon at every level and age range. Striving for clarity and critical self-reflection is imperative for the healing and forward progress of our society. This clarity and self-reflection are the needed grounding that can generate authentic dialogue, whether it be with a high school graduate who reads at a 5th grade level, but thinks they have a high school education or a self-proclaimed Marxist professor with a six-figure income who only mingles with members of the proletariat that sit in their class or when paid to speak at an event. I often wonder, what would Karl Marx have produced if he was seeking a pension on a tenure-track position with the institutional pressure of writing peer reviewed articles/books?

QUANTIFY

In my 20 plus years teaching, too many students struggle to make a distinction between the various terms used to quantify a unit of analysis, such as: a bit, some, many, a lot, most, majority, all. Not knowing the distinction between these quantifying terms, outliers are often used as the general rule or to dismiss an argument.

In relation to the pandemic and remote instruction, during a wellness check on a student who was chronically absent, the father shared, "My son hates remote instruction and people are tired of this shutdown, public schools need to reopen." I agreed and responded with the following, "There is no doubt that all people are tired of this shutdown, but I would argue that only a very small number are protesting." I then asked, "If schools reopened today, what percentage of the parents would actually send their students to school?" This father did not have a problem admitting that, "I had not thought of it from that perspective."

Statements such as "people are protesting the shutdown" cannot be quantified using the terms "most" or "all" of our society. In actuality, neither "most" nor "all" of society protested the shutdown. Similarly, though there are some people of color who distrust vaccinations for Covid because of what happened with the Tuskegee experiment (Elliott, 2021), making a general statement saying that most people of color do not trust the vaccine because of past government experiments such as the Tuskegee experiment, is equally misleading. Based on the percentage of POC who graduate college, I speculate that most POC do not know about the Tuskegee experiment. Furthermore, we cannot make this blanket statement and then argue for Ethnic Studies in k-12 because the current curricula do not cover the POC experience.

It is my belief that we do not teach students how to process information, how to think, rather, generally, students are told what to think. To complicate matters, the Netflix documentary, Social Dilemma (2020), does a great job at summarizing how social media further complicates this increasing social tension between right and left, pro-science and anti-science.

Another example, "We demand the reopening" does not translate into "All of society" and the term "we" should be unpackaged in a class discussion or assignment. Similarly, "People are tired of the shutdown" is distinct and should not be confused with, "People wanting to reopen in spite of the virus" yet certain media outlets regularly play with these terms, with people's emotions.

Similar to distinctions, placing a specific value on a quantifying term such as *most = over 50 percent*, can lead to clarity and establishes a parameter from which to engage in dialogue. If one thousand people attend an anti-shutdown protest, in a large metropolis such as Los Angeles, we must call it for what it is – *some* people are protesting.

CONCLUSION

The word "system" conjures an image of an advanced technological network that operates with minimal human interaction. While that is true for technological networks, human beings are the inner workings of social institutions. As a result, what works or does not work within social institutions is the direct result of human behavior.

The 2020 COVID-19 pandemic, among other things, exposed a deep fracture in the human network that operates public schools. Shortly after public schools transitioned to remote instruction, due to COVID-19, the physical shutdown provided plenty of downtime for those in power to critically examine the functions and dysfunctions of the matrix. From a classroom teacher perspective, it appeared that instead of developing forward thinking sustainable solutions, relevant to this modern epoch, time was spent planning the reopening as well as recreating the pre-existing fractured system by way of remote instruction. In the school district where I teach, teachers were not invited to participate in the solution process.

The overall rejection of science that occurred during the COVID-19 pandemic was no surprise. However, rejecting science during the pandemic was a stress test to our civilization. At the center of this rejection of science is the actual virus, often referred to as a hoax or bad flu by non-believers. In general, I strongly believe that the rejection of science is reflective of our overall floundering public schools. Sure, a small percentage are doing great but most are not.

The application of *context*, *distinctions*, and concise use of quantifying terms is as much for students as it is for educators. Teaching first generation k-20 students, at any level, is to introduce the individual/cohort to potentially life altering facts, concepts, and theories that will create tension in their personal lives. Over the years, it has not been uncommon for students to share that the class content caused friction at home, high school and college students alike.

Learning how to make distinctions is central to comprehending context. For example, my students frequently use the terms/concept "being a senior" and "having a senior level education" as if they are synonymous.

In secondary schools where I have taught, part of the students' context has been the ongoing tracking and overall classist and racist policies and practices that are part of the city and schools' fabric. Because it's part of the schools' fabric, the details are not always easy to identify by an untrained eye and many accept it as, "that's just the way it is." For example, while teaching at San Fernando High School (SFHS), a Los Angeles Unified School District (LAUSD) affiliate, the U.S. invaded Iraq and Afghanistan in response to the September 11th attacks on American soil. At SFHS, overnight all branches of the military ramped up their recruitment efforts in a way that most stakeholders either openly welcomed them (those who supported the invasion) or did not understand the disruption it caused to our daily instruction. A very small number of teachers openly critiqued the excessive military recruitment, as they walked into any class at any hour of the day without notice or appointment. I eventually expressed my concerns to administration, about the excessive military recruitment and brainwashing that occurred during the presentation. Administration pushed back and the friction led to a lawsuit, Gutierrez v. Rodriguez et al., mentioned in the book, Whitewashing War; Historical Myth, Corporate Textbooks, and Possibilities for Democratic Education (Leahey, 2010). I was reprimanded for engaging in public debates, during my off time, about the U.S. invasion in the Middle East and excessive military recruitment at SFHS which had a 60 % dropout rate. The case made it twice to the California Court of Appeals; the panel of judges ruled in my favor after the first hearing and dismissed the case after the second. Qualified Immunity was the premise for dismissing the case, arguing that administrators were unaware that they violated my Civil Rights; Qualified Immunity is generally used to defend rogue law enforcement agents who abuse their power. By dismissing the case, the court failed to establish precedence on, "Do teachers have the right to speak on matters of public concern during their off hours?" In the spirit of freedom of speech, "Will pro-science teachers have the right to speak on pandemic-related matters during their off time in a red state, county or school district?"

Language matters and has the power to shape our reality, our conscience. In a world in which anyone can post their opinions on the Internet, and by default, anyone can find an article to justify their beliefs, it is imperative that educators consider this new reality as the context of our times. In addition, this context is further complicated by the growing tension between the science versus religion/non-science movement that has plagued our political system. For these reasons, today more than ever before, I strongly encourage teachers to consider using context, distinctions, and quantifying terms as teaching tools.

"Adapt or die" by Charles Darwin

REFERENCES

Elliott, D. (2021, February 16). *In Tuskegee, painful history shadows efforts to vaccinate African Americans*. N.P.R. Retrieved from https://www.npr.org/2021/02/16/967011614/in-tuskegee-painful-history-shadows-efforts-to-vaccinate-african-americans

John's Hopkins Medicine. (n.d.). *COVID "Long Haulers": Long-term effects of COVID-19*. Retrieved from https://www.hopkinsmedicine.org/health/conditions-and-diseases/coronavirus/covid-long-haulers-long-term-effects-of-covid19.

Merriam Webster Dictionary. Retrieved from https://www.merriam-webster.com/dictionary/context.

CHAPTER TEN

Dear Educators

An Open Letter about How You Teach about Native Peoples

JEAN MENDOZA AND DEBBIE REESE

DEAR EDUCATORS

As former professors in Education, we know you are probably learning about diversity, inclusion, or multiculturalism, and we're pretty sure that you are not learning about Native sovereignty and why it is important. That's what our letter is about. In a nutshell, sovereignty means self-governance. Hundreds of years ago, Native nations were facing relentless European invaders who wished to take everything. They fought hard to protect their families, communities, homelands, resources on their homelands, and their status as nations of people with control of their lands. That fight led to diplomacy, and diplomacy led to treaties, agreements between individual Native nations and the invading European nations and, later, the United States. Those treaties are why Native people fight today. You might think we're using that word (fight) a lot. We are. People fight when someone comes to take what they have.

Native people are proud of what their ancestors did to fight against colonization and extermination. We don't know exactly how many Native Nations existed in 1776, but as of this writing, there are 574 federally recognized sovereign tribal nations. Citizens of those nations are determined to carry on the work their ancestors did to preserve and protect their status as nations, and the terms of those treaties. They were, and are, exercising their sovereignty.

Understanding Native sovereignty is essential to understanding the history of what is currently called North America. Sovereignty is a political and legal reality shared by no other minority or underrepresented group in the United States, and it forms the foundation for laws related to the rights of Native people. As an educator, you must take care to teach students about Native sovereignty. You're teaching children on the homelands or former homelands of Native nations. If you do not teach about sovereignty, you are erasing an essential aspect of Native existence, and mis-educating your students.

You may feel a jolt of resistance to some of what we say here. Words give comfort, or cause pain, depending on who you are. What might seem neutral to a white teacher may feel much different to a Native child. For far too long, schools have taught that Europeans "discovered" America. But Native people experienced that discovery as an invasion by forces that wanted to wipe them out. Children are often taught that Indigenous peoples were "warlike" when in fact Native people were resisting genocide by colonizers. Native people from those times are often presented as "primitive" and "uncivilized" because their homes, clothing, spiritual beliefs, and lifeways were different from what the colonizers had, but in reality, everything Indigenous peoples had and did on their homelands served them well. You may be thinking right now that your education didn't prepare you to be aware of how those words can miseducate about Native people.

For thousands of years prior to European arrival on what is currently known as North America, the thousands of Native Nations on the continent had complex diplomatic and trade relationships with each other. These relationships required Indigenous peoples to communicate across different languages and geographic locations, about matters ranging from the value of goods being traded to negotiation of alliances. These nations had systems of governance that could address conflicts that arose. When Europeans arrived, they entered into diplomatic negotiations with Indigenous nations and drew up documents that we know today as treaties. All of these relationships and negotiations are markers of Indigenous nations' sophisticated ways of being in the world.

Some popular approaches to teaching about diversity focus on comparing tangible aspects of culture across groups such as African American, Latinx, Asian American, and Native American. Critics refer to this as "the tourist curriculum." It highlights the visible (things like trinkets a tourist buys or the "exotic" foods they eat when traveling) while ignoring deeper, essential intangible elements that ultimately define a people.

Sovereignty is among those intangibles. Earlier, we mentioned treaties between Native Nations and with European Nations. Treaties are the outcome of diplomatic negotiations between heads of state. While all ethnic groups in the U.S. have cultural ways of being, the only ones that have treaties with the U.S. government are Native Nations. From the start, Native leaders had the power to negotiate on behalf of their nations. During treaty negotiations, tribal leaders made sure the treaties included language that protected their nation's rights to resources (like hunting and fishing) on ceded land and waterways. But several times during the 20th century when Native people exercised their fishing rights, they were threatened with violence by non-Native people, including animal rights activists and those who fished for sport or profit.

It was clear that some people did not understand the cultural, spiritual, and legal significance of those treaties, today. They are not relics of the past. As former director of the National Museum of the American Indian, Kevin Gover (Pawnee) puts it, treaties "enshrine promises" made between sovereign nations (in Harjo, ed., 2014, p. xi). The U.S. government made approximately 368 treaties with Native nations. Most of those treaties have been violated or ignored in one way or another by the government or others who want protected land or resources, but throughout their existence, Native peoples have fought for them and what they mean to tribal nations.

You may be familiar with the term "broken treaties." A lot of Native activism has focused on making sure people know that the U.S. has often failed to honor terms of treaties with Native nations. In other words, it has behaved in ways that deny the fact that a treaty is supposed to be a binding legal agreement between sovereign nations. Some people may think that the U.S. government has the power to end a tribal nation's existence, but it does not. It has terminated its relationship with some tribes, but those tribes still exist, and they have fought for their diplomatic status with the U.S. government to be restored.

If you're feeling overwhelmed, you aren't alone in that sense of confusion about treaties and sovereignty. We're talking about hundreds of tribal nations and hundreds of years of nation-to-nation relationships. We do have a good resource to help you. We suggest you read Suzan Shown Harjo's introduction to *Nation to Nation: Treaties Between the United States and American Indian Nations*. There, she writes that "None of the United States' treaties with Native Nations has ever been abrogated, even though most have been stretched to the breaking point, ignored, or all but forgotten." (in Harjo (ed.), p. 1) The rest of the book explains some of the complexities of treaties, and is worthwhile reading for educators, as well.

It's not surprising that the general population doesn't understand treaty rights, or Native sovereignty. Those concepts have rarely been a part of what schools teach about Native peoples and nations. One outcome of some court cases related to the fight for fishing rights was the creation of Native-developed materials that are mandated for use in some states' educational systems. Native parents in those systems are likely aware of those court cases. What people know is shaped by who they are.

Debbie is a tribal member (some nations use "citizen") of Nambé Owingeh, one of those sovereign nations. Debbie remembers her parents and grandparents talking about tribal elections. As she grew older, she realized that only tribal members could vote. She remembers that the state police could not come onto tribal land without permission from tribal leadership. She came to understand that elections and policing on Nambé lands were manifestations of the sovereignty of the Nambé nation. She realized that she had been living a sovereign life without being conscious of it. When she began working in teacher education, she saw that most curriculum materials misrepresented Native people and showed a complete lack of awareness about sovereignty. She realized she had to bring the concept of sovereignty into her work in a concrete way.

For Jean, who is white, understanding of Native sovereignty came through interactions with her Muscogee (Creek) husband and his family. She met tribal officials when their family visited the seat of the tribal government in Okmulgee, Oklahoma. She read the Nation's official newspaper and listened to her brother-in-law's stories of serving on the Creek Lighthorse, the tribal police force. She heard her husband's mother urge him to get their children enrolled as Creek citizens and began to follow legal arguments for and against citizenship for descendants of the Creek Freedmen. All of this made her see how the learning materials about Native people in her children's schools failed completely to address sovereignty.

We think it is vital that you bring sovereignty into your teaching! We strongly suggest that you begin by reading "Tribal Nations and the United States: An Introduction" on the National Council of American Indians (NCAI) website. It provides a crash course in understanding sovereignty. We recommend that you become familiar with the names of sovereign nations, by looking over the federal government's "Indian Entities Recognized by and Eligible to Receive Services From the United States Bureau of Indian Affairs." We think it important you know that the process of federal recognition is fraught with politics, as different entities leverage their political lobbyists to influence whether or not Native Nations are recognized as nations, and whether or not they retain rights and land that are theirs according to treaties. Also, missing from the list of federally recognized Indian Entities are a number of nations that the federal government wrongfully terminated in the 1950s. You'll find useful information about termination policies in *Nation to Nation*, which we referenced earlier.

It is important to know that there is a rise in groups that falsely claim to be Native. The websites they create may look and sound authentically Native. "Members" of these self-identified groups have sometimes gotten lucrative contracts intended for minority-owned businesses, defrauding taxpayers, undermining federal law, and taking business opportunities away from Native contractors. In 2019, the Los Angeles Times published an article about this, with the headline "Two tribes aren't recognized federally. Yet members won $500 million in minority contracts." Determining legitimacy is a fraught task for anyone, but an important one. If you come upon a site for a Native group, look critically at what they say about themselves. A give-away for fraud is if they have a fee to join and/or an annual membership fee. Legitimate tribal nations do not require tribal citizens/members to pay to be included on the tribal census.

In addition to fraudulent "tribes," individuals make false claims about their identity. For years, people thought "Forrest Carter," the author of *The Education of Little Tree*, was Cherokee and treated the book as an autobiography. In fact, he was a white man, a former KKK member, and speechwriter for a proudly segregationist Alabama governor. It took years for the truth to come out, and even now the book is often incorrectly shelved with autobiographies.

DNA testing has brought a new dimension to claims of Native ancestry. Family stories about a Native ancestor lead people to take a DNA test, thinking that will prove they are genetically Native (or whatever tribe the family story names). Those tests can show that a person had an ancestor on this continent but cannot specify a tribal nation. A DNA company's report that says a person has "Native American" ancestry does not mean they can say, "I'm Native!" and a company whose report tells you a specific tribal name is misleading you.

If U.S. policies had sincerely respected Native sovereignty over the centuries, questions about identity might not be an issue now! Too often the burden is on Native communities to say, "That author, artist, contractor, or politician, is not actually one of us. We have no record of them or their family." Many claims to Native identity are simply mistakes, not intended for personal gain. Fraud matters when those making false claims get funding or opportunities intended for someone with an authentic tie to a Native community. When we pose the question about identity, we are actively supporting and respecting sovereignty.

For teachers, claims to Native identity can present a special challenge when choosing literature for the classroom. We suggest that before you share the work of a writer who claims Native identity, carefully read what they say about their background. Then read reviews of their work and articles by others with expertise in tribal identity, to find out how their claims have been supported. Two good sources of books by Native creators are the list of titles that receive the American Indian Library Association's (AILA) Youth Literature Award, and the Best Books lists at American Indians in Children's Literature.

We hope the following topical "tips" will help you develop or adapt your lesson plans about Native peoples in ways that take sovereignty into account. For each topic, we suggest a children's or young adult book by a Native writer, that we think illustrates the issues involved.

BEGIN WITH SOVEREIGNTY

Show your students how sovereignty distinguishes Native peoples from other minority or underrepresented groups in the U.S. Have them find websites for Native Nations listed in the Federal Registry we referenced earlier, and study the pages related to tribal government. How is it structured? What services does the Nation offer to citizens? How does the Nation determine who is a citizen or member?

> Related Book: Between 1953 and 1964, the US government terminated the sovereign nation status of more than 100 Native Nations. Through all those efforts, Native peoples fought back. All of that is captured in Charlene Willing McManis's *Indian No More*, about an Umpqua family's response to their nation being terminated, and how tribal members fought to have their status as a sovereign nation restored.

BE MINDFUL OF TERMINOLOGY

When you teach about Native peoples, use the name of specific Native Nations whenever possible. "American Indian," "Native American" and "Indigenous" are used interchangeably when talking or writing about overarching concerns, but without fail, Native people emphasize the importance of being tribally specific. Native peoples are not all alike!

> Related Book: When you teach books by Muscogee (Creek) writer Cynthia Leitich Smith, name her Nation as you introduce her book. She has written about Native kids and families in picture books, middle grade and young adult books, and graphic novels. In *Jingle Dancer* (a picture book), you'll see a Muscogee (Creek) child in jeans and tennis shoes, interacting with a Native community as she gets ready to dance in a powwow for the first time. Smith's young adult novel *Hearts Unbroken* follows a suburban Native family as the teens navigate the theater department's production of *The Wizard of Oz*. L Frank Baum wrote *Wizard* but he also wrote editorials calling for the extermination of Native people.

WATCH OUT FOR VERB TENSE

There is a tendency to refer to Native peoples only in the past tense. Unless you are talking about history, say "Native people are/do/have" instead of "were/did/had," and when you are talking about past events, make sure you don't imply they no longer exist. When teaching about a tribal nation that was removed from their homelands, make sure students know where they are today.

Related Book: We suggest you share books by Marcie Rendon, an Anishinaabe woman enrolled at the White Earth reservation in Minnesota. Show students the White Earth website and use "is" when you talk about her, and her nation. Her nonfiction picture book, *Powwow Summer: A Family Celebrates the Circle of Life*, is about a contemporary Anishinaabe (Ojibwe) family on the powwow circuit. Rendon's short story "Worry and Wonder" in *Sky Blue Water: Short Stories for Young Readers* is about a 7th grade Native girl in a foster home. The Indian Child Welfare Act (ICWA) of 1978 figures in the story. ICWA's purpose is to curtail the decades-long, rampant anti-Indigenous practices of social service agencies removing Native children from their homes and placing them in foster homes outside their tribal communities. ICWA supports sovereignty by requiring those agencies to work with tribal nations to place Native children with someone in their tribe and family. In Rendon's story, ICWA enables the girl to stay with Native family members when her mother cannot care for her.

LOOK CRITICALLY AT THE CURRICULUM

Native peoples are Native all year long. Information and children's books about them should be included year-round. In many school districts, curriculum about Native peoples is limited to historical moments like Columbus Day, and Thanksgiving. It's possible to teach about historical events by linking them to present-day concerns. For examples, see the free online lesson plans about Indigenous Peoples' Day and Thanksgiving in our resource list.

To be well-informed about issues that directly affect Native peoples, read news media like Indian Country Today and Indianz, listen to radio programs like "Native America Calling" and become familiar with Native-authored books that win the American Indian Library Association's Youth Literature Awards.
Related Book: *We Are Water Protectors* by Carole Lindstrom (Ojibwe), illustrated by Michaela Goade (Tlingit), is inspired by ongoing Indigenous-led protests against the activities of energy corporations that endanger water supplies and other essential resources.

LOOK LOCALLY

Every home, school, town or city, is located on Indigenous land. What nation's homeland are you on? Use the online list of federally recognized tribal nations to figure out what nation your instructional materials should focus on. Have students find and use that nation's official website as a primary source. Look for resources about that tribe at the National Museum of the American Indian's *Native Knowledge 360° Essential Understandings About American Indians* website.

Montana's Indian Education for All, and Wisconsin's Act 31 pages (see links in resource section) can serve as models for what to do.

> Related Book: Read books by Native writers who create a strong sense of place. Eric Gansworth is an enrolled tribal member of the Onondaga Nation and his stories are set on the reservation where he grew up. His novels include *If I Ever Get Out of Here* for middle grade readers, and *Show Me Some Truth* for high school readers. Music lovers may recognize those book titles as songs. A music-lover himself, his books provide an opportunity to study his books within a rock and roll context.

Are you feeling overwhelmed? We've been in that place, ourselves, and though we've spent our adult lives studying how Native people are depicted in children's books and educational materials, we know there's still more to learn – especially about sovereignty. Be bold! Tell your colleagues and students what you are "unlearning" and learning. That can provide them with a space of safety and help them move out of their space of ignorance. Change is hard! But we hope our letter helps you make change in your teaching about Native peoples and nations.
With respect,
Jean and Debbie

REFERENCES

Harjo, S.S. (2014). *Nation to nation: Treaties between the United States and American Indian Nations.* National Museum of the American Indian.

Indian Education in Montana. (n.d.). Office of Public Instruction. https://opi.mt.gov/Educators/Teaching-Learning/Indian-Education

Indian Entities Recognized by and Eligible to Receive Services from the United States Bureau of Indian Affairs. Federal Register, The Daily Journal of the United States Government. Retrieved February 27, 2021 from https://www.federalregister.gov/documents/2021/01/29/2021-01606/indian-entities-recognized-by-and-eligible-to-receive-services-from-the-united-states-bureau-of

Martinez, N. (n.d.). *Rethink Columbus, A lesson plan for Indigenous Peoples' Day.* Beacon Press. http://www.beacon.org/assets/clientpages/IndigenousYALessonPlan1.aspx

Martinez, N. (n.d.) *Origin narrative: Thanksgiving.* Beacon Press. http://www.beacon.org/assets/clientpages/IndigenousYALessonPlan2.aspx

Tribal Nations and the United States: An Introduction. National Congress of American Indians (2020, February). https://www.ncai.org/about-tribes

Wisconsin First Nations: American Indian Studies in Wisconsin (n.d.). Retrieved February 27, 2021 from https://wisconsinfirstnations.org/

CHAPTER ELEVEN

Black Lives Matter at School

A Conversation with Jesse Hagopian

Jesse Hagopian and I spoke about the Black Lives Matter at School movement that began in Seattle and has spread across the country. We started by talking about Jesse's early experiences at school where he became aware that school was not a safe place for him as a mixed-race Black student, and that he only began finding meaning in education in two university classes, one about feminist theory in film and the other on the Black experience post WW II. From there we talked about his career as a teacher and the path that led to Black Lives Matter at School.

Jesse: I started teaching in Washington D.C. after college and I taught in a school in Southeast D.C. I would drive by the White House and 10 minutes later I'd cross the Anacostia River and be in one of the most impoverished and segregated neighborhoods in the country. I learned way more than I taught during those three years. It was an experience that's forever shaped who I am, and you know those 5th graders are some serious teachers. My first day of teaching I assigned each student to take home a brown paper bag and to come back with something that really told me something about who they were. I told them don't just put a favorite game or two in there, but to think about what shaped you and find something that can really reveal something about who you are. I definitely wasn't ready to ask that question as I found out the next day. The first girl pulled out the driver's license of her father and she said she carried it with her because her dad had been locked up in prison and that it helped her remember him. The next boy pulled out a picture of his dad who had been shot and killed that summer and every single student had a picture of a loved one who was either dead or in jail. I was in a panic, it was overwhelming. I knew it was going to be challenging but to have to figure out how to be a trauma counselor and a teacher and the many other roles I had to figure out was a lot.

And then the first research assignment I ever assigned those students was to study someone in history that they felt had helped to make the world a better place and they created a poster and they turned them in, and we were going to present the posters the next day. When we came back all the posters were destroyed because it had rained in my classroom. There was a hole in the ceiling I didn't know about and there was a half inch of standing water all over the floor and the posters were completely water-logged and illegible. I wheeled an industrial size garbage can under the hole and put in a work order, but that hole was never fixed for the 3 years I taught there.

This was also the same year that attacks of 9/11 happened, and we saw the smoke from the Pentagon rising from our classroom window and that was terrifying, but what was even more terrifying to me was to see the speed at which our government could mobilize an untold fortune to go bomb people around the world but couldn't fix a hole in the ceiling of my classroom just a few minutes from the White House. The only resources provided for them if you can call it that were police officers. Students were jacked up against the wall. One day I had a student who was taken in the back of a cop car, and they were screaming at them, "I arrested your dad last week and you're going to be next if you don't act better in school." This was the situation that taught me that we need to not only transform pedagogy in the classroom to be empowering of students, but we have to transform the policy and the structure of our society in order to nurture our youth rather than criminalize them.

Doug: I'm sure you didn't feel ready to do what you did but it's clear how badly the kids needed you, and you obviously were providing a safe place for them to come with that hurt, the pain and that honesty in their lives.

Jesse: I did the best I could.

Doug: Did you have allies at the school or were you kind of traveling alone?

Jesse: There were some incredibly dedicated educators, loving and kind, but this was also the year that the No Child Left Behind Act came online and so, all of a sudden, the narrative that was rolled out was that the problem with the public schools are the teachers. not the lack of resources, not the holes in the ceilings of classrooms, not the libraries that only have books from like the 60s. It was this big smoke and mirrors game to hide the deep inequities in society and blame the people who are trying their best to hold the system together. It was really hard to see all of us being blamed for a school system that we didn't create.

Doug: And that school system existed within the larger, inequitable system that created and maintained those unequal schools. What got you to move beyond doing what you were doing in the classroom? I would say that good teaching is activism, but what got you to become an activist beyond the classroom?

Jesse: My experience in seeing these gross inequities and institutional racism made me want to get active in transforming the system. I knew I had to take action and help expose the situation and figure out ways to organize and fight back. I got active in the union. I actually started organizing with Liz Davis, who just passed away unfortunately in a car accident. She was a rank-and-file teacher like me at the time. She later became the president of the union. We and other militants in the union began organizing, trying to get our union to become a force for social justice, and one of the first big events that let me know that this was the way to go, happened when the school district announced they were going to cancel our raises. They said there's just no money for the raise, and I'm like really, in the world's richest country, in the capital of that country you're going to cut the raises that you negotiated in a contract and signed your name to? The union organized a rally and we helped to mobilize members to go down to City Hall. We had a big rally in the circle and as the speakers began agitating people in the crowd got more and more upset and they started chanting "No 9% October one, no work October two." The crowd spilled out into the street and started blocking traffic and that wasn't enough. They blew past the gates of City Hall and went into the building and marched up to the mayor's office. They hastily shut the door and locked it, but just that reverberating chant off the walls inside the building of "No 9% October one, no work October two" just made me feel powerful. Lo and behold the next week they found the money. I learned a lesson from a young age that if you organize collectively and you say, "we're going to shut the system down if we don't get what we are demanding" that you can have a large influence and that's really a lesson that I've tried to take with me through all my work.

Doug: Let's move to Black Lives Matter at School, which you have been so instrumental in bringing to schools in Seattle and around the country, but first I would like to begin talking about Black Lives Matter. There's so much misinformation about what Black Lives Matter is about I wonder if you could talk some from your perspective about Black Lives Matter.

Jesse: Black Lives Matter is a continuation of the long Black freedom struggle that's gone on in this country. It's gone by many names. It's gone by abolition, it's gone by reconstruction, Civil Rights, Black Power and now Black Lives Matter. It's gone on for more than four hundred years because that's how long the enslavement and structural racism that have been forced upon Black people who were kidnapped and brought to this country in a genocide perpetrated on my ancestors. There will always be a new iteration of that freedom struggle until the structures, the inter-related structures of capitalism and white supremacy are brought down.

And what I think is truly remarkable of Black Lives Matter that is an advance from the previous eras of the Black freedom movement is that the Black Lives Matter cry for freedom takes an intersectional approach to understanding how we get free. The founders of the BLM global network are Black women, a Black immigrant woman, and two Black queer women who understand that we have to center the most marginalized people in our community, that all Black lives matter, not just Black, cis, hetero men. We have to actually fight to make sure that Black trans lives matter, Black women's lives matter, Black disabled lives matter, and that we can build a movement for the most oppressed as a way to free everybody. So there is a universalism that is really inspiring and just incredible to see how this Black freedom dreaming is freeing us all.

Doug: That's one of the things that has really struck me as well. The intersectional awareness, not just of the range of population but also the intersection with capitalism. That deeper understanding of how it is all connected and how powerful that is.

Jesse: Yes, it's incredible to see and in many of the earlier iterations of the Black freedom struggle, so often Black men were centered even though much of the work and important organizing that was done by Black women or Black queer folks. They were often made invisible. I'm hoping that this round of struggle can correct for those problems because if we don't, we can't win. We won't actually defeat the oppressive structures we are trying to bring down.

Doug: I was talking with someone a while ago who said that what is most important to our movement is to not get splintered. That we find a way to stand together because that's where our power is.

Jesse: Yes, solidarity is the key to winning because the richest one percent in this country are hoarding the wealth. You have like five people on the planet who have the same amount of wealth as the lowest three point five billion; that is an obscenity that is causing so much of the pain and suffering for so many of us. But, why don't we just go, as the bottom 3.5 billion of humanity, why don't we just go and take that wealth and use it for the benefit of humanity. The problem is that racism and sexism and heterosexism and xenophobia and ableism are dividing us all, so you have people thinking that the problems in our society are Muslims and terrorism and you have politicians scapegoating Black people and saying that's why you have crime and immigrants are coming and stealing your jobs. As long as you have racism as a tool to divide, we will never have the solidarity needed to wrestle the wealth away from the richest people in this country. They are making lives worse for everybody in the country. Even the majority of white people in the country would do far better if they were able to see through the racist myth they've been taught and see how their liberation is bound up with all of ours. For the first time white men's age expectancy has gone down in this country as the drug crisis ravages white communities as well and you have millions of white

children living in poverty. And racism is one of the key tools they use to pit poor and working people against each other rather than to form common bonds. Until people develop a racial consciousness the solidarity needed will never be possible.
Doug: How did you organize the BLM at Schools movement in Seattle?
Jesse: John Muir organized themselves. They have an incredible community there. They had some really talented and dedicated educators, and they formed a race and equity committee at John Muir Elementary and in the fall of 2016 they decided they wanted to do something special to celebrate their Black students' lives. This was coming off of a summer with the killing of Philando Castile and Alton Sterling. They wanted to let their Black students know they were loved and supported and that this was a place that would help them heal from their trauma. They organized an event with parents, and with a group called Black Men United to Change the Narrative. A really powerful educator named DeSean Jackson helped to organize it, and the art teacher named Julie Trout designed a tee shirt that said, "Black Lives Matter, We Stand Together, John Muir Elementary", with a beautiful picture of a tree with the many branches coming down together into the one trunk.

When the media ran stories about it the white supremacists heard that they were going to wear these tee shirts and hold a ceremony in front of the school where they high-five their kids on the way into the school, and Black families would be out front celebrating their youth. They started sending hate mail to the school, and one particularly hateful person made a bomb threat against John Muir elementary school. The school district officially cancelled that event and they brought in bomb sniffing dogs that morning to see if the threat was going to be carried out. And to the credit of the community the event was held, but it was a lot smaller than it would have been. And that hurt my heart, and it was particularly upsetting that these violent white supremacists could disrupt this joyful celebration of Black children.

My friend Wayne Au, whose son went to Muir, put me in touch with some of the educators at John Muir and I invited them to a meeting of the Social Equity Educators, the rank-and-file union caucus that I'd helped to found and organize and we came up with the idea of passing a resolution in our union declaring that October 19, 2016 would be Black Lives Matter at School day. And not only that we stood in solidarity with John Muir, but that we called on every teacher to go to school wearing a Black Lives Matter tee shirt.

The resolution passed, but then I was really worried that, you know it's easy to vote for something but then come the day how many teachers are really going to put those shirts on and teach lessons about the Black freedom struggle and Black Lives Matter? And then we had to launch a serious organizing campaign and we partnered with the Black student unions in the NAACP, and we even got the endorsement of the Seattle PTSA. We held press conferences and we organized a t-shirt distribution operation. We had distributed over 2,000 t-shirts and many schools made their own shirts and some teachers had their own so that we estimate there was around 3,000 educators out of the 5000 that day wearing the shirts. It was just an eruption of solidarity. It was so beautiful, one of the most moving days of my life. We held our evening rally at Washington Hall, and we had Black student performances, poetry and spoken-word and a roundtable discussion about what changes needed to occur in our schools and the media covered our event and it went on national news.

The most beautiful thing happened next which is that the educators in Philadelphia saw what we had done, and they took it to the next level; they made it a week of action and broke down the 13 principles of the Black Lives Matter Global Network in the teaching points for each day of the week. It was so moving to me to see other educators build on what we have done and then they presented at a national "Free Minds Free People" conference that summer and the idea was out. Educators all over the country who attended that conference wanted to take that up and so the following year we organized conference calls, and this was in the days before Zoom; we were just on the phone, the olden days. The following year we organized the first national week of action for Black Lives in the Schools and this past year we celebrated our fourth year of a week of action, and it actually tripled in size. Thousands of educators in communities all over the country were reaching tens of thousands of students with intersectional anti-racist lessons each day of the week and organizing around our four basic demands: Ending zero-tolerance discipline; hiring more Black teachers; implementing Black studies and ethnic studies; and funding counselors not cops.

Doug: This may be pretty hard to summarize, but when you think about the impact that doing this has had on the kids and teachers, what kind of impact has it had? How would you say this has changed things?

Jesse: Well, maybe I could just read you the words of one of my students; he sums it up the best. Israel Presley was one of my students in my world history class and in my ethnic studies class and I interviewed him for our book Black Lives Matter at School, and he said during the week of action,

> I learned that Blackness could be part of every subject in school. I finally was being taught things about myself. I learned about Black contributions to science in science class. I had a math teacher at Garfield who did excellent work. She didn't use math to talk about the negative statistics about Black people, no, she used math to talk about the possibilities that we could achieve. It felt very powerful. Black Lives Matter at School has shown us that our community can organize ourselves to a fight and to celebrate ourselves and our accomplishments. We are no longer living in a history of defeat we are living in a future of success.

I just feel like tens of thousands of students have had their identities affirmed and know that there is another way to organize education that's about fighting for a better world. We have had concrete victories around some of our demands. You know it was very controversial when we took up the demands of funding counselors not cops and then in the wake of the murders of Breonna Taylor and George Floyd and Tony McDade and so many others, the uprising that swept the country last spring and summer really helped to produce a new consciousness. Police were swept out of the schools in Minneapolis and St. Paul and Denver and Oakland and Charlottesville, and I'm proud to say in Seattle, and you know that's a huge victory for us. Ethnic studies programs are being fought for and won in communities around the country. Black Lives Matter at School in no way takes credit for all these victories but we're one part of a broader freedom struggle that has helped to advance these causes. There's some incredible educators here in Seattle, people like Tracy Castro Gill, John Greenberg and Rita Green who organized with students in the NAACP Youth Council and helped to win ethnic studies in the Seattle Public Schools. We held a Black Education Now rally this summer and as part of the Black Lives Matter uprising and that helped to push forward a brand new Black studies program in the Seattle Public Schools so we are definitely impacting the education system in some real ways.

Doug: Finally, what do you think young people need to know, to learn in order to move forward with the best resources and energy they can and how can we how can we do that?

Jesse: The first thing I want to say is I think it's instructive to look back in history and understand why and how the public schools were set up in this country as a starting place. To know that the school system is deeply contradictory in this country. I defend the public schools from the corporate education reformers who want to inundate the schools with high stakes testing and want to privatize the schools with charters and bust the teachers' unions but at the same time that I defend the public schools I also know that they are a very contradictory institution in that they were set up with contradictory impulses. On the one hand you have the industrialists who wanted an institution that could integrate a growing urban working-class into a highly inequitable economic structure and train them to accept their lot as low-wage workers in their corporations. The public schools were a very important tool for these industrialists to gather together the large numbers of immigrants coming from other countries and train them to believe that America was the freest place on Earth and that they should feel lucky to be here and that they should follow all the directions that are given to them by politicians and by bosses. And on the other hand, education has always been a demand of mass social movements. Black people have fought for access to education from the time when it was illegal to be literate and you could be tortured or killed if you were caught trying to educate yourself. From the time that Black people built the public schools across the South during reconstruction, to the time building Freedom Schools and Liberation Schools during the Civil Rights and Black power era, education and access to free public schooling has been part of the struggle as well. That's why I think public schools are such important sites of resistance because that contradiction produces change. Everything that we're promised from the schools, that if you work hard and get good grades and do your homework that you can have a good life just aren't true. It wasn't true for Tamir Rice just like it wasn't true for Emmett Till. All over the country that's why schools have become sites of resistance. That's why Black Lives Matter at Schools is growing, that's why teacher strikes in the red state revolt occurred, and then teacher strikes in L.A. and Chicago, our own strike here in Seattle. Educators know that that system isn't really living up to the promise that we were told it can be.

I think that our fight to transform public education has to have two main goals. The first one is fully resourcing the public schools. The fact that the schools are funded by property taxes so that the richest neighborhoods get the best educational resources is an obscenity that has to change in the world's richest country. We have plenty of money to make sure there are not holes in the ceilings of classrooms, to make sure that there is a nurse and social worker in every school, and every school has wrap-around services for healthcare and after school programs in enriching curriculum. The other thing besides the resources and the wrap-around services is what the kids are actually learning, and I think we have to completely transform the purpose of education and the way we conduct pedagogy. For the American public school system and the people who run it, their goal for the public schools is to help America compete in the global economy. I think we need to make school about solving problems in our society, so we need to help students identify problems in our society and then help them find collective solutions to those problems. To do that I think we need to radically reimagine how schools are set up so that we end the segregation of subjects.

What if we got rid of math and science and social studies and language arts and instead, we had a class called *Should we defund the police*? There's a live question that everybody is debating in our society that would grab our kids' attention and they would sit up straight and would be interested in a way they never were in the classes we have. Then through that lens of that real life problem we could teach math by teaching the city budget and learn about the fact that four hundred million dollars are being spent on the police in Seattle, far more than any other part of the budget and they could analyze that and discuss it and re-work the budget around their own priorities. They could learn history by learning the history of where police came from out of slave patrols and strikebreaking brigades in the north. They can learn language arts by writing poetry about resistance to police brutality or writing speeches about how they think the budget should be formed and delivering those speeches to the city council. I think that kind of an education that's focused on liberation, that's focused on solving problems will engage our students in a way that they are and also help us achieve a better society.

FOR FURTHER STUDY

Au, W., Hagopian, J., & Watson, D. (2018). *Teaching for Black lives*. Rethinking Schools.
Garcia, L., & Davidson, C. (2020). *What we believe: A Black Lives Matter principles activity book*. Lee and Low.
Hagopian, J., & Jones, D. (Eds.). (2020). *Black lives matter at school: An uprising for educational justice*. Haymarket Books.

CHAPTER TWELVE

Evolving Higher Education for a New Consciousness

YVES SALOMON-FERNÁNDEZ

INTRODUCTION

The influence of young people on all facets of life including our collective social and environmental consciousness, voting, and philanthropy has been the subject of many recent publications. In the historic election and reelection of the first African-American president of the United States, Barack Obama, analysts credited the increased voting rates of Millennials as a significant factor (Robillard, 2012). Young people's heightened consciousness vis-à-vis social, environmental, economic, and political issues coupled with the changes in demographics taking place in the U.S. and around the world are shaping the evolution of higher education.

In the fall of 2019, led by Greta Thunberg and young activists across the globe, young people organized global demonstrations to bring attention to climate change. Working with older generations, Gen Alphas, Gen Zs, and millennials mobilized large groups from their local communities and focused our attention on the warming of the Earth and the need to reverse human-induced damage to our planet. Regrettably, in November 2020, the United States officially withdrew from the Paris Accord, reneging on commitments to reduce greenhouse gas emissions and fund climate research, among other agreements. This was a disappointment in light of our young people's clarion call just a year prior, but it did not stop them from joining and leading around other causes and engaging in social action. Amid a pandemic, people across the globe took to the streets to protest against racism, declining race relations, and police brutality in the United States in the spring of 2020 following the death of George Floyd. Once again, around the world, young people were a strong voice advocating for equitable treatment of all.

Since the turn of the 21st century, we have seen tremendous displays of courage by young people. This is the age of Malala Yousafzai, Autumn Peltier, Naomi Wadler, Angy Paola Rivera, and Greta Thunberg. Young people growing up today are acutely aware of the challenges we face as a society. Climate change, gender parity, growing income inequality, disparate access to healthcare based on income and identity, rising college debt, racial disparities, and advancing democracy are among the issues that higher education should prepare them to confront and address as they enter adulthood. From their activism around these and other issues, it is clear that young people today imagine a different world, one that is more socially and environmentally sustainable, and where every human has a fair chance of success. Increasingly, young people are demonstrating, through their activism and philanthropic support for related causes, that they have the will to create that world (Orfield et al., 2019). As institutions of higher learning, the onus is on us to educate and prepare these young people as society will soon rely on their leadership and citizenship. It is our responsibility to create environments that equitably enable students and educators to learn and co-create knowledge within and outside of their chosen disciplines. Further, it is to ensure that students acquire the skills they need to secure employment and enjoy fulfilling careers post-graduation and empower them to participate as informed and engaged citizens in their communities. This chapter will focus on how higher education needs to evolve to (1) remain relevant for these young people; (2) equip them with the knowledge, skills, and disposition to succeed; and (3) support them in making local change with a global impact.

YOUNG PEOPLE TODAY AND HIGHER EDUCATION

Every generation has seen its young people serve as the conscience of its time. With the advent of technology, the speed, and effectiveness with which young people have mobilized themselves and others have been both magnified and accelerated. Today's youth have demonstrated an appetite for using technology to strengthen their organizing, leadership, and advocacy. For young people today, the fast-changing world of technology presents an array of opportunities. While the technological divide still exists between the haves and the have-nots even in highly industrialized countries, young people have shown adeptness in connecting geographically distant populations across communities and across the globe.

In some ways, this current generation of youth is unique in terms of the means of organizing that it has at its disposal. The availability of cell phones and body cameras to capture events and injustices just in time is a unique asset for this generation, and it allows them the opportunity to raise our awareness and consciousness of events around police brutality and other acts of injustice. Similarly, technological advancements like artificial intelligence, virtual and augmented reality, big data, block chain technology, the Internet of things, and many industry-specific advances have improved our capacity for improved workplace efficiency and economic prosperity. As a sector, higher education bears the responsibility of ensuring equitable access to opportunities and the achievement of equitable outcomes for students, so that as a society we can all share in the economic prosperity of our country.

The generation of young people that we are educating now and will soon educate is the most diverse that our nation has seen. The youths in the United States are different, in many ways, compared to the generations that preceded them. In 2018, the Pew Research Center announced that the "post-millennial" generation of 6 to 21-year-olds, meaning the generations considered Gen Z and Gen Alpha, is the most racially and ethnically diverse (Fry & Parker, 2018). The Pew calls Gen Z "the leading edge" of our country's changing racial and ethnic make-up. A quarter of Gen Z youth are Hispanic while 14% are black, 6% are Asian or Pacific Islander, and 5% are some other race or two or more races. At 22%, they are more likely to be the children of immigrants rather than immigrants themselves. Concerning Gen Alpha, they are predicted to be even more diverse than any prior generation. It is in this context that our country is expected to become minority White by 2045 and a racially plural nation. This has implications for both the students whom we educate and how higher education approaches teaching, learning, and the student experience.

There are other trends worth noting with this population of youths. With high school drop-out rates that are significantly lower than Millennials', parents that are more educated than any prior generation, and a higher propensity toward joining higher education than entering the workforce, these two generations are cited as being on track to be the "best educated" group of young people in our country. This is a positive outlook as our national economy becomes increasingly knowledge-driven. The aggregate trends also show that young people and their families are realizing the importance of a post-secondary degree. Indeed, the data show more career success and income mobility are associated with more advanced post-secondary education. According to the Bureau of Labor Statistics, the median earnings for someone with just a high school diploma is $38,792 compared to those with an Associate degree with $46,124, or a Bachelor's degree at $64,896, or a Master's degree at $77,844. Professional and doctorate degree holders earn a median salary of nearly $100,000. In addition to ensuring that our country has an educated citizenry, which is critical for a democracy and civil society, post-secondary education is also associated with lower unemployment rates and many positive income and lifestyle benefits (U.S. Bureau of Labor Statistics, n.d.).

Historically and even more contemporarily, higher education attainment and other opportunities have not been equally accessible to all. While the aforementioned trends and projections, at the aggregate level, are encouraging, when disaggregated a more nuanced picture emerges that has implications for equity and the continued economic prosperity of our country, especially as we become more plural. The existing empirical evidence shows that public schools in the United States are becoming increasingly more segregated by race and income[1] and significant inequities exist in college going and completion rates of White students versus students of color (National Center of Education Statistics, 2019). Further, our colleges and universities are not always adequately equipped to serve the diversity of students entering our institutions. To ensure more equitable access to opportunities that can lead to more equitable outcomes for all young people, our public school systems and higher education institutions must adopt policies and practices that support racially and economically disadvantaged students. Moreover, their faculty and administrative ranks must reflect the diversity seen within the student body and provide training that can help strengthen the levels of cultural dexterity among individuals to better serve students. Colleges and universities must serve as vehicles for achieving equity. We can begin by asking to what extent are we prepared to effectively educate the diversity of emerging leaders of our democracy, planet, non-profits, and businesses?

EVOLVING HOW AND WHAT WE TEACH FOR MODERN TIMES

As an industry, higher education is entrusted with preparing young people for both an evolving global economy and for citizenship in a racially plural democracy. Colleges and universities must ensure that young people develop and master the competencies that will enable them to succeed in their careers and as educated citizens. The student experience both inside and outside of the classroom must acknowledge and build upon students' interests, identities, heritages, and lived experiences. Our programs of study must offer students choices that will have market currency and ensure that they can participate in a changing economy immediately and in the years following their graduation. Moreover, our academic programs must provide the foundational knowledge and skills to allow them to

---

1 https://www.civilrightsproject.ucla.edu/research/k-12-education/integration-and-diversity/harming-our-common-future-americas-segregated-schools-65-years-after-brown

thrive and learn how to learn for many of the jobs for which we are preparing students have not yet been invented. Our graduates will be creating the jobs that they will have. In the context of the Fourth Industrial Revolution, they will be working with and alongside robots, and our curricula must help them hone uniquely human skills.

The Fourth Industrial Revolution refers to the current era of technological change that differs from prior periods of tech breakthroughs in terms of scale, speed, complexity, disruption, and transformation to our daily lives and in our professional lives. Advances in artificial intelligence, augmented and virtual reality, the Internet of things, autonomous vehicles, and the availability of a wide range of tech-enhanced consumer goods are evidence of the impact of the current tech revolution. In preparing college graduates to work and contribute to this new world, the World Economic Forum (WEF) has identified ten critical competencies needed for success in the workplace.

1. Complex problem-solving	2. Critical thinking
3. Creativity	4. People management
5. Coordinating with others	6. Emotional intelligence
7. Judgment and decision making	8. Service Orientation
9. Negotiation	10. Cognitive flexibility

WEF has extensively investigated the jobs that robots will displace as part of this evolving technological revolution. As this happens, new jobs will emerge that rely more on human cognition than manual labor. Thus, our higher education system must prepare students for careers that do not yet exist and prepare them to create new jobs and nurture an agile and entrepreneurial mindset to accommodate change of their work function and evolution of their knowledge base and skill set.

In addition to fostering an evolutionary mindset, Joseph Aoun, in his book Robot Proof calls for integrating the humanities with the more technical disciplines to create what he coins "the humanics." He presents the "humanics" as a model to understand and transcend the technological world by focusing on skills that increase students' capacity for creativity and mental flexibility. He argues for higher education to emphasize learning the "new literacies," which include technological literacy, data literacy, and human literacy. Aoun advocates for education that promotes curiosity and how to learn, think critically, solve complex problems, and collaborate with others. He also contends that undergraduate education should marry theoretical with experiential learning. The president of Northeastern University, an institution best known for its cooperative work-based learning approach called "coops," Aoun argues that in a world where artificial intelligence allows for robots to take on an increasing number of human functions and tasks, we must focus on teaching students the uniquely human skills, that are more complex and that also help protect them against robot displacement, and more broad skills.

As we evolve into a world where humans coexist with robots, higher education must prepare students to create and innovate in technology and within their disciplines. Colleges and universities must also help them develop and improve their uniquely human skills. Human cognition, adaptability, and flexibility become increasingly important as society continues to experience rapid technological change.

PROMOTING TEACHING AND LEARNING THAT VALUES ALL STUDENTS

Beyond the economy for which we are preparing students, our pedagogies and our course content must consider who we are teaching and the domestic and international contexts in which they are living and working when the world is globally interdependent. Technology knows no barriers. It allows us in the U.S. to work with folks across countries, languages, and cultures, not to mention how our country is becoming a racial plurality.

When it comes to the curriculum content, there is much room for improvement in our current higher education system. In the United States, across K-16, our public and higher education sectors have been criticized for not acknowledging the histories, struggles, and contributions of many diverse populations. Our education systems continue to perpetuate White-dominant perspectives that omit, erase, and undervalue the identities and lived experiences of students of color, students who are members of the LGBTQ community, and women, among other identities. A re-imagined higher education is one in which, at minimum, the curricula accurately teach the histories, contemporary contributions, and events in ways that are accessible, objective, and unbiased. At best, the curriculum is decolonized.

A concept worth extending beyond teacher education preparation at the undergraduate and graduate levels and more broadly into preparation for all of those wishing to teach in any discipline is culturally relevant teaching or CRT. Ladson-Billings (1994), who coined the term, describes it as "a pedagogy that empowers students intellectually, socially, emotionally, and politically by using cultural referents to impart knowledge, skills, and attitudes." Gay (2010) adds that CRT "uses the cultural knowledge, prior experiences, frames of reference, and performance styles of ethnically diverse students to make learning more relevant and effective."

College and university professors, generally, are not prepared to teach in the academy. Thus, they fall back to teaching the content that they were taught and in the manner that they were taught in their disciplines. As most of the teaching staff in the academy is White, institutions of higher education risk perpetuating White-dominant perspectives both in content and pedagogy. In the same way that Cochran-Smith, Gleeson, and Mitchell (2010) in their article on preparing classroom teachers to teach for social justice, argue that the former should prepare pupils to "develop basic skills as well as deep knowledge and the attitudes and values necessary for participation in a democratic society – opportunities that have historically been reserved for the privileged," college and university professors should also be prepared in contextualizing their subject matter content and embrace pedagogies that promote similar outcomes for post-secondary education.

At Greenfield Community College, we are explicit about centering equity in all of the plans and strategic goals that guide teaching, learning, and operations of the College. Through book reading clubs, asset-based participatory action research projects that engage students, faculty, and staff in inquiry focused on equity and student success, we are able to gather, analyze, and use systematic data to inform our policies and practices. These are in addition to disaggregating institutional research data. By providing opportunities for cross-cultural engagement among White and non-white students and employees, space for reflection, and training, our college engages in examining how our policies and practices can decenter whiteness, promote equity, and achieve equal outcomes for all of our students regardless of their identities and lived experiences.

CONCLUSION

Young people across the globe are increasingly demonstrating that they are ready for leadership. Among higher education's challenges today is to create environments that are diverse, inclusive, equitable, and that foster a sense of belonging for all. Students across the identity spectrum need to feel that they are represented, that they have mentors who look like them and whose lived experiences are similar to theirs. Our curricula and pedagogies must acknowledge the histories and contemporary events and contributions of all and should integrate educational technology in ways that expand access to those for whom access is limited and for teaching effectiveness. Our approach to higher education must also make room for more personalized, multi-disciplinary learning, and for experiential learning to allow students greater opportunities to combine classroom-based theoretical learning with applied, hands-on practice and to prepare for living and working within a diverse society and alongside robots. Higher education must promote learning that is inclusive and that empowers students broadly.

REFERENCES

Cochran-Smith, M., Gleeson, A. M., & Mitchell, K. (2010). Teacher education for social justice: What's pupil learning got to do with it?. *Berkeley Review of Education*, *1*(1), 35–61.

Fry, R., & Parker, K. (2018, November 15). *Early benchmarks show "post-millennials" on track to be most diverse, best-educated generation yet*. Pew Research Center. Retrieved from https://www.pewresearch.org/social-trends/2018/11/15/early-benchmarks-show-post-millennials-on-track-to-be-most-diverse-best-educated-generation-yet/

Gay. G. (2010). *Culturally responsive teaching. Theory, research, and practice, second edition*. Teachers College Press.

Ladson-Billings. (1994). *The dreamkeepers. Successful teachers of African American children*. Jossey-Bass.

National Center for Education Statistics. (2019, February). *Indicator 23: Postsecondary graduation rates*. Retrieved from https://nces.edu.gov/programs/raceindicators/indicator_red.asp

Orfield, G., Frankenberg, E., Ee, J., & Ayscue, J. (2019, May 10). *Harming our common future: America's segregated schools 65 years after Brown*. The Civil Rights Project. Retrieved from https://www.civilrightsproject.ucla.edu/research/k-12-education/integration-and-diversity/harming-our-common-future-americas-segregated=schoopls-65-years-after-brown

Robillard, K. (2012, November 7). *Study: Youth vote was decisive*. Politico. Retrieved from https://www.politico.com/story/2012/11/study-youth-vote-was-decisive-083510

U.S. Bureau of Labor Statistics. (n.d.). *Career outlook*. Retrieved from https://www.bls.gov/career-outlook/subject/education_level.htm

SECTION FIVE

WHO SHALL TEACH THEM?

The demographics of the United States are changing, an indisputable fact that is predicted to lead to the U.S. becoming a so-called majority minority country by mid-century, with non-Hispanic Whites projected to be slightly under 50% of the population. That trend has accelerated in recent decades, especially with young people.

> In 2019, for the first time, more than half of the nation's population under age 16 identified as a racial or ethnic minority. Among this group, Latino or Hispanic and Black residents together comprise nearly 40% of the population. Given the greater projected growth of all nonwhite racial minority groups compared to whites – along with their younger age structure – the racial diversity of the nation that was already forecasted to flow upward from the younger to older age groups looks to be accelerating. (Frey, 2020)

This is even true in the traditionally white, middle-class suburbs around our largest metropolitan areas. Whites are now at 48% of students in public schools in those suburbs (Chen, Yukiko Furuya, Harwin, & Herold, 2021). The economics of the suburbs are changing rapidly as well, as 40% of students are now eligible for free and reduced lunch. "We" are not who we used to be, and our demographics will continue to shift away from a white, middle-class country that still defines, for many, who the U.S. is, or should be.

There is one area of our population that has remained relatively stable, demographically, and that is the public school teacher corps. Roughly 80% of public school teachers are white, and nearly 80% of those teachers are women. This means that there is an increasing demographic gap between students and teachers in our classrooms, and that gap raises significant questions about what that means for public education (Geiger, 2018).

Wayne Au and Jesse Hagopian made very clear in my conversations with them that having teachers of color were crucial to them finding a place for themselves at school, and for finding their own voices and validity. I never had a teacher of color in my K-12 experience, rarely had a classmate of color, and almost never taught in a building that had more than one or two teachers of color, even in buildings where most of the students were Black or Brown. The fact that our schools are re segregating, by race and by class means that the gap between teachers and students will continue to widen, and the gap between communities of students will also widen (Mattea, 2019). As the demographic gap widens between teachers and students, what does that mean for the education our students will receive, and what, if anything does that suggest about actions we might take.

We've just taken a brief look at what we need to consider about the content they will need. Who will be their teachers? What will they (their teachers) need to know and be able to do if they are to be successful at teaching in a transformed educational system? What's most important about teaching and about those who are engaged in teaching, and how can we recruit, encourage, educate, and support those who teach? We clearly can't expect those currently teaching in schools, who have been trained within existing teacher education systems designed with the state's focus and requirements in mind to be able to seamlessly transition to teaching content they likely do not know, or to connect with the full range of students within their classrooms whose stories, cultures, histories, and concerns they don't know. This does not mean that many of our current teachers can't make the transformation advocated by the authors in this book, but it does mean that it won't happen without significant professional development, ongoing support, and time. And when it comes to recruiting and educating new teachers who will be active participants in the educational transformation, there needs to be significant changes in who we invite, encourage, and accept into our teacher education programs, significant changes in what they learn/experience in those programs, and significant changes in how they are supported and nurtured while they are in those programs, and while they are in their early years of teaching.

There are three chapters in this section focusing on the teachers we need. The first is from Jan Maher, who advises that "if we are to be effective guides of and models for young people, we need to cultivate certain dispositions *first of all* in ourselves," which will enable us to more effectively work with our students. Educators who know themselves and are practicing and modeling the dispositions they want their students to develop are most likely to be effective in reaching them, and in having their students trust what they are teaching.

The second features Alyssa Arnell, Linda McCarthy and Leo Hwang sharing their stories of becoming social justice educators. Each describes the ways in which their challenges as young people helped to shape their views on and passion for justice and led to them becoming the teachers they are and how those experiences are crucial to them being able to connect with and understand their students.

I have a conversation with Professor Wayne Au in the third chapter, talking about who we need to be teaching our young people if we want fundamental change to happen. It is a topic that I've worried about all through this book project, and I was looking for someone to speak with about it. Wayne is an internationally known professor, author, and activist. He served as an interim dean at his university and is an involved parent, so he has insights from many different vantage points, and he is a tireless advocate for justice and for decentralizing education away from a Eurocentric focus. He is deeply engaged in helping to bring change to the teacher education program on his campus and has both thoughts and questions of how we move forward in finding, educating, and holding on to the teachers our children need.

REFERENCES

Chen, X., Furuya, Y., Harwin, A., & Herold, B. (2021, March 17). *The dramatic demographic shifts resharing suburban schools: 7 Key data points to know*. EdWeek. Retrieved from https://www.edweek.org/leadership/the-dramatic-demographic-shifts-reshaping-suburban-schools-7-key-data-points-to-know/2021/03

Frey, W. H. (2020, July 1). *The nation is diversifying even faster than predicted, according to new census data*. Brookings Institute. Retrieved from https://www.brookings.edu/research/new-census-data-shows-the-nation-is-diversifying-even-faster-than-predicted/

Geiger, A. W. (2018, August 27). *America's public school teachers are far less racially and ethnically diverse than their students*. Pew Research Center. Retrieved from https://www.pewresearch.org/fact-tank/2018/08/27/americas-public-school-teachers-are-far-less-racially-and-ethnically-diverse-than-their-students/

Meatto, K. (2019, May 2). *Still separate, still unequal: Teaching about school segregation and educational inequality*. New York Times. Retrieved from https://www.nytimes.com/2019/05/02/learning/lesson-plans/still-separate-still-unequal-teaching-about-school-segregation-and-educational-inequality.html

Walker, T. (2018, June 8). *Who is the average U.S. teacher?* NEAToday. Retrieved from https://www.nea.org/advocating-for-change/new-from-nea/who-average-us-teacher

CHAPTER THIRTEEN

Disposed to Democracy

JAN MAHER

The United States, once considered among the world's most functional democracies, slipped during the years 2016–2020 into the category of "flawed." The rating, by The Economist Intelligence Unit, "is based on ... the electoral process and pluralism, civil liberties, the functioning of government, political participation, and political culture."[1]

Adding to these issues that were public and known when the rating was announced are the recent revelations of how relentlessly our 45th president pressured the Department of Justice and dozens of state election officials and others to overturn the results of our 2020 free and fair election. To make matters even worse, several states have already passed legislation making voting more difficult and making it easier for the will of the voters to be overruled by party partisans in power.

We are leaving our children and their children to face a world of climate change, gun violence, pandemics, political instability, a dizzying rate of technological change, on the precipice of losing our democratic institutions. What dispositions will serve them as they navigate the uncertainty we are bequeathing them? Who should help them to develop and learn? And can we find our way back to be among the world's strongest democracies as we confront this future?

1 Democracy Index 2020 – Economist Intelligence Unit (eiu.com)

I believe the old adage "if you aren't part of the solution you are part of the problem" applies. We all need to participate, honor the pluralistic nature of our society, and foster a culture that champions democratic ideals. I suggest as well, that if we are to be effective guides of and models for young people, we need to cultivate certain dispositions *first of all* in ourselves, develop the skills to express them, and then, as we continue to attend to our own growth, we will be better able to guide the young people in our lives. Otherwise, we are in danger (and our children are in danger) of simply passing on the dispositions that brought us to this state of affairs in the first place.

If we value democracy, and I sincerely hope that all who are reading this do, there are some dispositions and their associated skills that are urgently needed that it will serve us and our children well to cultivate. I will address three that I feel are of particular importance.

DISPOSITION NO. 1: TRUTH SEEKING IN AN AGE OF DISINFORMATION AND CONSPIRACY NARRATIVES

"A lie can travel around the world while the truth is still lacing its boots up." This adage, variously attributed and misattributed, has been around in one form or another since 1787 but it has taken on particular importance and urgency in 2021.[2]

Two lies that went viral in 2020 have proven particularly damaging to our democracy. One claims that Covid-19 is no worse than an ordinary flu and that public health warnings to wear masks and socially distance are intended to control our behavior and rob us of our freedoms. Another asserts the 2020 election was rigged to steal the victory from incumbent Donald J. Trump. With the 45th President as the highest profile promulgator of both, these big lies spread rapidly, persist, and have even gained ground in some communities as I write these words nearly a year later. Both have major consequences that threaten the unity that we presume when we speak of the *United* States. Approaching one millions dead, still counting, and with large swaths of the country in the grip of a resurgence due to the Delta variant and the steadfast opposition of so many to vaccination and masking. Insurrectionists attacking the Congress on January 6, 2021, and a substantial percentage of Trump supporters, egged on by members of Congress, persisting in the belief that it was a peaceful demonstration even in the face of sworn testimony from Capitol police first responders and a plethora of video images from police body cams as well as the phones and video cameras of the protesters themselves.

---

2 A Lie Can Travel Halfway Around the World While the Truth Is Putting On Its Shoes – Quote Investigator

We cannot sustain a functional democracy on lies. We cannot effectively deal with crises that threaten our future on a foundation built of deceits. The disposition to want to know the truth is paramount to negotiating our collective future(s), but it is not, in and of itself, enough. We need the skills to sort truth from falsehood. That skill set includes critical thinking, but also the skill of knowing what we don't know. We need to be clear about why we think we know what we think we know, and honest with ourselves about whether what we think we know is supported by facts, and not just opinions. It includes listening, really listening to others. It includes looking not just once but twice, three times, or more before we leap, and searching always for multiple points of view. It requires, too, that we are aware of our own biases and of the seductive appeal of having them confirmed. It requires that we be aware of how falsehoods can take hold on social media platforms and how we can fall victim to them. Artist Erin Babnik has summed up this process in a post on Facebook cautioning about the spread of conspiracy narratives:

> While you may not think that you're susceptible to these theories, you should at least be aware of how they spread…
> They will make a post that makes no claims and draws no conclusions. Instead, they post a provocative, alarming question or else a pondering phrase meant to pique your curiosity and to send you searching for more information …
>
> 1) The question itself will contain some very specific statistic or morsel of information that will lead you directly to their theory if you use it as a search term.
> 2) The question will be vague but alarming and will be accompanied by a series of links. These links will have no rational connection to each other and are likely to come from a variety of news sources, some of which you may even trust … the pattern of connection suggested by the list of links leads to something much "larger".
>
> In either case, the goal is to get you hooked … You follow the crumbs and come to a conclusion that you have been led to "find", a conclusion that will seem to connect the random dots … it's a Eureka moment that provides a rush and that drives the need to learn more. It makes you feel connected to that conclusion because you researched it on your own – you "get" it. The conspiracy theory gives a feeling of being smart enough to have figured it out, to see what other people don't see.
>
> The susceptible person then makes wider searches and comes into contact with other people doing the same. It snowballs, and eventually beliefs form and take root.
>
> …These theories are attractive to some people because they appear to give some sense of order to otherwise confusing times, or they give a feeling of importance and power to people who feel sidelined (i.e. they feel "in the know" when most of the world is "brainwashed"), or they provide a social network to someone who is lonely.

She concludes, " ... just keep your wits about you. Stay curious because curiosity is a key element of creativity, but also stay sane!"[3]

Another realm where disinformation is seeded and spread is in headlines. Some of them are headlines that directly quote the disinformation – because it is attention-grabbing (clickbait) – and others are headlines that mischaracterize the content below/behind the headline to grab attention by posing a rhetorical question. "Is the moon really made of green cheese after all?" it might tease us. But if we read the article, we find it may have nothing to do with green cheese and more to do with some actual discovery of a particular mineral on the moon. The person who simply skims headlines (or consumes memes rather than actual news) may hold on to the impression that someone has turned up proof of a green cheese moon. The next thing you know, wide swaths of the population think NASA is hiding something from us.

Another headline tactic is to quote the most outrageous thing a well-known political figure has said whether it contains a grain of truth or not. Media figures and social influencers may amplify it. Untethered from truth, it trends on Twitter and TikTok, sweeps across Facebook, takes root on lesser-known social media sites that cater to conspiracy fears.

In the marketplace, or battleground if you prefer war imagery, of ideas, democracy is threatened by those who would, wittingly or unwittingly, spread lies and disinformation. Each of us has a role to play to make sure we take the time to ferret out the truth of a matter and refrain from spreading anything but that truth, even if we are tempted by something that confirms our own biases.

In our K-12 and college classrooms, we can construct learning experiences that underscore the importance of seeing a situation from multiple points of view in order to have a more truthful understanding of it. From books that encourage young readers to look again at images that appear to be one thing at first, and another when you turn the page, or zoom in or out, and games such as "Telephone," to classroom meetings and talking circles, to simulated town meetings and authentic original research, there are activities that at each age level help to inculcate the skills we need to sort fact from fiction.

DISPOSITION NO. 2: EMPATHIZING IN AN AGE OF US AND THEM

Empathy is feeling what others feel. Elements of it seem to be hard-wired. Mirror neurons cause us to display physiological responses to seeing others in certain

---

[3] Babnick, E. (2021, January). *To my young and curious friends.* posted on Facebook, quoted with permission of the author.

states as if we, ourselves, were experiencing what they are. This human capacity to "feel with" others is an integral element that binds us together in social groups. The flip side of this is that research indicates we are also capable of indifference and even pleasure at the pain of others if we perceive them to be *outside* our group.

In a pluralistic society, with a democratic system of governance that presumably functions for the common good and yet has devolved into dysfunctional partisanship, it can be a challenge to forgo *schadenfreude* in favor of empathy. However, it is worth remembering that rejoicing at the ill-fortune of others who are in the same systems we are comes with inherent contradictions and pitfalls. When we perceive others rejoicing at our misfortune we harbor resentment, perhaps experience humiliation, possibly plot revenge. Why would the victims of our own glee not do the same? And how does this advance the common good in a democratic society? (Hint: it doesn't.)

Enemies of democracy, both foreign and domestic, are shrewd at exploiting the power of media, and especially social media platforms, to pit us against each other. Yet, we cannot sustain a democracy when the population of the nation bitterly sorts itself into unyielding categories of us and them.

Educational consultant Lucinda Garthwaite contemplates the potential power of practicing thinking of "us" in ways that include "those whose experiences, beliefs, behaviors and perspectives vary wildly from mine, even people who would do violence to those with whom they don't agree, including, perhaps, me." She asks, "How would that change my day-to-day, or my actions in the conscious service of social justice, equity and nonviolence?" She concludes, "That simple level of care can lead to understanding, compassion, the possibility of relationship. History offers plenty to suggest that understanding, compassion and relationship – on balance with a stalwart insistence on justice and nonviolence, is indeed a powerful recipe for change."[4]

We can each practice this in our own ways when our first impulse is to reject another's feelings or position out of hand. We can remind ourselves of the adage "hurt people hurt people" when we feel hurt ourselves and when we see others who are hurting. We can model for the children in our lives an ethos of respecting the lived experiences and feelings of others even and especially if and when we disagree with the conclusions they have come to as a result of those experiences.

We can practice, too, through engagement in the points of view of people whose experiences differ from our own. Empathy for others increases when we have real-life interaction with them. Not only that. Research has shown that even imaginative engagement, such as reading literary novels (character-driven) increases empathy, as does experiencing the arts in general.

---

4 Garthwaite, Lucinda, April 2, 2021, *Intersections*, the newsletter of the Institute for Liberatory Innovation, Montpelier, VT

In the United States, we can practice the "us" in U.S.

In our classrooms, we can help our students experience the power of the group by having them work in groups and teams, but groups that change members every few weeks. We can debrief this process and engage them in thinking and feeling about what it means to be part of a team in ways that pit them against others versus part of a team that cooperates toward a shared goal. We can ask them to consider all the teams and groups they are part of, and what the very largest ones are, up to, including, and perhaps even beyond "human." We can ask them to identify the ways they were most helpful to their groups, the ways others were most helpful, and the behaviors and attitudes that led to their groups being less successful (without naming names). We can offer them the opportunity to engage in debate while advocating for a point of view with which they disagree, to challenge them to represent the "other" side of a question. And we can both model our insistence that everyone in the classroom is listened to with respect and full attention by engaging in that listening and attending and intervening quickly when that is not happening.

DISPOSITION NO. 3: RESILIENCE IN AN AGE OF CONSTANT CRISES AND ACCELERATING CHANGE

The Covid-19 Pandemic brought an extraordinary level of challenge to a world already facing increasing climate catastrophes. In the United States, we can add the stresses of extreme partisanship in our political life, the social unrest and upheaval that attend our long-overdue and still uncertain reckoning with racial injustice, and the rapidity with which many traditionally held values were challenged by changing social mores.

Our bodies and brains are designed to handle intermittent stress but now suffer from levels of chronic stress that produce numerous negative health and learning consequences.

The intense stress and rapid change of 2020 took a great toll. The Kaiser Family Foundation reports that anxiety and depressive disorders, substance abuse and overdose deaths, and suicide rates were significantly higher compared to 2019,[5] and National Commission on Covid-19 and Criminal Justice (NCCCJ) reported

---

5   The Implications of COVID-19 for Mental Health and Substance Use, Nirmita Panchal, Rabah Kamal, Cynthia Cox Follow @cynthiaccox on Twitter, and Rachel Garfield Follow @RachelLGarfield on Twitter. Published: February 10, 2021 Kaiser Family Foundation website, retrieved at The Implications of COVID-19 for Mental Health and Substance Use | KFF It is worth noting that other sources report the suicide rate as having gone down 5% during 2020.

that domestic violence in the United States rose by 8.2%. Particularly at risk were communities of color, women, young people, low-income people, and essential workers, but a significant majority of all Americans of all ages, ethnicities, and income levels experienced heightened anxiety and depression.[6]

A vibrant democracy depends upon informed citizen engagement. A population overwhelmed by depression and anxiety is ill-equipped to maintain the eternal vigilance that is said to be the price of liberty.

To negotiate the relentless stress and challenges of rapid change, we need to find moments of rest, of peace, of safety in our lives. Only in these spaces can we slow down, indulge in the best kind of "slow thinking," the term psychologist Daniel Kahneman coined to describe a deliberative effortful thinking rather than defaulting to our "gut" responses,[7] be open to new ideas, and solve problems.

Educator Erika Huggins, reflecting on the importance of self-renewal to keep our energy and spirits up to keep making good change in the world, notes:

> The human body is a little ecosystem. We can't keep pushing it without giving it nutrition, water, and rest, without giving it a way to clear the emotions that accumulate over time, especially when you're out there on the front lines. If we don't recharge our batteries by taking care of our minds, our hearts, our bodies, we won't be able to be in it for the long haul.
> So, when I think of the front-line people, wherever they are in the world, whatever that front line is, I think about the breath – how important it is to pause and breathe. Even if you have an hour to sit somewhere and be in nature or walk in nature, which is very, very important. Or hang out with children or look in the eyes of a baby. You can at least sit for two minutes and just become aware of your breath and the power of it to help you reset.[8]

We cannot sustain a democracy if we don't know how to renew our energy to confront the continual challenges we face. People worn down seek easy answers and are vulnerable to the promises of autocrats. Resilience requires rest and recuperation.

In our learning spaces, too, we can have times for rest and reflection, whether it be naptime in pre-school, stretching together to warm up for the day in an elementary classroom, practicing "wait time" and the "think" part of "think-pair-share" discussions in middle and high school, or inviting a moment of relaxation

---

6   National Commission on Covid-19 and Criminal Justice, February 23, 2021, Impact Report: Covid-19 and Domestic Violence, retrieved at NCCCJ - Impact Report: COVID-19 and Domestic Violence Trends (counciloncj.org)
7   See Daniel Kahneman's book *Thinking Fast and Slow* for in-depth discussion of how we don't always know what we think we know.
8   Tapper, C.M. (2020, July 16). *A former Black Panther Party leader reflects on her revolutionary work*. Zora. Retrieved at Ericka Huggins: The Former Black Panther Party Leader Talks Black Lives Matter

as students enter our classrooms by playing music or having a thought-provoking quote on the board for them to contemplate during a short period of silence.

We cannot be passive in the face of forces that push high stakes tests, mandate policies that devalue our children's experiences and subvert critical thinking, and underfund programs that support the physical, social, and emotional well-being of our children. Even as we strive to create the best possible circumstances for learning and caring inside our classrooms, we must be leaders outside our classrooms as well. And keep remembering to breathe!

In much of the literature I've seen about managing the stress of rapid change, writers reference the idea of reminding oneself of one's own core values. As we the people of the United States move into our shared future, let us continually remind ourselves of the core values set forth in the Preamble to our Constitution. Let us remind ourselves that the "us" that is the "U.S." is an ever-expanding, increasingly inclusive pluralistic society. Let us practice being "us" in order to sustain our democracy and teach our children well. Starting in our homes, our neighborhoods, our classrooms, our social gathering places (both virtual and in real life), let us model justice, domestic tranquility, the common defense, the general welfare. Let us secure the blessings of liberty to *all* of ourselves and *all* our posterity.

CHAPTER FOURTEEN

Finding Our Paths to Social Justice Education

ALYSSA ARNELL, LEO HWANG, AND LINDA MCCARTHY

INTRODUCTION

For several months, we, the three authors, met once a week to share stories about our evolution as social justice educators. While we come from different backgrounds and are different ages, we have each pursued a career in academia, motivated by a desire to address social injustice. Different identities and experiences have shaped our lives, but we share a common understanding of social justice and a collective desire to make an impact on the lives of our students. We are Korean, Black, and White, all raised in the United States. We are cisgender heterosexual, bisexual, and gay. We are from the northeast and the south. Together, our ages span two decades. We were raised upper-middle, middle, and lower middle class. While we each found our way to the field of education, we share common values of equity, access, and empathy.

As social justice educators, we view our roles in education not just as passing along discipline-specific content but communicating a framework for understanding the world around us, and the social dynamics within it. We ask our students to examine their own positionalities and the experiences that have led them to our classrooms. We model the curiosity and humility indispensable for learning, while striving to help students develop a set of values and their own voices. We foster a sense of agency and a responsibility to civic duty. We do all of this through a social justice framework which equips students with a lens, a voice, and an understanding that their life experiences are intrinsically linked with the world around them.

Each of our stories illustrate that the path to becoming social justice educators often meanders but is shaped by the connections we make with others. Our paths include histories of feeling isolated or marginalized, looking for reflections of ourselves in the communities around us. We reached out for guidance from those whom we saw as mentors. We sought out our own stories in literature, finding connections in the social metaphors of literary giants. We were affected by significant historical events, recognizing their impact on our own communities. None of these paths led us directly to our calling as teachers, but the learning we gained from experiences along the way is infused in our practice. We all have been fortunate to achieve careers where we can empower students and influence change in our communities. Yet we maintain humility, understanding that we always have more to learn and that we will never stop growing as educators.

ALYSSA

I fell in love with history in the summer before my junior year of college, when I reluctantly took a summer course on the Civil War that changed the way I viewed history. It was the first time that I learned about slavery in a deep and meaningful way. My paternal grandmother raised me on stories of her own experiences in the Jim Crow South, and the oral histories of our family's past that had been carried down through the few generations from slavery. I suppose part of my younger disconnect with the past is related to the ways in which the U.S. History has been told. Traditionally, U.S. history was collected and taught in ways that often relegated the experiences, contributions, and collected memory of non-Whites to the background landscapes of stories and scenes that, in turn, put White leadership, experiences, and culture in the forefront.

It was not until I took that class on the Civil War that I made the connections between my own experiences and the larger history of the culture and society in which I lived. I went through a Renaissance that took me through a period of Black militancy. Beyond that was a reckoning with the Kingian philosophies of universal love. I continued my education with mentors who guided me towards a deeper understanding of civil rights. This education set me on a path of community engagement and civil rights enforcement in South Florida.

Miami-Dade County is a large county covering over 2,400 square miles of land. It is also one of the most populous counties in the country and home to people from across the world. I moved in very diverse cultural circles during my time working in civil rights advocacy. I read stories about civil rights to Haitian children, participated in celebrations for queer people of color, and provided disability sensitivity training for city employees and private management companies. I traveled to the southern edge of the county to talk to groups of newly arrived immigrants and visited high schools to remind pending graduates that they were protected under civil rights laws. In all these communities, people shared intimate stories of struggle, resistance, bravery, and triumph. It was the first time that I lived and worked among such richness of difference. And yet, as I learned more about what makes us all unique, a new understanding began to dawn on me. I began to see how much we all have in common.

The intimacy of my experiences with others whose realities and struggles were different from my own helped me learn to see past my own perspective. I became aware of some stereotyped messages that I internalized as a young person. By helping others fight injustice, I also grew in my capacity to appreciate the world and my place in it.

This was not a lonely journey. I was never without my advisors. Academic mentors steered me towards the writings of MLK, Angela Davis, and James Baldwin. These historic voices shaped my appreciation for social justice activism. In my civil rights work, community members opened their circles and spaces to me so that I might learn about community engagement. Local representatives and business leaders gave me their time and helped me learn to communicate in ways that might effect change. There were obstacles, of course. But struggle is inherent in the experience of living.

It was not long after President Obama was elected that something began to happen more and more often: police were shooting Black men in and around Miami. In 2010 and 2011, city police shot and killed seven Black men over the course of 7 months. I worked in these neighborhoods. I was in these communities. I spent most weekends at open-air community fairs distributing information on civil rights and speaking at homebuyer workshops and community events. These were my friends and neighbors, and we were all mourning and somewhat fearful.

We drove slowly in our neighborhoods to ensure we would not be pulled over. It was about this time that I was stopped by an officer who approached my car, screaming and accusing me of swerving in traffic and crossing several lanes to almost sideswipe his vehicle. I was so stunned that I was silent. After all, I had been in one lane for several miles. He then demanded, "Do you even speak English?" To which I replied, "Yes officer, I do. I am just confused by your accusations." He seemed surprised and told me that I should be very careful on the roads and stormed off. I often wonder what would have happened that day if I did not speak English.

There was a new focus and sense of urgency that washed through the nonprofit world in South Florida during this time and new initiatives and targeted work emerged. I saw increased partnership opportunities with companies like the Boys and Girls Clubs and local schools. So, in 2012, when one of our own local teenage boys was stalked and murdered in Sanford, Florida while walking home from buying sweet tea and Skittles at the local convenience store, it was devastating for our community. George Zimmerman, the neighborhood watch coordinator for the Sanford community, had been instructed by police to stay in his car when he called to report a suspicious person walking in a hoodie, but he ignored those directions. He stalked Trayvon Martin and then shot him while the two struggled on the ground. He was charged with murder and pled not guilty under Florida's *Stand Your Ground* statute. Our community held out hope that the courts would deliver some justice. Instead, on a Saturday evening at 10 p.m. in July 2012, the news broke that Zimmerman was found not guilty. It was unbelievable but not surprising that the news broke at such a late hour when people would not be able to immediately react.

The following Monday, I was in the small satellite office that I shared with my colleague who was a Black father of two teenage boys. I will never forget how he looked when he arrived that morning. His eyes were puffy and red. His voice trembled as he described the conversation he had with his two sons the day before. It was not safe to travel alone. You could not cover your head with a hoodie. You could not be out in the evening. You could be targeted for your race. You could be killed for no other reason but their fear and racist suspicion. That same week, I was offered an adjunct teaching job at Dillard University in New Orleans. It was a 75% decrease in my pay. I would have to live off my savings for a while. I would have to break my rule on quitting a job without having secured another full-time position. But I would be teaching at a historically Black college in the city that felt like home. It was the easiest decision.

There is a different cultural complexity in that part of Southern Louisiana. New Orleans, itself, is an intricate mix of French colonialism, Haitian and African originalism, and Cajun wonder. It is a Black city and a European city. It was also the site of large-scale federal failure and practical abandonment.

When I began teaching at Dillard, I found that many of my students were ill-prepared to engage in academic research. Because of the lack of governmental intervention after Katrina, many spent their childhoods in neighborhoods that did not have libraries, leaving them unprepared to navigate such college resources. I would take them over in small groups and we would wander the aisles and examine different books of interest. Over time they began to trust the safety of our classroom. Repeatedly, my students would find connections in our class content to their own lives and would share stories about their experiences during Hurricane Katrina. I would often find myself pausing the class content in order to make space for students to talk about the trauma of that time. Some sat for days on the rooftops of local businesses and homes waiting for rescue. I saw students comforting each other – supporting each other through illness and loss. I watched them celebrate good fortunes together. I came to understand a deeper meaning of community building and community outreach.

There is a real responsibility in higher education to ensure that students not only learn the content of a given discipline, but also become empowered in their voice and their reasoning. I learned that this was a process of creating brave spaces where we made connections based upon commonalities; my students trusted each other to be honest, truthful, and respectful of difference; and we all learned in those moments how to support each other. It was not always easy. Many sad and painful truths were shared, but we were brave, and we faced it together. I thought this experience was unique to the place and the moment, but I was wrong.

When I moved to Western Massachusetts to develop a history program at a community college, the demographics of my students changed dramatically. The move brought me to the poorest county in the state and it did not take long for me to realize that these students lacked certain academic skills. What I once saw as a regional and racial issue became one of class. I started to see an even deeper connection between institutional power and community impact. Embedded within class are the issues of race, gender, nationality, disability, age, and identity. Within class is a shared common experience of struggle and marginalization that transcends one group identity. I still find myself walking small groups of students to the library to show them how to do real in-person research.

In the summer of 2020, the lynching of George Floyd painfully rocked our country. The images of a defiant police officer slowly killing a helpless man was one of a history of moments of awakening for this country. I think about all the students and neighbors that I have so far been blessed to know, guide, and learn from. I wonder about how they navigated this painful moment and the movement that was part of the aftermath. I wonder who marched. I wonder who grieves even now. I wonder if my small role in their development has helped them in the ways that I hope.

What does it mean to be a social justice educator? We see a social justice framework in education as both a process and a goal (Adams, et al, p. 1). As educators, we make intentional choices to highlight content that pushes students of all backgrounds to reflect on their assumptions about the world. Through an examination of historical patterns, social forces, literature, and research methodologies, we all strive to engender agency and empathy in ways that strengthen marginalized voices. We interweave the narratives of divergent voices within our content so that students who rarely see people like themselves represented in higher education, see themselves reflected in the stories that we share and the lessons that we teach. We lead those with privilege to an understanding of their role in constructed hierarchies and nurture a sense of responsibility to contribute to social change.

While the content of our disciplines vary, there is also significant overlap. Social issues and inequities are fundamental to who we are and how we evolved as a country. They are interwoven in our shared history, the same way that the analysis of literature weaves together history and social issues and helps us understand our world better.

In addition to content, we identify the skills of empathy, agency, and critical thinking as foundational to fostering students' capacity to be productive members of society. Part of our role as educators is to help students recognize the institutional structures of society that contribute to theirs and others' oppression, because once we can recognize this, we can then understand and take action. Making sense of the past helps us to contextualize the present so we can improve the future. By increasing our understanding not only of facts, but of our human experiences within these contexts, we aim to raise awareness of our collective responsibility to each other.

To this end, we teach critical thinking skills as the foundational tools for analyzing history, society and literature. Evaluating evidence and integrating new information with prior assumptions makes room for this critical thought process and becomes part of the way our students navigate their worlds. We train students to consume and synthesize information, identify subjectivities, and discern fact from fiction.

Ultimately, our classrooms are a microcosm of society beyond the walls of higher education. Most of the dynamics that operate in our world eventually show up in our classrooms. We give students the opportunity to practice new skills, to try out new language, to envision new ways of relating with people different from them, and to envision systems that reflect the values of equity, social justice and respect. We humbly hope that our students are transformed by their experiences in our classrooms and that they will become motivated to take what they learn and transform their communities, families, and workplaces.

LINDA

I teach my sociology students that there is no such thing as objectivity, and that anyone who claims to be objective is willfully ignoring their own positionalities. Instead, I encourage them to recognize the lenses through which they see the world, and to identify the social identities that have shaped their biographies. As a White lesbian woman, my own identities have been integral to my journey toward a career teaching sociology. Sociology is an ideal discipline that encompasses a study of society, examination of one's positionalities, and a sense of responsibility to better the world. It never fails to bring me joy that I get to discuss social issues and inequality with students as part of my job. I cultivate both the *sociological imagination* and something called *sociological mindfulness*. In the first, I want students to understand that their lives are shaped by larger social forces, and that this historical moment and their own biographies are intertwined. None of us are as independent as we believe. In the second, I want students to understand how they are connected to others and that their individual choices impact others. Though we are socialized to think otherwise, no one person's life exists outside this context. The most important concept that I teach students is that everything is socially constructed. And, if we created this, we can also change it.

My own biography was defined by feeling marginalized, isolated, and in search of community as a young person. I was bullied by kids from my neighborhood for being different. I couldn't pick up on social nuances and often broke the rules without understanding they even existed. I verbalized thoughts that others knew to keep to themselves. I couldn't detect what I needed to do to be just like everyone else. My attempts were sometimes blunders that made me more of a target than I'd already been. Increasingly, instead of looking to other people for connection, I found myself in the stories of others, and never left home without a book. This feeling of being an outsider has kept me ever aware of how my students might feel, in an educational system that does not support or expect their success. I never saw myself in my teachers, so I feel a responsibility to be honest and genuine in the classroom. I feel a special responsibility to LGBT youth and to those with gay parents or siblings; I recognize that I might be the only lesbian professor they ever have.

I began reading *The Boston Globe* regularly when I was about 10 years old. One of my favorite parts was *Confidential Chat*, which was a combination of *Dear Abby* and a recipe swap. They fielded everything from people seeking sewing patterns, to what to do with stacks of old magazines, to people wondering where to bring their pet bird for medical care. It was a community – letters were printed and readers would write in with their advice. Before the Internet, this was a primary way for readers to find information for any problem, great or small. You name it, there was someone asking about it, and someone was there to respond with a solution. I imagine I loved this partly because I saw people connecting with one another and finding common ground.

One of the best decisions my parents made for me was to send me to a YMCA summer camp for girls when I was 10. There, I met children from working class cities like Roxbury, Dorchester, Mattapan, and other places I had never heard of. I had the opportunity to make friends with children of color for the first time. Instead of feeling like an outsider, I felt like an insider; people knew my name and wanted to engage with me. Everyone was different, and for the first time, I felt seen somehow. I returned to that camp for 4, 6, and then 8 weeks, over the next five summers. It was the most diverse environment I was ever in as a child and, truth be told, these were the best summers of my life.

My last summer at camp, when I was 15, there were rumors that Cathy Jacobson had been seen kissing another counselor in Chalet. I was confused. I felt I was supposed to express disgust, and I probably did, but I was also secretly intrigued. My best friend and I would often lie on the tennis courts at night, the concrete still warm from the sun, looking up at the stars, smoking cigarettes. We talked about everything, and eventually we tentatively addressed the rumored lesbian activities at camp. It felt like just gossiping, but internally, I was trying to conceive of a world where I might be gay.

Arriving at boarding school that fall, I couldn't shake the idea that people could be gay. Was I? Though there was a school psychologist available to the student body, asking for help was not a skill I had developed. Instead, I investigated on my own. At night at the library, while I should have been studying history or math, I stood in the stacks trying to absorb what I could about what being gay meant and how I would know if I was. Although I found some information about "the homosexual lifestyle," I wanted to know about real people. I wanted to know about gay people.

One day in late fall, it dawned on me. There, in my beloved *Boston Globe*, in the *Living* section, was a possibility. I wrote to the readers of Confidential Chat and asked, "How do you know if you are gay? Where do you meet gay people? I think I might be. What should I do?" My letter was printed, I was shocked to see it, but there it was, on page 3 of the *Living* section. It seemed innocuous enough, that one paragraph, those few questions. But one day, some weeks later, I stood in the school mailroom with *The Globe*, and there it was again. My letter. But this time, *The Globe* had published it on the front page of the *Living* section, as a feature story about gay youth. This was 1982, when many gay people were shunned and disowned by their families. And way before gay and lesbian people were featured on television in any positive roles. The feature story called attention to the isolation of gay youth (me) and made suggestions for how our society could better support them.

And then the mail came. Letters upon letters. Advice, encouragement, cautions, Psalms. Many elders in the gay community wrote supportive, "It will get better" letters. And some cautioned me that while they too were attracted to the same sex when they were young, they knew enough to turn away from those feelings, and that I should too, that life would be better for me if I resisted these feelings which veered from the natural way of God. On the whole, the letters were mostly supportive. They suggested I go to BAGLY (Boston Area Gay and Lesbian Youth) in Boston, but that felt about as possible as going to Mars. I never went to Boston on my own; I was a young 15, sheltered in the suburbs. I couldn't imagine getting there or finding a building somewhere in the city with gay kids talking about their lives. Without access to transportation, or independence from my parents, I was at a loss as to my next steps. So I took none. I kept the letters in boxes under my bed, and occasionally laid them all out to review my options again.

I never came out in high school. With no support, no community, and a profound terror about this possibility, I laid away those feelings like the letters under my bed. I found a boyfriend (or, he found me), which helped me to fit in better, which was always my primary concern. It wasn't until I encountered lesbians again, 8 years later, that these feelings found their way back into my consciousness.

As a college transfer student mid-year, the choice of available classes was limited, and I ended up in a Women's Studies class called *Contemporary Issues*. In that class, my world was transformed. Among other issues, I learned about sexual harassment and assault, date rape, domestic violence, and the wage gap. This course led to more, and to a Women's Studies major, where concepts like intersectionality, white privilege, and feminist theory equipped me with an analytical lens to help me make sense of the world around me. Classes like African American Women Writers, Feminist Theory, Chicana Studies, and Feminist Theology not only introduced me to alternative understandings of history and society, but illustrated that learning is most powerful when one sees one's self in the material.

In my *Mothers and Daughters in Literature* class, I was taken off guard by the three friendly lesbians who spoke openly about their sexuality. Lesbians. All my memories of camp and being 15 and my letter to *Confidential Chat* came flooding back to me with a mixture of fear and recognition. Serendipitously, I began to see advertisements posted around campus for a Coming Out group that was starting soon. On the scheduled night, I found my way to The Feminist Alliance's office in the Student Center. Walking down the hallway, I was overcome with a physical terror, but I managed to get myself through the doorway. Inside, I found a community and a path to fully embracing my sexuality.

I was introduced to activism. I helped organize and lead *Take Back the Night* marches. I got involved with protests against the Gulf War, and participated in actions against Rocky Flats, where they made plutonium triggers for nuclear bombs. With these groups, I learned about consensus building and affinity groups. I was surrounded by people who also cared about inequality and injustice. I began to recognize the connections between my own experiences and the world around me.

After college, I studied Sociology in graduate school where I was trained in classical theory and methods. Instructed to find a fieldwork site for my master's thesis, I began facilitating at a gay youth support group. My thesis focused on the connection between identity and community, and on the importance of feeling part of a community. I knew from experience how isolating it was to feel so different from everyone else. At the time, I thought the gay youth group was simply a convenient site to conduct my fieldwork, but it was undoubtedly an opportunity to be the role model I never had.

As a doctoral student in the Social Justice Education program at the University of Massachusetts, I learned how to teach about racism, sexism, classism, and other types of oppression. I learned about the importance of both process and content, and, like my college Women's Studies courses, experienced much of the dynamics in the classroom that we were reading about. In the classroom community, we learned not only from the books we were reading, but from each other. We spent intense time together in weekend workshops where there were tears, there was conflict, and there was resolution, sometimes. I observed the skill with which our professors handled and in fact elicited the strong emotions that come from experiencing social injustice.

Today, when I teach sociology, I am relaying content about the theories and concepts important to the field, but I am also cultivating an environment in which experience plays a critical role in our learning. Balancing the emotional and cognitive processes that unfold when delving into difficult topics such as racism, classism, mass incarceration, or nationalism is challenging; it necessitates a group dynamic that centers empathy and acceptance. Creating a brave space where students are willing to take risks and reveal their perspectives is an intentional process. Students will not engage with difficult ideas and with each other, if they do not feel there is room for their stumbles. Students need to be able to raise their hand and blurt out the wrong answer or find a space where they can ask the question that they cannot utter out loud. And, they need to find the place where they can see themselves as belonging in a community they believe in and are willing to fight for.

How do we promote social justice education? We create democratic classrooms with intention, where students actively participate in their own education through problem solving, rather than the passive model of education where students are merely vessels into which information is deposited. In our classes, we value collaboration, individual responsibility, contextualized personal experiences, responsibility, social change, and personal growth. This kind of collective learning often invokes feelings of cognitive dissonance; students come to recognize that the world doesn't actually work as they had been taught to believe. Helping students unpack that confusion is essential for understanding how they are growing. To do that, we create brave spaces for learning where we welcome the affective in the classroom. It is a key way that teaching in a socially just manner differs from traditional pedagogies.

A social justice curriculum is designed to acknowledge, honor, and call forth students' feelings and emotions, and to share these truths as an inherent part of the learning process. In addition, emotion-based learning is considered to be of equal value as discipline-specific theories and ideas. In practice, this translates into an emphasis on the validity of emotional responses to cognitive-based material, and reliance upon critical questions to examine the influence of power and privilege on the perspective of the author, reader, student, and teacher.

As part of our pedagogy, we balance the emotional and cognitive aspects of learning, along with the process (in the classroom) and content (our course material). We establish a learning environment that allows for personal and academic growth. We recognize that students sometimes have personal reactions to course materials, and we attend to those reactions. We respond to the individual students' experiences, while calling attention to systemic and structural forces that shape those experiences.

Group dynamics can affect learning in meaningful and destructive ways, so we attend to the dynamics that develop among students. This requires flexibility and patience and a willingness to cast aside a learning plan in favor of addressing the current moment. We notice and name whose voices are elevated and whose are missing. We allow space for mistakes and stumbles. We support interpersonal interactions that lead to new learning. By viewing conflict as a learning opportunity, we demonstrate that growth can emerge from misunderstanding, if it is addressed in a constructive way. In sum, sometimes the most powerful learning experiences emerge from dynamics among the students in the classroom.

We hope our students see us as whole, fallible people, who have also gone through stages of development and paths of learning. We share with our students that we are all life-long learners and that the more we learn about ourselves, the better we are able to understand how we relate to others.

LEO

In the introduction to *How to Be an Antiracist,* Ibram Kendi writes, "Even now I wonder if it was my poor sense of self that first generated my poor sense of my people. Or was it my poor sense of my people that inflamed a poor sense of myself?" (6) and I am struck with the realization that like Kendi, in my earlier years, I adopted the racist thinking that I was surrounded by and that permeated American society in the 1970s and 1980s. For the longest time I thought I was struggling against racism and racist stereotypes, but the reality is, I had internalized those stereotypes and expectations to the point that I believed that I might be able to craft an entirely new identity that was separate from my lived reality. "Racist ideas make people of color think less of themselves, which makes them more vulnerable to racist ideas," Kendi continues (6). I was very vulnerable.

Racism against Asian men in the 1970s and 1980s had several different stereotypes (Asian women experienced additional layers of stereotypes that were no less destructive). The first was that of the foreigner who was intruding in the spaces of "real" Americans. This sentiment ranged from the, "Go back where you came from!" statement in its mildest form, to the more acerbic sense of Asians as the dehumanized enemy in war where we became, "Chinks, gooks, and Japs." In any case, it was clear that Asians were outsiders and did not belong.

The second stereotype was that of the association of Asian with junk. Made in Japan, Made in China, Made in Korea, Made in Taiwan – those were the stickers on cheap toys, small cars, and unreliable electronics. The anthropomorphized version of this was of Asians as untrustworthy, inscrutable, unfair, cowards and cheats. In its mildest form, it was a joke about cheap products and the highly inflected, "What a bargain!" exclamation. At its most vicious, it manifested in incidents like the killing of Vincent Chin in 1982, a Chinese man who was beaten to death by two Michigan auto workers who blamed him for the success of the Japanese auto industry.

The third stereotype was that of the shamefully inept Asian immigrant that appeared in countless films of the time period. In a mild form, it appeared in the simple Korean peasant characters in the television show *M.A.S.H.* but the most archetypal figure was that of the character Long Duk Dong in *Sixteen Candles*. He represented the utterly bumbling Asian man who lusts after unattainable white women, who find him so unsuitable that the joke is that the man is delusional for even imagining that he has a chance with them. The character is emasculated as a comic gag. It was a cultural phenomenon to have one Asian eunuch buddy in a whole generation of popular movies from *Goonies* to *Fargo*. It made watching movies with white people very uncomfortable.

Stereotype four was the kung fu master. On Boston area TV, in addition to the beloved Bruce Lee films and the *Kung Fu* show reruns, there were the seemingly endless reels of overdubbed Chinese martial arts films and early Japanese manga cartoons. While I watched these shows and movies with rapt attention as they were the only representations of Asians in mass media that were not based in stereotypes, my White peers all saw them as additional fodder for highlighting my difference. They would mouth extra syllables in a pantomime of overdubbed talk while teasing, and of course make the high pitched, "Hi-ya!" sounds of kung fu while kicking the air or making karate chops. It was humiliating to have the one cool and masculine depiction of Asians in popular American culture be coopted and once again made to symbolize the foolish foreigner.

The last stereotype was the model minority: the Asian student as being preternaturally good at math and science. The model minority stereotype is the essentialist racism that Asians are good at these things because that is how their minds work. It is the idea that all Asian kids should become doctors or engineers. It is the idea that the Asian student will behave, will submit to hard work unquestioningly, and will follow any authority figure because they are essentially obsequious.

There are more stereotypes I didn't recognize at the time, or that have evolved since, but these were the images that obstructed my imagination as a child and teen. Because I allowed myself to be shaped by the society around me and did not have the tools to think critically about their impact, because I consumed the mantras of racism, and because I did not have a lot of models or guidance on how to see myself differently, an entire continent of people were amalgamated in my mind to have certain specific traits. I could not imagine alternatives to these images, and I was left to form an identity in response to them. I did not have a strong enough imagination to envision a different kind of Asian masculinity and sexuality. Instead, I saw myself as part of that pan-Asian stereotype and I thought the only way to fight against it was to try to exist outside of those expectations. I did not allow myself to be whomever I wanted to be: I had to be the opposite of these models I saw in the media. I had to be able to respond to bus stop taunts with something that denied the validity of their teasing. I didn't define myself by who I wanted to be, or what I felt might be my preferences; instead, I defined myself in relation to what I was not. In so doing, I also defined myself as "not Asian" and "not Korean," because to be Asian or Korean would mean trying to fit into the American stereotype of Asians or Koreans. I was not going to be the fool, I was not going to be the scapegoat, I was not going to be the nerd. Instead, I was going to misbehave, I was going to be rebellious, I was going to lift weights and play football. I was going to reject the emasculation of the Asian body by becoming hyper-masculine. I was going to hang out with the troubled kids and smoke cigarettes. In all these actions, I ended up denying the existence of my own heritage and sense of self in order to remake myself in what I was convinced was an entirely independent identity, but in reality was a full embrace of the assimilationist ideas of what mainstream White American visions of cool and desirable were.

When I look back at my childhood, my adolescence, my young adulthood, I see the ways this lack of imagination manifested in my life and limited its potential richness. It was not only a fear of embracing White stereotypes, it was a fear of embracing my own identity, and ultimately who I would allow and not allow myself to be. Eventually, I was able to move beyond those limitations. I have been able to learn to recognize and deconstruct socially constructed stereotypes in media and recognize what, of these, I have internalized, and then, explore how I can move beyond these stereotypes and start inhabiting the sense of self that is not inhibited by a lack of imagination.

Kendi explains a similar revelation:

> I feel free to move in my imperfections. I represent only myself. If the judges draw conclusions about millions of Black people based on how I act, then they, not I, not Black people, have a problem. They are responsible for their racist ideas; I am not. I am responsible for my racist ideas; they are not. To be antiracist is to let me be myself, be my imperfect self (p. 205).

Like Kendi, I take responsibility for my own racist ideas, my own lack of imagination. This lack of imagination hindered not only me but hinders people throughout our educational systems. I see reflections of my former self in our students as they seek some kind of connection in their lives. How do they make meaning out of who they are becoming? We can work to address this through an educational system that is designed with a social justice agenda. We need to explicitly privilege racial justice, and integrate a fluid understanding of how to foster and support imagination in our LGBTQIA students, in our students with disabilities, in students from different economic backgrounds and religious faiths. We need to support imagination in all our students.

We do this through an attention to the individual, through a practiced posture of continual self-reflection and exploration so we can better understand how our own failures of imagination were shaped. And we do this through a willingness to listen to stories – the stories of our future doctors, engineers, scientists, musicians, poets, painters, politicians, and playwrights. As we look at our curriculum and our individual courses, where do we encourage these stories? How do we support the sharing and learning that comes from these stories? Our students can reach their full potential only when they have access to the entirety of their capacities. When our students' imaginations and images of themselves are constrained by their experiences of racism, homophobia, sexism, or any other form of discrimination, we are failing as educators. In contrast, when we can witness the transformation that happens when a student is able to realize a full sense of self, when an imagination is unbound, and when they feel safely heard both inside and outside of themselves, that is truly transformative teaching. We can do this by helping students learn to value themselves and value others. To help increase students' imagination by increasing their vocabulary with which they can describe themselves and their experience in this world. Once students can recognize themselves as valid and valuable permutations of humanity, then they can begin to fulfill their potential.

CONCLUSION

It is difficult to forge an identity that is true to one's self and to pursue that vision, and yet it is crucial to finding a way to flourish in life. We have each been confronted with choices, and without the educators who helped us see ourselves, those choices could have led us down long lonely paths, dead-ends, or circular driveways. We were each lucky enough to have encountered the right degree of mentoring, support, and independence. We found ways to integrate those things that are most important to our identities into careers that bring our lives meaning because we are able to help students navigate some of the same challenging paths we have trodden.

In this chapter, we have revealed some of the foundational experiences that have shaped us as people and educators. Each of us has offered a story shaped both internally and externally, by context, history, and community because, while we may walk different paths, we have been led to similar standpoints, undergirded by a set of values established by our experiences, impacted by our mentors, and filtered by our own unique perspectives. At the heart of these shared stories are a few commonalities of note. Like the students that we now teach, we were molded by our college experiences. Our good fortune came from finding those educators who taught us to look for ourselves in the narratives that we embrace.

In academic spaces, we found paths to our callings as social justice educators. We found ways to love ourselves. We were taught a new way to look at the world that gave us active agency and helped us to work within our compassion as we defined our own teaching philosophies. It is this agency that we hope to teach to others: the ability to step beyond the forces that wish to shape us in one uniform image, and instead imagine a diversity of possibilities and futures that are not pre-determined by the expectations of stereotypes.

Being an educator is a responsibility that we each take seriously. We recognize that we may be one stop along the way for our students, who are on their own journey towards their chosen goals and the goals that they will awaken to in our classes. To truly be available to our students, social justice education requires that first we learn to appreciate our own value. Only then can we guide the path for our students to do the same.

FOR FURTHER STUDY

Adams, M. (1997). *Teaching for diversity and social justice: A sourcebook*. Routledge.
Kendi, I. X. (2019). *How to be an antiracist*. Random House Publishing Group.
Schwalbe, M. (2018). *The sociologically examined life: Pieces of the conversation*. Oxford University Press.

CHAPTER FIFTEEN

Transforming the Teacher Corps

A Conversation with Wayne Au

Doug: When you think about the teachers who were the best teachers for you, what leads you to identify them?
Wayne: What all these teachers did, is they helped me make sense of and understand the world and connect with that criticality part. I think the value of education is as much about context as about anything else. And what I mean by that is, when I was at Garfield, and in Mr. Davis's classes, it was the late 80s, there was a rise of African, Afrocentric stuff happening in hip hop, and Do the Right Thing [Ed: the Spike Lee movie], there were conversations about race, and what was happening in the world, and so that class became an avenue for processing and thinking about the world. And so it met a particular need, and helped me to make sense of what was going on in the world. And the same is sort of true all the way through, even when I got to Evergreen [Ed: State College]. Gail Tremblay helped meet some of those sense making questions about who I am, and race and culture and just politics generally. In my doc program I spent my time making sense of "The Academy", and so I would say Mike Apple, and the stuff he introduced me to, and the community that we had built there really spoke to the kinds of things I was sorting through in my own life, and my own thinking.
Doug: I want to move us into thinking about what makes a good teacher. What are some elements that go into us identifying them as good teachers?
Wayne: One is, I think there's an ethos of care. And not to put it in economic terms, but the first word that comes to mind is investment. I mean, someone

who's committed to the connection between the teacher and the student. And for me, it was less so about being committed to academic development, right? I think all those folks I named were all invested in me learning. They all wanted me to learn, and they were committed to that, but I feel like they more cared about me as a person, both my physical care and well-being. I think all these teachers were caring people in that respect, but I think good teachers also care about who their students are in the world. They want to see them go out into that world as strong people who understand what's happening in very critical ways and who want to be alive and be present in their communities. I know we tend to glamorize the idea that we want our kids to become activists and go out and like, do this world changing. But I think, given the state of the world, the amount of trauma and where things are at times, what people are struggling with, I think good teachers want to see their kids be healthy, and carry on healthy lives, whatever that means, and so there's the care around that as well. And then that obviously spreads to community, care for community. If you're going to care for your kids, and care for your students, then you have to be caring about their home lives, what their community is like. I also think good teachers might see their students as individuals, but they don't see them individually. They understand that they are part of relational networks, that are also important to be tending to.

Doug: What I'm hearing is that these teachers also hold an awareness that school is part of a larger picture. It is not a closed system where we only are concerned with what happens in our classroom within our four walls. But if you're going to be healthy out in the world, you have to understand the world.

Wayne: Yeah, absolutely. And you can't be healthy in here without understanding the world. I think good teachers do see schools as part of a broader system and a broader network, and a broader web of relations. The other piece of that is, then, it's really about helping students have some critical sense-making of their contexts, and what their realities are. I think good teachers, and the teachers that have impacted me are grounding us in context and helping us understand things in ways that we didn't before and making sure that that understanding is really applied to our own lived experiences. It's one of the things I appreciate about the Rethinking Schools stuff is the whole idea that you start with where students are at. What does that mean as a foundational concept, because they're at where they're at in terms of cognitive skills, and social emotional health, but they're also at where they're at in terms of their context, in terms of what's happening in their communities.

Doug: And we have to recognize how many different communities and contexts we have in any one classroom. How do you help that range of students appreciate and respect and acknowledge each other's worlds in ways that say we're in this together, in the same ocean but we're not in the same boat?

Wayne: We are. And that's the thing is to say that if we're helping students understand the web of relations that includes the web of relations between each other.
Doug: So, given that, and the size of the challenge, how do we best do that? If we want people to learn the kinds of things you're talking about, how do we best structure things so that we can support them to do that? What are some things you've seen that really lead us in that direction?
Wayne: Well, the first thing is who we recruit to become teachers. Who sees teaching as a viable profession, as something worth doing? And we have some inherent headwinds built into that because, some of the most critically conscious folks who I want to become teachers had bad experiences in schools. We know about white supremacy and settler colonialism, and that schools perpetuate these things. And so, if we want more teachers of color, or folks who've experienced and can speak critically about this stuff, we want them to become teachers. But why would they do that? They're like, why would I want to become one of the enemy? I understand that; that's totally, absolutely valid. But it's become clear to me that we are not going to, we can't train ourselves about equity, about diversity, we can't train ourselves to where we need to be with the existing teacher population. I think that might be a little bit cynical, or a little bit sad to say, but based on my experience, I feel that pretty strongly these days.

Some of the best teachers I've seen came into teaching as a political act; they went into teaching, for very specific reasons. And they had a consciousness about the world that was critical to begin with and in many ways, the teacher education programs became an obstacle for them. I'm trying to think through these days about who do we get to become teachers? And then the question after that is how do we create programs that can support their success in the process?

Doug: We know that many of the hoops connected to getting into and going through teacher education programs are going to keep many of those folks who are best at connecting with students and connecting students to the world from making it through to become teachers. And we know that, given the hyper focus on testing and test prep, some of the more aware, creative, and passionate potential candidates are choosing not to go into teaching.
Wayne: Right now, we're trying to work on a pipeline for ethnic studies majors to have a clear pathway and an easy pathway to become social studies teachers. In part, because the rise of ethnic studies means that we need more ethnic studies teachers, but in part, because the folks who major in ethnic studies are the folks who have that really strong activist, anti-racist, critical consciousness about the world. And those are the folks that we need to get in now. But then, what are the cohorts going to look like? There are things that we need to do to support our teachers, because we already know, students of color, in particular, and other minority students end up having bad experiences in their cohorts, especially if

they're in a numerical minority in those spaces. We have to have conversations about the kinds of communities we build, having folks doing affinity groups to support minoritized students. And then the other piece is thinking about our coursework. How are we decentering whiteness, how are we centering, you know, marginalized voices in the content that we're bringing into our teacher classes? I think this has been an ongoing project for a lot of programs. One thing that is happening in Washington State is "Since Time Immemorial" is now required to be taught in all schools. And so here's a space to focus on indigenous and native sovereignty, and what that history is from a native-centric perspective. Getting these kinds of courses built in so that it makes them the norm, makes them par for the course. And we do see that work happening. But it becomes really difficult because if you don't bring in the right student, okay, so we take a generic student, can we help them become what they need to be? And how far can we move them, what's their zone of proximal development? That's a really hard thing to judge, because we need teachers and we're not going to get all these ethnic studies folks to become teachers. And some of them may not be good teachers even if they are ethnic studies majors. We still have to help them learn how to be good teachers.

I think for me, I want my teacher education students to really understand their students. The whole idea of starting where students are at has to be taken to such a degree of seriousness to them, and they don't really get that, especially in secondary education. I think we tend to have a harder and harder issue because everyone's like, "I'm a history buff, I'm going to become a history teacher." They're interested in the subject; they're not necessarily interested in the connection with the students. Elementary tends to be obviously more connected to students. But, getting them to take seriously that if you're going to be a teacher, you need to understand your school context. And your students' context, what's the history of the area? What have their experiences been? These are all the things that good teacher ed programs should be attending to, for their students, because our teachers won't be good if they can't connect students with their contexts in critical ways. And so, really trying to center that work into the teacher education programs is critical.

And then the other piece, it gets so complicated, the other piece is then placements. We struggle with this all the time. And I know everyone does know. Because for one, the current teaching force is, you know, predominately white. It's, usually about 80% white women, right across the board, although there's probably a few more men in secondary.

What would it mean for us to recruit the right students into our programs, have our program structured in this way that really focuses on critical engagement with understanding students and society and communities, and then put them in a placement that doesn't match that? They might be with a white cooperating teacher, and there's plenty of good white cooperating teachers, but to take for instance, when a radical student of color, if I had my imaginary ideal student coming from ethnic studies through our program, great community, great cohort, and then plop them in a predominately white district with a white cooperating teacher, that would not match what their intent was for why they were becoming a teacher. And so that's getting these placements that are really community based, that are more diverse in terms of teaching force, and who they're working with. And also more diverse in terms of the student, the student communities are working with, that's the next sort of disconnect. But that's the third piece of this puzzle that needs that needs to happen.

Doug: I'd add a fourth piece, which is being part of a teacher education faculty, some of whom get it and most of whom don't. Many did their doctoral work in a specific subject area, and that's more important to them than the students they are working with, more important than the larger context of white supremacy or Euro-centered education, which is linked to what you were saying earlier. You have to start with the students and an awareness of the outside world and the politics and critical thinking. Finding a coherent and focused community of teacher educators is not the given.

Wayne: And yeah, the retention piece becomes huge, right? And how do you survive that thing? Because then you're in this institution, and we know who leaves. And so what you're saying is absolutely right.

Doug: If we focus on what kids need to learn, how might we set things up so that we're most likely to be successful in helping them learn it? It might look like some of what already exists, but it might not.

Wayne: Yeah, I feel like in terms of teacher education really what you're pointing to is the need for a kind of inquiry learning that future teachers need to really engage with. Instead of us answering that question for them, we need to have them go explore, what do my students need to learn? That's part of the point of the education piece of it, the teacher preparation stuff, right? They need to go ask those questions. What do my kids need to learn? What are their basic needs? And are they being met? I feel like that would be the space where the curriculum in teacher education comes in, is it based on that kind of inquiry? Is it really pushing students to ask those questions, push our teacher education students to ask those questions of their students or of current k-12 students? So that they can sort of come to that understanding on their own as they think about who they are as teachers.

Doug: Given the restrictions within teacher education, how do we educate future teachers to be aware of those context issues you've talked about here?

Wayne: What I think about is the work that radical teachers' unions have done. There's a space where you can have a community of educational colleagues who actually understand that the school is part of this broader web of life and relations.

And in doing so, the advocacy work they do becomes not only about their own work conditions, but also becomes about the conditions for the community. I see a fair amount of organizing around that, most recently in Chicago, where they negotiated for vaccines for their students, as part of their last contract negotiation. Here was the Chicago teachers' union, looking at community health as an issue, because they understood that community health was directly related to the health of their members. And so that was part of the negotiation. The same thing was with the stuff around Black Lives Matter at School, and some of the racial justice organizing that's come through some of the more radical teachers' union stuff, also recognizing that racial trauma, and white supremacy is impacting the communities of their students. They're organizing for things that they know can help ameliorate and help build resistance and survival in that context. And so they're seeing racial community health, too, as part of what they're fighting for. And so those are a couple of spaces that I think are sort of beyond school and outside of the institution in a way that does that work.

Doug: I wonder if zoom is helping in any way, just because it makes it more possible to reach beyond the limits of your community to find out there are voices like yours.

Wayne: Yeah. So maybe, there's a potential to use that in the future. You also point to some other spaces where it doesn't have to be union connected. That's just one example. But sure, there's certainly plenty of community organizing that teachers get involved with, like, you raise the stuff about the MCAS and the opt out movement. In fact, I did two MCAS things this last spring, talking about white supremacy in the history of standardized testing, that were really parent oriented, and community activists oriented. And so most definitely, there's other organizing spaces outside of the unions, where I think teachers can also take up broader sorts of issues-based things that are really aimed at that community.

Doug: And are there models going on now? I know you're doing some interesting things at UW Bothell. What kinds of things are you doing and/or seeing that gives you some hope?

Wayne: Well, in terms of teacher education, the idea of pipelines for teachers of color, I think, is really good. And there's even folks who are doing pathways teaching starting in high school. Margarita Blanco in Denver, for instance, has a whole pipeline where she starts working with largely students of color in high schools, and helps get them into the study of teaching and helps create pathways through undergrad in an audit to teaching. So I think those are hopeful. I'm hopeful about the work we're doing to work around similar pipelines, but more around the kinds of students we have at Bothell, the kinds of politics that are in certain majors and moving those into the school day. We get to descend upon a school with 25 or 30 future teachers who get to go be in classrooms and work with students very closely for a good portion of their methods classes. And the reason why I am drawn to that as a model is because it shows what happens when you really embed teacher education into the lives of kids, in particular school lives of kids, and what does that do? I think that is a really strong practice as well.

Doug: What are your relationships with the teachers in the schools you descend on? How do you work with them?

Wayne: These are all partnerships that are developed, agreed upon ahead of time. We don't surprise people, you know, to just show up. These are all partnerships. And really, we work in a way that is a true partnership, because we want to do things that are benefitting the school community as well. It's a mutually beneficial arrangement. And we're really working towards that model for everything, including our secondary programs. Those are some of the main models that come to mind. I haven't seen too much in terms of stuff that's sort of truly revolutionary, like, teacher ed is sort of going in this other space. You know, I like to think we're trying to work towards that at UW Bothell, but because we have the faculty, and we're small enough where we can make those changes, we can tack pretty easily and make those kinds of shifts. Let me just say it's hard because teacher education is highly regulated. And so, we're not free to do just anything, we have to work within state requirements for certifications and that kind of stuff.

Doug: I get the limits of teacher certification requirements and hoops. Part of what I'm pushing here is, if those requirements weren't there, if you could make that radical shift, what would it look like? You know, if you had your dream here..."

Wayne: If I had my dream, besides all the other stuff around class sizes, and resources and schools themselves being adequate, yeah. I would have space for my students to work in community centers, I think in some non-school contexts, where they got to see those kids not in a school context. And where they got to understand their students more as community beings, and not just school community beings. They'd have to do the school stuff too. They need to understand schools, and how they work. But I feel like one of the things I would really reach for would be for our students to really be engaged in student communities in meaningful ways. You know, so whether it's working with community centers, just trying to understand students' lives and what would that really mean?

Doug: When you think about students leaving your program, ready to teach, what do you want them to carry with them?

Wayne: I want them to carry with them a critical disposition, because teaching is a practice, and it's something to develop, and you get better at it across time. You're only going to be able to do that if you have a level of self-criticism that you're willing to take, critical self-reflection and growth. I want them to have that also, that kind of self-reflection because it requires that they are always working to improve their practice, to understand students better, to create curriculum that engages their students better. And to do that, your students are always changing, the world is always changing, you're always changing, so that means there has to be an ongoing commitment to self-growth and self-development that you have to undertake as a teacher.

Doug: Lots to think about. Anything else come to mind?

Wayne: No, not immediately. It's hard. I think the older I get the idea of transforming the system of education systemically feels more and more difficult. It feels like I'm becoming a hardened cynic.

Doug: What some of the folks who've been writing for the book are advocating is going back to freedom schools, saying, we can't do that in this context that is so full of "No". So how do we create contexts that are smaller, and more able to pivot, and create spaces that don't have anybody looming over our shoulders so that we can actually do the work. Even people in teacher ed programs who are drawn to finding a place where you can meet outside of a school context to say, let's take it further or find some context that allows for the real work to happen, even while you're learning how to be part of the club.

Wayne: It makes absolute sense that the freedom school thing is, I mean, I've seen more of that, obviously. And whether teacher education can somehow or within teacher education, if we can move that way, recognizing there are places we can't go in the formal setting, because those in control won't let that happen. Clearly public education is serving those in power. Yeah. So, we have to go around that structure in order to really challenge it.

FOR FURTHER STUDY

Wayne has listed four organizations that are focused on social justice and racial justice, and that recognize the link between schools and community. I have added three of his books for those who want to explore his work more directly.

Au, W. (2009). *Unequal by design. High stakes testing and the standardization of inequality*. Routledge.

Au. W. (2014). *Rethinking multicultural education: Teaching for racial and cultural justice*. Rethinking Schools.

Au, W. (2018). *A Marxist education*. Haymarket Books.

Rethinking Schools (rethinkingschools.org) is an organization of educators that puts out journals and books focused on social justice, racial justice, and student-centered education. Their materials are written for teachers by teachers.

Zinn Education Project. (zinnedproject.org). The Zinn Education Project promotes and supports the teaching of people's history in middle and high school classrooms across the country. Based on the lens of history highlighted in Howard Zinn's best-selling book A People's History of the United States, the website offers free, downloadable lessons and articles organized by theme, time period, and reading level.

Education for Liberation/Free Minds Free People. (https://fmfp.org/).

Abolitionist Teaching Network. (https://abolitionistteachingnetwork.org/).

Abolitionist Teaching Network's mission is to develop and support those in the struggle for educational freedom by utilizing the intellectual work and direct action of Abolitionists in many forms.

SECTION SIX

THINKING ABOUT FREEDOM SCHOOLS

Many of the authors in this book lament the restrictions or challenges of bringing an honest and fully student-centered education within the confines of the public education system. They note that the restrictions on what content is to be taught, how students and the schools are assessed through high stakes testing, who the teachers are and how they are assessed as candidates, and the oppressive oversight of the state, which is invested in keeping the current system in place compromise what can and does happen in schools. It seems that schools are designed to keep students from knowing a more complete and accurate accounting of our collective histories more than they are to help them learn it.

When considering how else we might help to support our young people to learn what they most need to learn and practice many people look back to the Freedom Schools of 1964, which took place in Mississippi during Freedom Summer. Organized by the Student Nonviolent Coordinating Committee (SNCC), volunteers, many from the North came to work with African American youth to provide them with the opportunity to learn in settings away from the repressive "school" experience they received in Mississippi schools.

"SNCC's Charlie Cobb thought, 'let's use their education,' and in December 1963, proposed an education program–Freedom Schools–for young Black Mississippians, who suffered in an educational environment that was 'geared to squash intellectual curiosity and different thinking.' Such a program would empower young people 'to articulate their own desires, demands, and questions' and 'to find alternative and ultimately new directions for action.'" (SNCC Digital Gateway, n.d.). The classes took place almost anywhere; in church basements, backyards, in people's houses, or outside under trees, and were carried out under the constant threat of violence, that often proved to be more than a threat. The content of the classes was co determined by the teachers and students, and the focus was on what would most serve the young people.

These Freedom Schools offered young African Americans the opportunity to experience a real education geared toward them gaining knowledge, skills, and power that would enable them to act on their own behalf and on behalf of their communities. Many of those educated within the Freedom Schools became activists in the Civil Rights movement and helped to bring voting rights and freedoms to African Americans throughout the south.

Historian Howard Zinn noted the revolutionary nature of Freedom Schools, saying

> The Freedom Schools' challenge to the social structure of Mississippi was obvious from the start. Its challenge to American education as a whole is more subtle. There is, to begin with, the provocative suggestion that an entire school system can be created in any community outside the official order, and critical of its suppositions. (Zinn, 1964)

Zinn added in his article on Freedom Schools:

> One teacher spent a whole hour with his students discussing the word "skeptical." He told them: "This is a Freedom School and we should mean what we say. We should feel free to think as we want, question whomever we like, whether it's our parents, our ministers, our teachers, yes, me, right here. Don't take my word for things. Check up on them. Be *skeptical*". For these youngsters it was a new way of looking at a classroom. (Zinn, 1964)

Caroline Whitcomb, an educator based in Georgia has researched education of African Americans in the south and her chapter re introduces us to Freedom Schools, both as history, but also as a current and powerful approach to educating young people. While citing the Freedom Schools of 1964 she also tells the story of a "freedom school" being currently held in Oakland, California as a model of what could be happening for more of our students. She notes the power, depth, and passion of the learning that goes on in these class sessions, which are held outside of any formal school or state structure.

REFERENCES

SNCC Digital Gateway. (n.d.). *Freedom Schools*. Retrieved from https://snccdigital.org/inside-sncc/culture-education/freedom-schools/

Zinn, H. (1964, November 23). *Schools in context: The Mississippi idea*. The Nation. Retrieved from https://www.crmvet.org/info/641123_sncc_zinn_schools.pdf

CHAPTER SIXTEEN

Freedom Schools

CAROLINE WHITCOMB

Who Am I?

by Sandra Jo-Ann O., Hattiesburg

Who am I, let me see,
Am I a dog or am I a bee?
Am I a maniac who's out of her mind?
I think I know and I'll tell you
I'm not the girl I used to be.
Who am I? I have to know
So I may tell it wherever I go.
I'll tell it to men of all the land,
I'll tell it to kids who shake my hand,
That I am free and it shows,
To everyone all over the land.
Who am I? I'll tell you now,
I'll have to find words, but I'll tell it somehow.
I am a Negro who fought her best
To earn her freedom and deserves to rest.
So do as I did, and you'll be free,
Just don't hit back, and you'll win

Your rest. (Student Nonviolent Coordinating Committee, 1966, p. 18)

Do you hear the power in her voice? Can you sense the setting of her jaw, envision the determined look in her young eyes? These are the words of a child who has been transformed, educated, liberated.

In Mississippi, in the summer of 1964, roughly 3,000 Black students, primarily ranging from ages 10 to 18, attended the 41 Freedom Schools created by the Council of Federated Organizations (COFO). The Freedom Schools were part of COFO's massive civil rights campaign in the state. Despite the sweltering heat and promised violence by white Mississippians, seven hundred college students descended upon the state with the purpose of educating Black children and registering Black voters.

Sandra Jo-Ann was one of the students who participated in the Freedom School project. Despite Mississippian hell, Black children voluntarily attended the schools. The knowledge they gained was life-altering.

> As part of leadership training ... the students discussed the role of freedom schools and the need for blacks to preserve their own culture rather than uncritically adopting white cultural values. In addition, students were offered courses in creative writing, drama, art, journalism, and foreign languages. (Carson, 1981, p. 120)

The summer's impact was captured in the pages of a small book, *Freedom School Poetry* (Student Nonviolent Coordinating Committee, 1966), a book that demonstrates the power and beauty of liberatory, transformative education.

Sandra Jo-Ann had been educated, not schooled. There is a marked and often overlooked difference between the two. Education requires a form of departure, separation. Michel Serres (2006) words it this way,

> A rending that rips a part of the body from the part that still adheres to the shore where it was born, to the neighborhood of its kinfolk (...) to the culture of its language and to the rigidity of habit (...) no learning can avoid the voyage. Under the supervision of a guide, education pushes one to the outside. (Serres, 2006, p. 8)

When we push beyond what society wants us to believe, beyond the traditions which empower a few and oppress the majority, we discover the unveiled world. This discovery, this journey results from authentic education. "Real education lays hold of the soul itself and transforms it in its entirety by first of all leading us to the place of our essential being (Wesensort) and accustoming us to it" (Heidegger, 2005, p. 157). Education liberates. Education creates an understanding of who we are, past the labels ascribed to us and the labels we ascribe to ourselves. Education cultivates the hope and love necessary to think critically about societal ills and to envision and evoke change.

Schooling, on the other hand, provides skills, not transformations. Schooling is the memorization and regurgitation of theorems. It is the diagramming of sentences, the reading of classics, and the dissection of frogs. It is indoctrination into veiled societal systems that maintain the status quo, undergird power structures, and support racism, classism, sexism, and capitalist individualism. Our public education system maintains our caste-like society, continually wounding those who need our help the most, our children. This "democratic," "Christian" nation has failed to understand when one of us diminishes, we all diminish. Our greedy individualism continues to ravage us from within. In a speech in 1900, W.E.B. DuBois stated, "Either America will destroy ignorance or ignorance will destroy America" (*The Niagara Movement's "Address to the Country*," 2021). We are on the cusp of self-destruction.

No one wants to believe they have been "schooled." Americans want to believe we have been educated, liberated, that we are in touch with our inner being and the world at large. We want to believe we are free. We believe education is the "great equalizer" and that the public education system affords an opportunity for everyone to reach their full potential and, at least, achieve middle-class status. We've been conditioned to think those who aren't successful simply didn't apply themselves, they rejected the bootstraps of publicly funded education. This is not to say all educators spend their careers schooling children. There are, and historically have been, teachers who seek to educate and liberate their young charges. However, educators such as this remain few and far between.

George S. Counts (1932, 1978) writes, "To refuse to face the task of creating a vision of a future America immeasurably more just and noble and beautiful than the America of today is to evade the most crucial, difficult, and important educational task" (p. 51). The questions before us, not just those of us directly involved in education, but all of us, are how do we break the systemic schooling cycle and offer our children a new vision, real vision? How do we educate children to become those capable of creating a future more just and noble for themselves and future generations?

Let's return to Sandra Jo-Ann and her poem. Sandra Jo-Ann wants her readers to know she has seen the world and herself unveiled. She has seen past painful labels, past fear, past childlike thinking, and despite the hell of the summer of 1964, entered a world of activism, freedom, peace, and rest. We are left to wonder, what brought about this change in Sandra Jo-Ann? How did she overcome the Mississippian deficit ideology forced upon Blacks in the state? How did she free her mind from the pain of being told she was the equivalent of a dog, an insect, a maniacal being, and recognize her true worth? What fueled her fearlessness and inspired her to declare her freedom to *every man* in the state? Who convinced a child, who without doubt, had witnessed horrific racist violence to believe in the power of nonviolent protest? She certainly was not taught to think this way in the haphazard educational institutions providing a sharecropper education to Black Mississippians. Sandra Jo-Ann's poem is powerful; in fact, *every* poem in the book is beautifully written and often imbued with strong liberatory rhetoric.

Sandra Jo-Ann and around 3,000 other students' lives were transformed by the knowledge they gained in the Freedom Schools. As we witness the terrifying rise in racist murders and brutalities, the incendiary rhetoric of a president, the response of his supporters, the storming of the US capital, and the massive and ever-growing number of segregated, high-poverty schools, our need for change is dire. The nation's trajectory must be disrupted, our children liberated, and our future salvaged. We need a generation of Sandra Jo-Anns. We need Freedom Schools.

COFO recognized the necessity of reaching and educating Black students in Mississippi. The work occurring in the schools was intentional as was the targeted population. Historical examinations of the Movement and its continued impact often fail to recognize the significance of the Freedom Schools and the students who attended them. When we fail to examine the Freedom Schools and the students, we fail to understand this powerful example of grassroots activism, and, in many ways, fail to understand the Movement itself. The thousands of children who were educated that summer became an army of activists who ignited flames of activism in their communities. Jon N. Hale (2018) suggests an examination of the Freedom Schools,

> illustrates the dialectical relationship between the local and national context. Though marginalized within contemporary discourse and typically overlooked by civil rights movement scholars, the local development of the Freedom Schools enabled the growth of federal educational initiatives that transformed public education by the mid-1960s. (pp. 2–3)

The year before his assassination, Dr. Martin Luther King, Jr. (2010), published his final book, *"Where Do We Go From Here: Chaos or Community?"* I believe one of the answers to this still pertinent question is, to the Freedom Schools. From the nation's inception, there have always been centers of subversive, liberatory education, some hidden and others not. In Raleigh, North Carolina in 1808, John Chavis ran a secret night school to educate free Black children. At the turn of the 20th century, Jane Addams' Hull House instructed and informed poor immigrants in Chicago. In the 1950s, Septima Clark and Esau Jenkins began citizenship schools on Johns Island, South Carolina to teach adults to read so they could pass the discriminatory voter registration exam. Freedom Schools offer a "unique, politically oriented curriculum through a progressive student-centered pedagogy" (Hale, 2016, p. 16). Freedom Schools intentionally operate outside the public education system and provide students with a critical examination of history and systemic oppression, empowerment and community service training, and the methods and motives of activism. Today, we find a contemporary example of the freedom schools in Oakland, California, The Martin Luther King, Jr. Freedom Center.

Just over a year ago, Dr. Clayborne Carson of Stanford University invited me to join, via zoom, his weekly office hours. Along with the link, came two suggested readings, a speech and a letter written by Martin Luther King, Jr. Days later, homework complete, I joined the call. I was surprised to find around 30 young faces and a handful of seasoned ones staring back at me. Many of these students were far too young to attend the university. After a brief discussion of the readings by Dr. Carson, the children began to ask questions and engage in the conversation. I was awed. I blinked back tears. I messaged a friend to share what I was witnessing. These students were different, they were, even the youngest, eloquently spoken activists with insightful minds and incredible knowledge. They pondered King's work, contrasting it with his other speeches and those of his contemporaries, they wrestled with modern-day applications while demonstrating their extensive knowledge of history, politics, societal operations, and the ills plaguing them all. The numerous ethnic backgrounds represented created a beautiful kaleidoscope of color and perspective, an incredible picture of our nation's diversity. Before presenting Dr. Carson with a question, students greeted him and often acknowledged the thinking of the child who had previously spoken.

The Martin Luther King, Jr. Freedom Center, located in Oakland, California, was founded by East Bay community organizers in 1995. These organizers testified in support of legislation written by state assembly member Barbara Lee calling for the creation of a state-sanctioned center championing the life and legacy of Dr. King, non-violence, youth, and civic engagement. Students, from junior high through college, involved with the Freedom Center participate in civics-based leadership seminars grouped into three 8 to 10-week courses. The seminars, grounded on the science of non-violence, provide regular opportunities for students to engage with and learn from activists working in the labor, business, education, public and tribal sectors (Center et al., 2020). "Throughout the courses the students gain critical analysis skills, developing the capacity to identify a problem, trace why it exists, and identify solutions. This directly leads to the capacity to make contributions to legislative formulas and influence" (Center et al., 2020).

The first course, Civic Engagement,

> Develops one's voice and an appreciation for the value of basic civic engagement. Topics include: self-discovery, build up your cultural power, gratitude, be great through service, vision making and vision keeping, the power of nonviolence, creating power in your school, and self-transformation and the role of coaching. (Center et al., 2020).

The second course focuses on activist civics. Here, students learn about the "branches and roles of government, policymaking, advocacy, running for office, elections, marches, and rallies" (Center et al., 2020). The final course, community organizing, provides an in-depth examination of movement and organization building. Students consider the work and writings of Mahatma Gandhi, Richard Gregg, Cesar Chavez, Martin Luther King, Jr, and other activists (Center et al., 2020). They also study the organizational contributions of the Southern Christian Leadership Conference, the Student Nonviolent Coordinating Committee, the Montgomery Women's Club, and the Black Panther Party.

The profound impact of the Freedom Center seminars is akin to that of the Mississippi Freedom Schools. A 15-year longitudinal study of the program showed,

> 100% of the students participated in civic engagement, and 97.6% of the students increased or maintained academic grade, with 38% showing a significant increase. 100% of the students graduated from high school (or equivalent), 96.3% enrolled in community or four-year colleges, and 89% were conferred degrees ranging from AA to JD. (Center et al., 2020)

Over the past year, I have spent an hour each week listening to and learning from this group. These children have become my source of hope for our nation's future. I have no doubt a number of them will run for public office, continue their activism well into their adult years, and profoundly impact their communities and the nation.

One student described their experience in the program this way,

> I learned how to better connect with people, how to better speak in public through my heart and not just my head. I learned how to feel instead of how to only think. I learned that actions done first, before actually thinking, can have a profound effect on one's development. For better conduct leads to better character. But really I learned that everyone has so much potential, and that humans, though we at times consider ourselves different because of culture, experiences, work, school, etc., we really have so much in common, and that anyone if given a chance and treated with respect and dignity, and if willing to get out of one's comfort zone can transform one's self towards being better and towards a better world. (Center et al., 2020)

These are the words of a child who has overcome their schooling and gained an education. They have joined the ranks of Sandra Jo-Ann. In less than a year's time, this program transforms students' minds, hearts, and lives. The students' work is contagious, grassroots activism at its best. Their bravery, passion, love, and determination are fuel to my fire.

Liberatory, transformative education, not schooling, should be a universal human right. Yet, we live in a schooled society, a society increasingly and blindly plagued by the privatization of education. The public school system of today is incapable of training a generation of activists to fight for a more just and democratic society, a society that seeks to educate every individual. This training, as demonstrated by the Mississippi freedom schools, and the Martin Luther King, Jr. Freedom Center, must occur outside the walls of our schools and be available to all students, not just the marginalized. White middle-and upper-class students must learn to recognize the inequities embedded in their privilege and power.

They, too, need liberation, transformation. Humanity exists only in our relationship to others. The Freedom Center students recognize this and articulate the necessity to expand their program, share their knowledge, and invite other students, both within the state of California and around the world, to partner with them as they move forward. These students recognize where we need to go and are bravely, while continually pursuing education, walking, arm in arm, in that direction. The role of critical educators and activists is to provide similar opportunities to students around the nation, to prepare our young to change the nation.

What Does Freedom Mean?
By Madeline McHugh, Hattiesburg
Whenever I think about sunlight and fresh air, or peace and springtime, I think about men wanting to be free.

There are men who want freedom all their lives and never get it: there are men who have freedom all their lives and never know it.

...but I think men who know they are free and try to help other men get it show how precious freedom really is. (Student Nonviolent Coordinating Committee, 1966, p. 23)

REFERENCES

Carson, C. (1981). *In struggle: SNCC and the Black awakening of the 1960s*. Harvard University Press.

Counts, G. S., & Urban, W. J. (1978). *Dare the school build a new social order? Arcturus Paperbacks (No. AB 143)*. Southern Illinois University Press.

Hale, J. (2018). *The Freedom Schools: Student activists in the Mississippi Civil Rights Movement* (Reprint ed.). Columbia University Press.

Jr., K. M. L. D., Harding, V., & King, C. S. (2010). *Where do we go from here: Chaos or community? (King Legacy)* (Illustrated ed.). Beacon Press.

M. L. K. J. F. (2020, September 30). *Leadership seminars*. Martin Luther King Jr. Freedom Center. https://mlkfreedomcenter.org/leadership-seminars/

The Niagara Movement's "Address to the Country." (2021, February 23). Teaching American History. https://teachingamericanhistory.org/library/document/the-niagara-movements-address-to-the-country/

Serres, M., Glaser, S. F., & Paulson, W. (2006). *The troubadour of knowledge (Studies in Literature and Science)* (3rd ed.). University of Michigan Press.

Student Nonviolent Coordinating Committee. (1966). *Freedom school poetry, 1964*. Civil Rights Movement Archive, Inc. https://www.crmvet.org/poetry/64_fskool_poems-r.pdf

Thomson, I. D. (2005). *Heidegger on ontotheology: Technology and the politics of education*. Cambridge University Press.

SECTION SEVEN

BUT WHAT ABOUT ASSESSMENT?

Most of the public discourse around education in recent years has centered on assessment, most particularly around high stakes testing. There has been strong opposition to high stakes testing since the passage of No Child Left Behind in 2002, which made these tests a federal requirement and coupled results with punishments and consequences for schools and districts. There is no evidence that the tests have delivered the promised improvements in school performance and much evidence to suggest that they are bringing harm to many students, particularly those they were presumably helping, but that has not made any difference to those who support them. These data driven enthusiasts continue to ignore their own data as they keep pushing the testing policy, even during the pandemic.

The tests, which are a racially biased outgrowth of the eugenics movement, that make huge profits for the companies that produce them at the expense of the districts that have to pay for them, and which have served to shift decision making about education away from local teachers, administrations, and communities and to the federal government and states are still with us. Students were ordered back to in person schooling in the spring of 2021 to make sure they would be able to take their standardized tests, despite concerns around the safety of the students and staff, despite the absurdity of expecting students to take tests a week or two after returning from a year of schooling in isolation, living through trauma and loss, and even though the tests would not count. The fear was that if the tests were not given 2 years in a row (because of the pandemic) we might notice that they actually did not add any value to the education of our young people, which might support the arguments of those who would do away with them.

Proponents of the tests argue that without testing we would have no idea of how our students were doing, not trusting that teachers actually carry out assessment on their own. In fact, most teachers are assessing their students and classrooms every moment of the school day but testing advocates clearly do not trust teachers enough for that to be enough. Without standardized tests how would we know that our students were being well served, and that our tax dollars were being well spent? There are many responses to that, many ways that we could (and do) assess our students and schools that could improve the educational experience of our young people and reassure the public, and Jack Schneider, an associate professor of education at the University of Massachusetts offers his thoughts in the chapter that follows, but I want to take the opportunity here to suggest something more radical and less practical than what I've seen in any of the testing related conversations to date.

I think if we want to assess the quality of our educational system, we should look at the quality of the lives we are leading in our communities and across the country. Since the purpose or function of educating our young is to prepare them to live well and sustainably as they move to adulthood, we can assess how well we have done by how they (and we) are living. Are we meeting the needs of our population, are we living in a manner that is sustainable and that is allowing us to thrive as individuals and as a society? Are our people happy, satisfied? Are their needs being met? Are our cities, towns, and environment healthy and able to sustain us? Given our current situation it seems clear to me that, given this yardstick, our educational system is failing.

How else to make sense of our current situation? There is substantial evidence every day that we have produced a population that is ignorant of its history, that rejects science and critical thinking, that is able to be fooled by politicians and business leaders who offer blatant lies supported by no facts or evidence, and who have been taught to hate and mistrust anyone who does not think like them or look like them. The discord and anti-scientific stance pushed by the former president and political leaders of both parties, funded as they are by dark money, is leading us down a path to destruction, and too many of our "educated" adults are willing to mindlessly follow them, no matter how absurd or unsupportable their claims and pronouncements. What is most disturbing is that followers of these outlandish conspiracies, such as concerns that the vaccines contain computer chips, or that Hillary Clinton and her democratic cabal are running child pornography rings out of a non-existent basement of an obscure pizza shop, are more believable to them than are the findings of scientists who have devoted their lives to the study of climate, or pandemics, or population health. Since the goal of education is to support the health and survival of our society, the fact that graduates of our current educational system are rejecting what supports health in favor of that which is bringing us closer to our destruction, I'd argue that our educational system is failing us all, and not just those who drop out or get poor grades.

Creating a more functional, useful assessment system seems crucial to me, not just for the sake of our schools but also for our survival as a nation, and perhaps as a planet. We have to educate young adults who can think critically, who can look for evidence and research when evaluating claims made by politicians and corporate CEOs, and who have the confidence and skills to organize and stand up to false claims. We have to have a population that values each other and learns to work together for the common good. Our schools are one place where that learning can take place, and it is imperative that we take action while there is still time.

I spoke with Jack Schneider about assessment, focusing on what it can offer by way of truly serving all of our children. We agreed that there were significant problems in education, that many children, particularly from under represented communities were not well served by our current system, but agreed to focus on what possibilities a different approach to assessment could offer to public education.

Dr. Schneider argues that we should begin our assessment work by identifying what we value most highly and then assess our educational system in terms of how close we are to meeting our goals, informed by those values. He says that if we don't have assessment instruments that will perform that role, we should create them. To start with assessment instruments and then bend our educational system to fit the demands of those instruments is backwards, and frequently moves us away from what we value, to the detriment of all. Jack has been working to put some of his ideas into action in the state of Massachusetts and shares a brief look at the work he is doing. He is quick to point out that he recognizes that there are many alternative assessment approaches out there and encourages more so that there are a range of assessment options that can be chosen as a best fit for particular schools or districts.

CHAPTER SEVENTEEN

Assessing What Matters

A Conversation with Jack Schneider

Jack: I think, for me, the place that is always important to start is that we need to recognize that the things that we presently can measure constrain our imaginations with regard to what matters. I think that has it exactly backwards. We have to first figure out what we value and what we want for young people, and then figure out how we're going to measure that stuff. And if we can't measure it, then I think that that's a sign that there's work to do in terms of building tools, rather than that we need to set that value aside. We have too much evidence over the past quarter century that values do get set aside when we let our toolbox shape our actions rather than letting our values shape our actions.

Doug: Thinking about schools and education, what do you value for your daughter and other kids?

Jack: I say this as somebody who believes in school, and who thinks the public schools do an incredible job. I think, first and foremost, about art and music, because of how much they have enriched my life. I just think about how important these things are, which don't, in any way, for most of us advance our careers or our job ready skills. All they do is help us lead better lives. I say that with a little bit of irony in my tone. It's the same thing with regard to the way I appreciate literature. I think about the things that I love in my life that I either did or didn't encounter in school, and how important it is, particularly if we're thinking about kids who don't have every privilege and every advantage to ensure that they do encounter this stuff. Sports are another place. I found sport outside of school.

I was on a little league team and ended up playing baseball all the way through the end of college; it was a great passion of mine. And through that, I discovered other sports, that are still a part of my life and enrich my life. That should be a part of school for all young people. I could go on and on with examples, but I'll say one that I think about all the time, is going to school with different kinds of kids. I went to what has to be among the most diverse elementary schools in America. It was the lab school at UCLA, where they had very intentionally cultivated a student body that reflected Los Angeles, which then and now is a multicultural, polyglot city. I just took it for granted that everybody around me had the same value as I had, that we all had equal access to the truth, and that we all had something to learn from each other.

I think about this divide between the way things actually work and the way things ought to work, and schools are one place where we can try to close the gap between the way reality is and the way reality ought to be. Thinking about all of those things, including and perhaps especially the diversity of the student body, because ultimately what's more important than our ability to live side by side and to learn from each other, and you think about the great tragedies in human history which are a result of our inability to see each other as equally valuable and to build things together.

Doug: Given how you started our conversation, focusing on the arts and recognizing the diversity of humans on the planet, in some ways assessment is at the other end of the scale from that. I'd be interested to hear a little bit about how you found yourself coming to focus on assessment, and how that connects.

Jack: It's because of outrage, because I see how schools get rated, and what is left out in those ratings, and it's most of the things I care about. In fact, it's most of the things that most people care about. I am outraged when I see that there are school ratings that are tied to real estate listings, and that are steering people, not just towards schools that may not match their actual values and concerns, but away from schools that might help us build a better society. The way schools are rated presently with their focus on their standardized test scores. Knowing what we know about the relationship between proficiency rates and demography, we know that these readings are predominantly demographic data in disguise, and then we act on those. I think it undermines our values to act on that stuff.

I came to this work of trying to measure school quality by wondering whether or not it was actually possible to begin with what we value and then try to figure out if we can measure those various components of school quality. We can assess things like the racial diversity of a school, the economic diversity of a school, the number of minutes a typical student gets of art instruction, or music instruction, how varied the curriculum is, how culturally sustaining the teaching is at that school. We can measure, not with the kind of precision that we might measure the hardness of steel or the speed of a fastball. But that's because those things are pretty narrow and concrete as opposed to our values, which are often broad and somewhat abstract. But we can measure things like how happy kids are, and how safe they feel and whether or not they feel valued. And those are the things that I certainly want in schools for my own kid and for all kids. You often see these contorted arguments like, we ought to have recess because studies show that more recess leads to higher test scores. But I think that those kinds of contorted arguments are a result of the fact that we are not actually measuring what we value because I think most of us do value young people, we value them as human beings. Why should they have recess? Because we love them. Because they are children, and children deserve to play, whatever the impact on their test scores. And so, I came to this, again, out of outrage at the fact that the way we are currently measuring student learning and school quality leads to a world in which kids don't have recess in some schools, because it's viewed as a distraction from the academic core.

Doug: I don't want to spend a whole lot of time on what's wrong with high stakes testing because I think those arguments are out there. How can we use assessment to have schools more align with our values?

Jack: I think it's an important place to start, to think about what assessment is good for, because if we actually take that seriously, it very quickly leads to the realization that our current approach is failing to get us to what assessment can do. I generally think about two core audiences, families, and educators. These are the people who are closest to young people, and who have the most stake in young people. There's sometimes this rhetoric that if we don't have standardized tests, how will families know how kids are doing? And that to me just seems so disingenuous, because how did families know for the previous century and a half of American public education? They could tell from their kids coming home each day what their kids were learning. They could tell from looking at their student's assignments, by talking with their children's teachers. They could tell by looking at the written feedback that teachers had offered. That's not to suggest that the information that families were getting was perfect, but if what we value is communication to families, then we can see that students standardized test scores, reported once a year, and often not reported directly to families, or if they are reported to families at all are often reported in a way that is completely incomprehensible to them is not really serving them well. It strains credulity to think that this is being done on behalf of families. So, then we can think about, okay, well, what about this other audience of educators? And sometimes people will make the argument that this gives teachers and school leaders data around which they can make data driven decisions. I have yet to meet a teacher who said that they learned something from a student's standardized test scores that they didn't know from working with that student in the classroom. What are educators learning about students that is new? I think almost nothing.

It's pretty clear that our current approach is guided by two ideologies. One is a market ideology, that standardized test scores can function as the currency in a marketplace where we believe that schools get better from competition, and that education will be improved if parents act as shoppers. And there's no evidence that suggests that this is true. In fact, evidence suggests the contrary. And then the second ideology is one about control. That we believe it is the duty of those in power to exercise control over our educational system from afar, in some centralized manner. They of course, have no ability to see inside America's 100,000 schools. They need something reductive, something that can fit in a ledger in an Excel file, and so standardized test scores are useful for that. I think if we talk about what assessment could be good for, and what assessment currently is good for it again presents us with this divide between the real and ideal, which then may foster our ability to imagine alternatives.

Doug: So let's go there a little bit. I remember educational policy researcher Gerry Bracey used to say there is no such thing as a standardized test because there's no such thing as a standardized child. But recognizing the wide range of people we're dealing with and the diverse contexts in which children live and attend school, how can we think about assessment most usefully? It's a huge question. How do we start thinking about it?

Jack: I think that first, we need to think about what assessment is used for. And it serves multiple purposes. One is what I call short haul communication, communicating with people outside of the classroom but who are in the immediate environment and have a stake in particular kids, like families and other educators outside of the classroom. And then there's long haul communication. And that's like you're trying to communicate something about what students know and can do with people who don't necessarily have a stake in this individual student but may want to know that information at some point. College admissions committees, for instance, or future employers.

Then there's this entirely separate purpose of assessment, which is motivation. We use assessment to motivate kids in this country and in most countries. I see the logic to it, particularly if education is compulsory, forcing most children to do something that they probably wouldn't choose if they had their own vote in the matter. So how do you get them to do it? Well, you create a set of incentives and sanctions, carrots and sticks, and assessment plays a key role in this.

And then finally, there's this purpose of articulation, which is trying to stitch together a system in what is basically a non-system. We have 13,000 school districts which operate fairly autonomously from each other. We use assessment as a kind of common language in order to try to create a system where there isn't one, not from state to state, or from district to district, or even from elementary to middle to high school. I think it's just important to recognize we're trying to do lots of different things with the same core set of tools, the tools being grades, test scores and transcripts.

Now, let's have a serious conversation about, can we do better than this? Can we, for instance, communicate better in terms of the student him or herself? Can we communicate better than via grades, tests and transcripts? You bet we can. And there's a long history of alternatives there.

When I think about what assessment could be for young people, in terms of communication, we are limited only by our imaginations with regard to how we could communicate with a young person about their learning, or to the people who care about him or her. What it requires is an investment of time, and or resources. We know that it can be incredibly powerful when teachers visit students' homes and learn something about them and share something with families about how those young people are doing. People wouldn't often think of that as alternative assessment, but if we think about the purposes that we are using assessments for, all of a sudden, we can see that instead of a grade for this student, the educator is communicating with the family through the visit. Here's what this young person's strengths and weaknesses are. Here's how we can work together to support this young person.

Or consider motivation. What could we do instead of saying, gosh, you got a one on the AP test, you better work a lot harder? There are lots of alternative efforts there, like figuring out what kids actually care about, and giving them a little bit of discretion and freedom in schools to pursue those things, or, gasp, training teachers and encouraging them to help young people discover what is exciting and interesting and beautiful in material rather than just saying, well, it's in the state standards. It involves a lot of trust and respect, and that's not just for educators, it's also for young people. Trust and respect are the opposite of rules, and consequences and punishments. Instead saying, we are guided by a deep and abiding respect for you so you're going to be included in this process in a powerful and important and authentic way and we're going to trust that you're a professional, or that you want what's best for yourself, if you're a student. We're not going to be naive about this, but I think that there's a middle ground between saying let's just let teachers do whatever they want and let's let kids choose the curriculum.

I'll just add that, one more sort of framework for thinking about this is to think about three big values that I have in assessment, which are validity, democracy, and equity. Validity is the question of are you measuring what you are intending to measure? And we know that lots of our current assessments fail in that way. Are you measuring school quality when you sit kids down for a standardized test in two subjects? Well, probably not. And can we imagine a more valid way of measuring school quality? I think that all of us know well enough to say we can't just measure this narrow range of things if the construct we value is much broader than that. So that's validity. Democracy is, who's this for, and who's this by? And right now, I think we look at current assessment practices and we can say, if it's not really for us, or by us, who gets to make the ultimate determination? It's either an algorithm or a bureaucrat. It certainly isn't the people who have a stake in a particular school. Why not? Why don't those people have an opportunity to sit down with various kinds of information, including information from students and teachers, and heck, give them standardized test scores too, as a part of what they're looking at, and let them deliberate.

And then finally, the equity piece. We must at all times be attuned to that, because in any system, there is the potential to simply perpetuate the social order, that if we are not actively working to create a fairer world, we know that systems and structures more often than not, will just regenerate the world that we presently live in. And so we need to be really attuned to that when we're engaging in assessment practices, because assessment is a part of this cycle. If you aren't attuned to a whole group of people who are being left out of this or who are being unequally served in some way, if you're not measuring that, then at no point is there going to be a correction in this cycle.

Doug: The people who are currently teaching or administrating in the public schools are people for whom the system has worked well enough that they've chosen to stay in education, and to perpetuate it, if I can phrase it that way. And most have not been educated really to do the kind of assessment or the approach to assessment you're thinking about. So how do we help them learn to approach assessment in the ways that you are advocating?

Jack: I think that a big part of the work that we need to do always in education, is helping people see the water in which they swim, because education is an inherently conservative field. And by that, I simply mean that it tends to preserve itself as it is. This is not political conservatism, but the perpetuation of a status quo. And why is that? It's because we all move through the system before we then become empowered to change it. I won't use the word indoctrination because there isn't a kind of intentionality there. Instead, think about it as being inoculated against your more radical tendencies. Think about it as a vaccine for imagination, that will make sure that you don't have any ideas that are too outside of the norm. And again, this is not a vast conspiracy. It's simply how these self-perpetuating systems work, where you move through it, and you gain a sense of what a quote unquote real school is. And then there are these cooling out mechanisms for anybody who doesn't like it; they drop out or score poorly so they can't become teachers or administrators. Those who love it, and who succeed in schools as they exist, are then likely to want to stay there and want to remain involved. This is how culture works. And we can see this, particularly with teachers, where if teachers are not encouraged at some point in their pre-service training to simply understand their own proclivities towards keeping schools as they are, because they are a self-selecting group who have opted into returning to school, the place where they felt valued and successful, then they are far more likely to produce schools as they are. I'm not suggesting that we dump all the current teachers and go out and get all the students who dropped out and put them in charge. Instead, I'm suggesting that we all simply need to become a little bit more conscious about how this works. There are some things we want to keep and other things we probably don't want to keep, and there are things teachers do simply because that's what teachers do. There are things schools do because that's what schools do, and we parents often insist on it, because that's what a quote unquote, real school does. We want grades, right? We want our kids to come home with report cards. Many families say, I want my kid to go to a real school that prepares them for the real world. You hear them stand up for things that they themselves don't like where, you know, they'll say something like, nobody likes tests, but tests are just a part of life. We hate tests, but you've got to do them. Why do you have to do them? We have simply accepted it because we spent 13 years exposed to it.

Simply being aware of that allows us to then have better and richer and more imaginative conversations about what we want in our schools and what we are opposed to.

Doug: Can you talk about the project that you're carrying out now, in service to how can we do better by way of assessment?

Jack: We have a consortium here in Massachusetts, called the Massachusetts Consortium for Innovative Education Assessment. Right now, there are eight districts involved. It's really a kind of pilot project, a proof of concept that we hope will convince other people to either join on so that we can grow, or to spin off their own versions. I think my hope would be for both, that we would build a movement in which there wasn't only one alternative to the existing measurement and accountability regime, but there were a few and that they looked somewhat different from each other, and that they each had compelling reasons for being. And ours seeks to change how we measure student learning and school quality with regard to student learning. The focus has been on the use of teacher created, classroom embedded teacher-scored performance assessments in place of externally produced, machine-scored standardized tests. There are a few reasons for that. We're already measuring that stuff in the form of teacher assessments that happen in classrooms all the time. There are some things we need to do in order to make those more standard across classrooms such that one teacher's assessment of how a student is doing would be more or less in line with how another teacher would make that assessment. Training is involved in the creation of scoring rubrics, but it is possible. And this would mean that you simply don't need to spend as much time as we currently do on standardized tests and preparation for those standardized tests. And in addition to that, if assessment then is embedded in classrooms, now we can start imagining a much wider array of assessments that happens. And particularly if human beings are going to be rating them, we need not limit ourselves to multiple choice items. We can start imagining assessments such as science labs and sculptures and paintings and essays in a foreign language, all sorts of things that students produce in their classes as evidence of what they know and can do.

With regard to measuring school quality, we built a School Quality Framework that was informed first by research and national polling. And then was informed by focus groups we ran in multiple languages, with educators, school leaders, district leaders, and community members, the idea being that we ought to figure out what we all care about before we go around trying to measure anything, and that we all ought to have a say in that, including students. And believe it or not, and I was actually not surprised by this, we all tend to agree on the core things that schools ought to do. And that, no, it isn't simply about outputs, or outcomes. If students have access to arts and music education, for instance, that may produce better artists and better musicians and maybe we'll be able to measure it, but it's also just simply important that they have that access to begin with. And so we built a School Quality Framework consisting of inputs and outcomes divided into five major categories; teachers and leadership, school culture, resources, indicators of academic learning, and community and wellbeing. And then, when we're trying to measure how schools are doing on these five different categories, we use multiple measures from different sources, including actually asking students and teachers. It turns out that the people who spend 180 days a year inside a school building actually know something about how things are going. And the vision then is to build a better measure of school quality, not to produce some single score by which we would rate and rank schools, rather, to feed this information back to educators so that they can then be the kind of on the ground local policy experts who might say, gosh, we actually have a school culture problem that we weren't aware of. Let's design some interventions in response to that.

The School Quality Framework itself, even without measures can empower both educators and community members by giving them some common language to talk about the values that they're trying to advance. The data produced here, when given back to families can help families, not as shoppers buying schools, but as engaged members of the community who are interested in how the school is doing and who then might advocate for particular kinds of action or bring their strengths to bear and say, Hey, you know, can I help out in this regard? And then would also function as a replacement for existing state measurement accountability systems, which exist to ensure that schools are doing right by the young people in their care and the taxpayers who are funding them. I could envision an accountability system, a democratic accountability system where people come together, and they deliberate over how the school is doing. And it ends not with a rating for the school or the threat of closure, but with a plan for supporting that school, which then comes with resources from the state to try to enact that plan. So that's a brief overview of what we're trying to accomplish. And right now, I think just simply the fact that we exist is a win, because it enables people when they say, I don't like what's currently happening, and are then challenged with the question. Yeah, well, what are you going to do instead, can say, how about this thing? How about this alternative?

SECTION EIGHT

LEARNING THROUGH ACTIVISM

This section of the book briefly addresses youth activists who are taking action on behalf of themselves, their communities, and the planet. Youth activism isn't new. As Aji Piper (see Chapter 20) states in his testimony to a congressional committee,

> Young people are often on the frontlines of human rights abuses, experiencing the most severe impacts of bigotry, oppression, and violence, sometimes in their own homes and often at the hands of adults in positions of power who do not act in the best interest of children. They are also inevitably at the forefront of the movements that emerge to address these issues, as we saw in the Child Labor Law Movement or the Civil Rights Movement.

Youth activism in our time is most visible in the climate justice movement and also in standing up for racial justice, through movements such as Black Lives Matter. Locally, in our small town some of us gray hairs organized a rally in support of Black Lives Matter and got around forty or fifty people to stand together. Later that same day, youth organizers, working through social networks and media many of us elders don't know enough about, orchestrated a march and rally of close to two thousand, a rally that was well organized, peaceful, and effective. This march reminded me that many of the Civil Rights demonstrations and actions back in the day, such as the lunch counter sit-ins, the Black Panther breakfast programs, and marches were organized and carried out by students and other young people. Much of the protest and activism of the 1960s and 1970s, on a wide range of issues was led by students and other young people, often working in concert with older activists. This activism and collaboration between the young and supportive elders is often a powerful educational experience for all concerned. Occurring as it does outside of school contexts, we might not think of it as an educational activity, but there is strong learning to be done through passionate involvement with a cause or issue that matters to those involved. It requires and invites deep learning of content, skills, social relations, media relations, and a willingness to merge intellectual learning with action, and, as Aji Piper says, has frequently been instrumental in both bringing change and in educating a generation of activists and leaders. Caroline Whitcomb notes in her chapter on Freedom Schools that many of the young attendees of those Freedom Schools in 1964 became a generation of activists/leaders in the Civil Rights movement, and those young adults who were part of the movement, including those who taught or helped administrate the Freedom Schools are names we know from their decades in the Civil Rights movement.

My own experience, on a much smaller scale is that young people put so much more of their passion and energy into projects that have meaning for them, and when there is a tangible, real world outcome they dig a little deeper. Within a school context this can range from writing for a newsletter that goes home to parents and families, to practicing reading books they are reading to younger reading buddies, to actions that reach out into the surrounding community. For example, as a consequence of our investigation of homelessness after several of my third graders encountered homeless men in a nearby park, the class decided to make quilts for students who attended a school for homeless children. They researched the history and uses of quilts, studied quilt designs, helped to write requests for donations of material for the quilt, worked out the math related to the quilt squares, interviewed young people who were homeless and a counselor who worked with them, and spent hours working with adult volunteers who helped them to construct the quilt, which we presented to students from a class at the school for homeless children.

The students also took the lead in our school in organizing a community wide response to a severe earthquake in Japan while we were exploring homelessness in our community. They realized that thousands of Japanese people were homeless as a result of the quake and were determined to gather clothing and other items that might be useful to them. They had come to a deeper understanding of what it meant to be homeless and this led them to action.

Their passion and dedication for this project, and for other "real world" projects went beyond the usual, and their learning was deeper because it meant something to them.

I am highlighting two activists and actions in the following chapters as examples of out-of-school efforts that are deeply educational and inspiring and that provide another model for how we consider educating and supporting our young, by listening to them, by supporting them as they work towards their passions and concerns, and by recognizing that what we learn and what stays with us has to be linked to our deep caring and emotional investment.

Greta Thunberg is a youth climate activist whose Ted talk from 2018, *School strike for climate – save the world by changing the rules* went viral. Ms. Thunberg, then 16, was becoming increasingly well known around the world for her school strikes for the climate. She struck from school to sit outside of Swedish parliament in an attempt to get Swedish politicians to take decisive action to halt climate change. She was alone at first, sitting each day by the entrance to the Swedish Parliament, and later she was joined by other students who joined her strike out of concern for the health of the planet. They went on to form Fridaysforfuture (fridaysforfuture.org), a youth led organization that is now world-wide.

I have included the transcript from her Ted talk because her response to those who chided her for missing school raises the question that I quoted in the introduction:

> What is the point of learning facts in the school system when the most important facts given by the finest science of that same school system clearly means nothing to our politicians and our society?

What use is an education if that education does little to address the world's crises, and what good is learning "facts" if those facts lead nowhere? What is the lesson for the rest of us? Are the young people making the right choice by walking out of their classes in order to take education into their own hands and to then act on what they have learned? How else can we offer education such that it better meets the needs of our young people and of the moment?

The second action I am highlighting in this section is the lawsuit filed by 21 youth plaintiffs who are suing the federal government for violating their constitutional rights through its actions and inactions related to fossil fuels. Our Children's Trust, a non-profit public interest law firm gathered youth climate activists from around the country to be part of a lawsuit against the federal government. "Their complaint asserts that, through the government's affirmative actions that cause climate change, it has violated the youngest generation's constitutional rights to life, liberty, and property, as well as failed to protect essential public trust resources." (https://www.youthvgov.org/our-case). This lawsuit, *Juliana v. United States*, which began in 2015 against the Obama administration shifted their suit to the Trump administration after the election of 2016, and their actions continue against the Biden administration in 2021. Their suit demands that the federal government "offer both declaratory and injunctive relief for their claim – specifically, a declaration of the federal government's fiduciary role in preserving the atmosphere and an injunction of its actions which contravene that role." They had a hearing on June 25, 2021, to determine whether they can continue their lawsuit, which the federal government has resisted, stalled, and delayed through the courts over this 6-year span, and we await the results of that hearing as I write this.

While I was following the trials and tribulations of this lawsuit that the federal government and their deep pocket, fossil fuel friends resisted with every legal tool at their disposal, I also considered the learning experiences that the young people were gaining through their efforts. I made a short, probably incomplete list of what they had to learn and practice, not because they were assigned tasks, or for a test, but because they were necessary to carry out this action that meant so much to them. The list included the following: reading a range of complex and varied documents; writing addressed to various audiences in various contexts for various purposes; listening critically to legal arguments; working with others to plan and carry out the project; speaking in public, including speaking in a federal courtroom; traveling around the country; engaging in research in a variety of fields; making sense of statistics, graphs, and maps; learning about climate science and other related science content; working with a diverse group of people from around the country; working with adults, some of whom come from very different backgrounds and experiences from them; being able to communicate personal stories and science based facts to others; participating in public actions to help the public understand their case; dealing with the frustration of the government continuing to delay their case on questions of standing and other technical grounds so that they avoided having to confront the substance of the case; and more. It's hard to imagine a more powerful, integrated, and intersectional educational experience than this one.

I was drawn to this case both because of the power of featuring young people in the lawsuit, arguing for their health and futures in their own voices, but also because it was and is such a profound example of an educational experience that comes out of the passion and interests of the young people involved, and which focuses on having an authentic impact on an authentic, real-world problem. This is not a simulation; this is a real lawsuit filed in the real world and aiming for a real-world consequence that would benefit the entire planet. The 21 young people involved in the lawsuit have all chosen to be part of the action and have stayed with the suit since 2015, and their actions have already had real world consequences, inspiring actions of youth activists around the world and bringing attention to the climate crisis to a much wider audience.

I have included a conversation I had with Aji Piper, one of the plaintiffs in the case and follow that with excerpts from Aji's testimony before a congressional committee looking at the issue of climate change to share a sense of this young man and the scope of his learning and the lawsuit.

I've included this material for three reasons: The lawsuit is an extreme (beyond what most schools can carry out) but powerful example of how education can be if we really want our young people to gain confidence, knowledge, experience, and a sense of their own power to transform their world through their actions; the lawsuit has the potential for significant consequences and has inspired efforts from other groups around the country or world; and Aji is quite an amazing and inspiring young person who has aligned his actions with his values, and his testimony before this congressional committee shines a light on him, on the power and clarity of his argument, and is a testament to the learning he has gained.

CHAPTER EIGHTEEN

School Strike for Climate

Save the World by Changing the Rules

GRETA THUNBERG

When I was about eight years old, I first heard about something called climate change or global warming. Apparently, that was something humans have created by our way of living. I was told to turn off the lights to save energy and to recycle paper to save resources. I remember thinking that it was very strange that humans, who are an animal species among others, could be capable of changing the Earth's climate. Because if we were, and if it was really happening, we wouldn't be talking about anything else. As soon as you'd turn on the TV, everything would be about that. Headlines, radio, newspapers, you would never read or hear about anything else, as if there was a world war going on. But no one ever talked about it. If burning fossil fuels was so bad that it threatened our very existence, how could we just continue like before? Why were there no restrictions? Why wasn't it made illegal? To me, that did not add up. It was too unreal. So when I was 11, I became ill. I fell into depression, I stopped talking, and I stopped eating. In two months, I lost about 10 kilos of weight. Later on, I was diagnosed with Asperger syndrome, OCD and selective mutism. That basically means I only speak when I think it's necessary – now is one of those moments.

For those of us who are on the spectrum, almost everything is black or white. We aren't very good at lying, and we usually don't enjoy participating in this social game that the rest of you seem so fond of. (Laughter) I think in many ways that we autistic are the normal ones, and the rest of the people are pretty strange, (Laughter) especially when it comes to the sustainability crisis, where everyone keeps saying climate change is an existential threat and the most important issue of all, and yet they just carry on like before. I don't understand that, because if the emissions have to stop, then we must stop the emissions. To me that is black or white. There are no gray areas when it comes to survival. Either we go on as a civilization or we don't. We have to change. Rich countries like Sweden need to start reducing emissions by at least 15 percent every year. And that is so that we can stay below a two-degree warming target. Yet, as the IPCC have recently demonstrated, aiming instead for 1.5 degrees Celsius would significantly reduce the climate impacts. But we can only imagine what that means for reducing emissions. You would think the media and every one of our leaders would be talking about nothing else, but they never even mention it. Nor does anyone ever mention the greenhouse gases already locked in the system. Nor that air pollution is hiding a warming so that when we stop burning fossil fuels, we already have an extra level of warming perhaps as high as 0.5 to 1.1 degrees Celsius. Furthermore does hardly anyone speak about the fact that we are in the midst of the sixth mass extinction, with up to 200 species going extinct every single day, that the extinction rate today is between 1,000 and 10,000 times higher than what is seen as normal. Nor does hardly anyone ever speak about the aspect of equity or climate justice, clearly stated everywhere in the Paris Agreement, which is absolutely necessary to make it work on a global scale. That means that rich countries need to get down to zero emissions within 6 to 12 years, with today's emission speed. And that is so that people in poorer countries can have a chance to heighten their standard of living by building some of the infrastructure that we have already built, such as roads, schools, hospitals, clean drinking water, electricity, and so on. Because how can we expect countries like India or Nigeria to care about the climate crisis if we who already have everything don't care even a second about it or our actual commitments to the Paris Agreement?

So, why are we not reducing our emissions? Why are they in fact still increasing? Are we knowingly causing a mass extinction? Are we evil? No, of course not. People keep doing what they do because the vast majority doesn't have a clue about the actual consequences of our everyday life, and they don't know that rapid change is required. We all think we know, and we all think everybody knows, but we don't. Because how could we? If there really was a crisis, and if this crisis was caused by our emissions, you would at least see some signs. Not just flooded cities, tens of thousands of dead people, and whole nations leveled to piles of torn down buildings. You would see some restrictions. But no. And no one talks about it. There are no emergency meetings, no headlines, no breaking news. No one is acting as if we were in a crisis. Even most climate scientists or green politicians keep on flying around the world, eating meat and dairy. If I live to be 100, I will be alive in the year 2103. When you think about the future today, you don't think beyond the year 2050. By then, I will, in the best case, not even have lived half of my life. What happens next? The year 2078, I will celebrate my 75th birthday. If I have children or grandchildren, maybe they will spend that day with me. Maybe they will ask me about you, the people who were around, back in 2018. Maybe they will ask why you didn't do anything while there still was time to act. What we do or don't do right now will affect my entire life and the lives of my children and grandchildren. What we do or don't do right now, me and my generation can't undo in the future.

So when school started in August of this year, I decided that this was enough. I set myself down on the ground outside the Swedish parliament. I school striked for the climate. Some people say that I should be in school instead. Some people say that I should study to become a climate scientist so that I can "solve the climate crisis." But the climate crisis has already been solved. We already have all the facts and solutions. All we have to do is to wake up and change. And why should I be studying for a future that soon will be no more when no one is doing anything whatsoever to save that future? And what is the point of learning facts in the school system when the most important facts given by the finest science of that same school system clearly means nothing to our politicians and our society. Some people say that Sweden is just a small country, and that it doesn't matter what we do, but I think that if a few children can get headlines all over the world just by not coming to school for a few weeks, imagine what we could all do together if you wanted to. Now we're almost at the end of my talk, and this is where people usually start talking about hope, solar panels, wind power, circular economy, and so on, but I'm not going to do that. We've had 30 years of pep-talking and selling positive ideas. And I'm sorry, but it doesn't work. Because if it would have, the emissions would have gone down by now. They haven't. And yes, we do need hope, of course we do. But the one thing we need more than hope is action. Once we start to act, hope is everywhere. So instead of looking for hope, look for action. Then, and only then, hope will come. Today, we use 100 million barrels of oil every single day. There are no politics to change that. There are no rules to keep that oil in the ground. So we can't save the world by playing by the rules, because the rules have to be changed. Everything needs to change, and it has to start today. Thank you.

To view this Ted talk: https://www.ted.com/talks/greta_thunberg_school_strike_for_climate_save_the_world_by_changing_the_rules/transcript?language=en

CHAPTER NINETEEN

We Are Suing the U.S. Government

A Conversation with Aji Piper

Aji: I'm turning 21 this year. I've lived in the Pacific Northwest, the Seattle-Port Orchard region since I was around three. Our family had, from the jump, a focus on environmental responsibility, that you have a responsibility not to dirty the space that you're living in, to clean a place and leave it cleaner than you found it or leave it better than you found it. And that wasn't just applied to our material spaces, like inside our own houses or buildings and things, but also extends outside, beyond our houses. Too many people in our society tend to think our houses are different than the natural environment when there's literally no distinction. You know, we can't block the air travel at our property lines. It's not like we separate atoms and molecules or something like that. I think that's an important foundation.

Taking care of the environment. I pretty much always looked at it, like, I have knowledge, and it's a crucial topic, a topic which a lot of people are not educated about. And it was something that I had the power to attempt to change. So it wasn't one of those, "with great power comes great responsibility moments," it was just like, with the knowledge, I feel comes the responsibility to act on that knowledge. If you sit on the side with knowledge about what's happening, you are essentially complicit with what's going on.

Doug: And you said you started joining with others when you were 11.
Aji: Yeah, that was 11 years old.

Doug: Did your formal school bring any awareness, or was this entirely outside of school?

Aji: Well, for the most part it was entirely outside of that. The one teacher I ever encountered was in high school, junior year, taking a marine biology class. And because climate change has such an impact on ocean, the ocean chemistry. It's just one of those things that I'm always able to say, regardless of whether or not you believe in the hocus pocus or get confused by the political back and forth and misinformation about whether or not climate change is real, the truth is that a simple chemical equation is enough to show us that what we're doing is ultimately harmful to the planet. And that CO2 plus H20 equals H2C03, which is just water, plus carbon dioxide equals carbonic acid. And it's just that ocean acidification in a nutshell, three chemical symbols. Very easy, pretty straightforward and simple. My marine biology teacher talked about it because ocean acidification is a pretty obvious thing from the migration of Humboldt squid, who normally sit around the middle of California in terms of their northern reaches all the way down to Mexico and South America. All of a sudden, they're up by Alaska. We've got Alaska grizzlies catching Humboldt squid, which are not supposed to be up there. There's an obvious problem there.

Doug: What were the first kinds of things you did with your group when you were 11? What was your entry into acting with a group related to environmental issues?

Aji: The first entry was actually probably what I'm most known for in terms of small protest activism, which is singing with my ukulele. I did what they call the Plant for the Planet Academy, which is a day-long workshop where they simply catch you up to speed on climate change issues. Plant for the Planet has a simple goal of planting a billion trees. And so playing my ukulele and singing is what I started with. And then pretty much immediately afterwards, I was invited to speak at a rally against the oil trains that take tar sands and crude oil on our railways, because they passed through downtown Seattle. It was July 6, 2011, and one of those trains derailed and exploded in Canada. And then I think it happened like a couple more times. They ship these oil trains right up along the Salish Sea, right through downtown Seattle, right by all our waterways, our freshwater lakes. We said you need to get those trains out of our city.

Doug: How did you connect with Our Children's Trust?

Aji: I was with Plant for the Planet for a couple of years, mostly doing protests. But as we got a little bit older, there's more of a draw from the political side of things to try to get our politicians to act because you run into this feeling of, no matter how many trees I plant as one kid, I don't have the power to plant 100,000 trees or a billion trees for the state. I need the state to act on this. We were working on a couple of initiatives. One of them was related to getting warning labels on gas pumps, kind of similar to how you have warning labels on cigarette boxes or alcohol. And we were also trying to get some legislation passed to try and get the state to start reducing its carbon emissions. We were trying to get the Washington State Department of Ecology to update their recommendations to the legislature, because they've been talking since the 90s, about how their ecology standards have been abysmal. That's where we got in contact with Our Children's Trust. We got the runaround from the DOE and the legislature, so we sued them with the help of Our Children Trust, Andrea Rogers being our attorney. When Our Children's Trust decided to bring a lawsuit against the Federal government and asked around for any youth that were interested, I was like, Oh, yeah, sign me up. I definitely want to be a part of that because we were not making progress at the state level.

D: What was it like for you as a young teenager to go to court? And how did you prepare to go to court and how were you supported to do that?

Aji: I mean, court is kind of a crazy. I feel like most people's experience with what court is like comes from Judge Judy and other court shows on T.V. I also had these ideas of what court would be like. You know, "Objection, Your Honor", that kind of thing, Court is a lot drier than that. The language is far more academic, it operates much more in the realm of legal jargon, than it does the common and colloquial language. And at state court what we brought was a class action lawsuit, not a civil lawsuit where it's one person and another. So, as plaintiffs, we weren't sitting there, at two parallel tables, where we could look to the left and see the people specifically who were in charge. It's not like the governor was sitting there in court. It was just the court's attorneys and me.

It was such a valuable experience. It's one of those experiences that gives you a wider perspective in the world. It really gives you that extra weight in your step, it gives you that extra confidence, to just seek out and challenge things. And I think that is just one of those benefits that subtly affects the rest of your life. It's just a comprehensive kind of gentle increase in your standing as a young person.

Federal court was different. Federal court was a bit more intense, still dry. But federal court was the first time that the dryness got broken up, because my judge asked questions during the hearing. And then I also experienced deposition in federal court, which is also one of those things I feel everybody should experience it. It's super cool.

Doug: Once Our Children's Trust decided to sue the federal government, how did you prepare for that?

Aji: Mostly, what I did as a plaintiff is I gave a full and truthful account with my story and of the harms I believe I had received from the government. I focused not only on the harm they caused by neglecting to take positive action on climate change, but also on the deliberate, intentional acts they have taken, such as subsidizing fossil fuels, leasing out public lands for oil drilling and extraction, permitting pipelines and shipping routes. So the government has taken an action, a lot of actions for a long time.

What I did as a plaintiff was to talk about how I was harmed by their actions. And I feel like the gravity of it being against the federal government never really felt that important. A lot of people might feel intimidated by it, but, ultimately, a government is a function of the people. I just think it's a natural course for me to be able to speak to the federal government on the same level, because as a citizen, my rights, my needs, and especially because I wasn't just speaking for myself, but speaking as an individual who had been uniquely harmed amongst a group of individuals who had also been uniquely harmed. We are looking at a situation where we are all going to continue being harmed, not just the group that I'm in with the twenty other plaintiffs, but everybody is going to continue being harmed if we don't do anything. I feel like it's my right, an unalienable right to be able to speak to the federal government on the same level. They have no actual standing above me morally, there's no more moral importance between the federal government and one of their citizens because the moment you separate those two, you start drifting towards tyranny. When the government system undervalues its citizens and it no longer treats them with the respect that they're due, then we start slipping from the tenets we built the nation on, the tenets that we pride ourselves on holding throughout our democracy, like leveling the playing field, of giving voice to the voiceless and the meek masses. Where is the spirit of America when our government is the tyranny our forefathers were trying to escape? Then I just feel like it's the right given to me by citizenship to appear on the stage. So I never felt really that nervous about it. It's a pretty big deal. It's a high-profile case, you're talking in front of a judge who can literally decide the fate of the environmental movement for a significant portion of time, until it's too late. We can easily run into situations where it's just like, we're screwed, because the judges won't work with us, or judges can't understand it.

Doug: It's really the highest stakes there are.
Aji: I think it is. The court's input is exceptionally important in all kinds of cases. In fact, some of the cases that we've referenced in the federal lawsuit are like Brown v Board of Education, because of youth being a protected class, because there's specifically discrimination against youth. The people of America wouldn't have as easily. not that it was easy, but they wouldn't have as easily desegregated schools, if it weren't for a change in the Supreme Court, which is, you know, what we're shooting for. It is important to sway the hearts of the people, but as was evident in the 2016 election, and then the 2020 elections, it's easy to have huge portions of our population misguided. And so we need large policy change from an entity as powerful as the Supreme Court in order to jumpstart real change.
Doug: So this amazing group of kids, kids, in some cases, and some a little closer to adult status had a lot to learn. How did you go about doing that? How did the

lawyers you work with and other adults around help? What was most effective in that process?

Aji: Our lawyers were pulling together expert reports, scientific data and evidence from the government and everything like that. And then on top of that, what most of the plaintiffs did is we would read these expert reports, we'd watch expert report videos, and then we would just go to our lawyers if we didn't understand specifically, how it would affect the case. Or we could ask the experts themselves in several cases for more detailed explanations. That was probably the biggest academic learning impact directly, was literally just having access to hundreds of pages of world-renowned scientists and their life's work on our subjects, you know, ranging from economists, to epidemiologists, from the climate scientists to the ocean scientists to geologists. And then we would talk to each other; we've had regular plaintiffs calls throughout the six years of being plaintiffs and they are incredible.

The lawyers did a really good job of making sure that we understood what the case was about, that we understood the principle of, this is what we're suing for, this is what we're saying. They helped us understand the legal terms and also understand how to tell our personal stories. I think sometimes there is a tendency to take your personal story and kind of wash it with other people's personal stories so they can be thrown all together in a big pot. Look, we're all in this together, it's in our collective interest. Definitely, in terms of the lawsuit, it's more in our interest to show how our stories differentiate, because it's not just that we've been harmed exactly the same as everybody else, but there's also unique harm, you know, special health considerations of family members of plaintiffs, the loss of the natural resources that maybe we depend upon, the loss of stability in our lives, or the loss of family, or farmland, or the loss of their home through rising sea levels, because they live on an island. All of those are unique harms that not 100% of the population faces. And so that's why, you know, we bring them in court, because we've been uniquely harmed as individuals.

So, we would talk to each other, and then we have these expert reports. And it's just kind of like the combination of that, learning how to tell our stories to show that they're our own.

Doug: And how did you learn that? It may feel like something you take for granted now, but it's not simple, and it's even harder under pressure to do that. So you must have practiced.

Aji: It started with our declarations of harm, that our lawyers worked pretty hard with us. They asked us to write down the things that we had been harmed by specifically, our specific harm, things that we can point to in our lives that are damaged because of climate change. Like for me, the wildfire smoke. When wildfire season comes in the Pacific Northwest, it gets particularly bad, in fact, so bad last year, the smoke was all the way across the country from coast to coast, smoke in New York from the West Coast. I don't personally have lung problems, but my mom does have some issues with her lungs, she has some complications with her health that make her significantly more at risk, and that's a direct harm to me. Those declarations were the first part of the learning.

And then the second part was preparing for deposition. The way our lawyer has worked with us for our harms is, we'd write it out, and they would help us revise it. And they'd be like, okay, so this is a general harm. Is there a way you can point out more specifically how this harms you? Not just wildfire smoke in my air? Why does the wildfire smoke hurt you? Which I think is a great learning opportunity, understanding how to contextualize the world specifically, so other people understand how you yourself are being harmed. And then using that, in order to further the promotion of everybody's rights. And then I studied other people's depositions. I literally sat down and watched a couple of hours of deposition from different experts on my case and other plaintiffs who had been deposed. It was a great foundation.

For me, it was the scrutinization of my complaint, or my declaration of harm that was included in the amended complaint. And so, essentially having to go through and defend each point on my declaration of harm was a pretty enlightening process, having to show how they were all related to each other. And then also, I guess another lesson from the deposition is it's okay to not be an expert. That was an important one that we gain expertise through experiencing the field. I was only freaking 17 at the time I got deposed and a 17-year-old is not going to be an expert on climate science and fire science and epidemiology. I'm not going to be an expert on ocean biology, and in ocean chemistry.

Doug: But you're an expert in the harm you were experiencing,

Aji: I was an expert in the harm that I was experiencing. And I was an expert, by the knowledge that I had, period. I didn't need to have read 50,000 pages and done six years extensive studies on the state of our climate, in order to tell people that I read a paper from James Hansen, who is a world-renowned climate scientist who has done that work, who has read upwards of 50,000 pages, and done years and years of science work. And through reading this and other papers, I know that the knowledge that I have is enough for me to tell you what's wrong. And to have confidence in my own knowledge. I think that's probably one of the most important lessons that could be taught to young people, how to work with the knowledge they have and know, and be able to say, sure, I'm not an expert on this thing. I don't have to be an expert. At this moment I'm young, that's the whole point of being young and growing and going into a field. And learning is the whole point of doing these things. Gaining knowledge, and having knowledge is never a bad thing. Without any knowledge, I would have been in a far more passive position. I think that is still an important takeaway that can be taken from it.

Doug: It also sounds like you came away feeling respected by your peers, and by the lawyers you worked with, who respected you enough to trust that you could tell your story and that they could support you to do that. But they believed in you and that your story was worth telling.

Aji: Yeah, also that I came to respect my own story more. Just because somebody else in the world is suffering worse than you are doesn't invalidate your own suffering. Just because somebody else in the world has more expertise than you do doesn't invalidate your experience and you're the only one who knows the validity of your own story. And yeah, I think that's it, in a roundabout way. It's about respecting my own story. So yeah, respecting your own stories, and having your peers and adults, role models who respect your story as well just allows you to move with more confidence.

Doug: When you're not wrapped up in the case, how has it affected you moving through the world and the rest of your life to be involved in the case?

Aji: It's kind of hard to quantify the impact of an experience as large as suing the U.S. government in a courtroom in front of a federal district court judge with a defendant panel comprised of not only the Department of Justice attorney, but also three attorneys representing over 600 fossil fuel companies who, due to their own business interests feel that the cases are an actual threat to them, and they intervene. It's impossible to describe the weight and grandeur it instills in you fighting for such a righteous cause, but also the weight in the opposite direction of grandeur, the somberness and sadness of the situation. This is not just about the immediate harm that's a problem and we need to do something about it because it is harming our younger generations.

I would say that besides those intangible lessons of how to tell your own story, of pursuit of academic knowledge, of respecting your own story, you know, not needing to be an expert and everything of allowing yourself room to grow. Besides those which, it's unfair to say that it hasn't had an effect beyond those because I could be in an entirely different place in my life, mentally, emotionally, financially, all of it just by not having those experiences and so I'm not sure how accurate it is to say that it's only that. I haven't really pursued a field in which my environmental lawsuit would be a decisive factor in getting me an entrance or giving me some leeway to progress further in or a door opening opportunity. I'm an electrician, and I install solar panels, so I'm still kind of pursuing that renewable path and getting people renewable energy.

Doug: And my final question is, as we think about the generations coming after you, and think about how we can be most useful to them, helping them learn what they need to know so that they are in the best possible position to act on their own behalf and on behalf of their communities and planet. Are there lessons that we can share, or think about those of us in education who are hoping to do better?

Aji: I think there are. I know that it's hard from the perspective of a teacher to influence the life of a student outside of the classroom. Students oftentimes separate classrooms from the world; this is the class world, and this is the real world. And even some of that language bleeds through when we say oh, you're going to graduate high school and get out to the real world. I think, even if it's just one teacher, teachers all around can help reduce the idea that there's a difference between the environment that you think of, when you think of a forest, and your house, there really isn't much difference. There should be no distinction between how we treat those two areas. And that we should treat both of those areas with respect. I think by helping contextualize the world as a more cohesive place, rather than separated into the human world of progress and the natural world that we have to protect and understanding that all of it is just one planet, like you don't get to hurt the natural world without hurting our human world, and hurting our human world, subsequently, also hurts the natural world. It's not two separate dimensions. It's one planet. They are together, they're inseparable.

And I think that that principle is the foundation of having a more sustainable economy. And that if all of our students growing up now were able to hold that principle as a core tenet , as a truth of their world, that helping the environment is also helping my community, that helping the environment is also helping myself and helping my community that would make a difference. And when you start with the idea that there isn't a big separation between what we usually consider separate aspects, I think it helps people in the same way that learning multiple languages allows you to understand another language easier. It primes your brain when you don't have this, when you're able to just slowly phase out some of this hard, divisive language that we have about our world, you start allowing other things to mesh together as well. For example, the idea that helping my neighbor, what might seem like it's just out of the goodness of my heart to no benefit of my own, most people won't recognize that, generally, helping a neighbor creates a stronger sense of community, creates a stronger community. And thus, you create a stronger support system for yourself. So directly helping a neighbor, whether that's your neighbor across the street, or, you know, whether your neighbor's more in a principle of like, maybe the neighboring city, or the neighboring state or the neighboring country, that helping neighbors, helping people around us helps ourselves, because we live in a much larger community, then maybe people are used to thinking about. Once we stop separating the parts of our world with divisive language, we're able to mesh those ideas a lot easier.

CHAPTER TWENTY

Aji Piper's Testimony before the U.S. House of Representatives Select Committee on the Climate Crisis (Excerpts) (April 4, 2019)

Chair Castor, Ranking Member Graves, and distinguished Members of this Select Committee, Thank you for inviting me to provide testimony to your Select Committee on the Climate Crisis. My name is Aji Piper. I'm 18-years-old. I love vanilla bean ice cream, snowboarding, and writing songs on my ukulele. I love my family and my friends and my home near the Puget Sound in Seattle. And I am suing the United States government for knowingly causing climate change as the largest historic contributor to the problem and for continuing, even now, to make a dangerous situation worse.

I have been reading climate science literature since I was 13-years old. I have also been studying what my governments have done about the climate crisis during my lifetime, and even before I was born. For much of my life, I saw climate change as a problem that would be solved by adults in nice suits in a faraway Capitol. But as I grew up, and the coal and oil trains kept rolling through my hometown of Seattle, and the oil tankers kept sailing in and out of Puget Sound, I became apprehensive.

The late summer skies over Seattle now regularly fill with wildfire smoke, people walk around in gas masks, our ocean waters around my hometown are acidifying and rising, and yet there are still politicians in Washington, D.C. talking about climate change as if it is an issue to debate and still talking about promoting fossil fuel energy as if the pollution from that energy source is not dangerously destroying the one planet we've got, and the lives and futures of children along with it. I got to a point where I felt like I could no longer wait for the solutions to come from the Capitol or the adults that are responsible to protect young people like myself.

I am one of the 21 Youth Plaintiffs in the constitutional climate lawsuit, Juliana v. United States. Our complaint asserts that, through the federal government's affirmative actions in causing climate change, it has violated my constitutional rights, and those of my generation, to life, liberty, property, and equal protection under the law, as well as failed to protect vital public trust resources. While I am not a legal expert, nor a climate scientist, and I only recently came of voting age, the goal of my testimony is to explain my perspective on the most consequential and far-reaching issues of our time, an issue that all three branches of this government are duty bound to address.

****

As a young black man, I have grown up with the long-lasting consequences of unconstitutional discrimination from government-sanctioned and -engineered segregation. My childhood was shadowed by trauma from an abusive father. The trajectory of his life was formed in part by generational trauma of unlawful discrimination. Generations of black families have lived with the lasting legacy of government-sponsored racial discrimination, not just in the South, but in places like Seattle, where white suburbs formed out of federal government policies with restrictive covenants on housing developments and federally guaranteed loans to homeowners that only whites could take advantage of. Cities across the country are segregated because of these federal policies that were finally declared unconstitutional after World War II by the Supreme Court, and that this branch of government attempted to redress decades later in the Fair Housing Act of 1968. But the damage had been done and the legacy of that unconstitutional government conduct remains today in the color and shape of our communities, the makeup of our schools, the voting districts, and the disparity in those who were able to acquire home equity and wealth and those who were not. Unconstitutional systemic government actions have long-lasting social consequences. Innocent children inherit those legacies.

In response to decades of unconstitutional discrimination, in May of 1963, thousands of children led marches through Birmingham, Alabama to demand the desegregation of the city in a movement now known as the Birmingham Children's Crusade. On the first day of the protest, hundreds of children were arrested. By the second day, police officers tried to stop the marches by using fire hoses and police dogs to attack the children. On May 10, 1963, within 1 week of the first march, the city acquiesced to the children's demands, agreeing to desegregate businesses and to free all who had been jailed during the demonstrations. These youth stood at the forefront of one of the most pivotal moments in civil rights reform in the United States, using non-violent protest as a means to advance human rights.

Young people are often on the frontlines of human rights abuses, experiencing the most severe impacts of bigotry, oppression, and violence, sometimes in their own homes and often at the hands of adults in positions of power who do not act in the best interest of children. They are also inevitably at the forefront of the movements that emerge to address these issues, as we saw in the Child Labor Law Movement or the Civil Rights Movement.

Climate change is no different. My generation, and generations to come, have the most to lose from the sweeping impacts of climate change. As a result, youth throughout the world have taken the lead in the movement to address this existential threat. Just last month, over a million students the world over walked out of class to demand urgent and sane climate action from the adults in charge.

The entrenched federal government policies of orchestrating, promoting, supporting, subsidizing, sanctioning, and permitting a fossil fuel energy system will perpetrate as long-lasting harm on generations of innocent children as did this body's legal sanctioning and promotion of segregation. When government sanctions and controls a system that unconstitutionally deprives children of their basic fundamental rights to life, liberty and property, that system must be dismantled, and it is up to all three branches of this federal government to act now while there is still time to uphold the rights of my generation, to stop the perpetuation of intergenerational injustice.

I became a climate activist because I know that it is my moral responsibility to do everything in my power to stop catastrophic climate change. Your generation and the ones before you, sitting in your seats in positions of power, have decimated our planet. My words stand before you, representing the voices of millions of children, youth and future generations, who are trying to clean up the mess of our forebears. For years, the federal government and the same adults who created the disaster have marginalized us. No more. Climate change is here now. Waiting for the future is already too late.

It is clear: Without youth leadership and a constitutional guidepost, legislative efforts won't save us in time. The Executive Branch won't even fully admit climate change is real, and its leaders do the bidding of the fossil fuel industry. Half measures and incrementalism will only modestly delay the worst impacts of climate change. If we want a future worth living, all three branches of our federal government must recognize our unalienable rights are at stake and work with the youth at the forefront of this movement, to guarantee that the constitutional right to a stable climate is recognized and protected in the United State of America.

Forget about being on the right side of history. If there even are history books, it will be because of the efforts that we are taking today. Be on the side of young people right now. Act as if our fundamental rights to life, liberty, property and equal protection under the law are as important as yours, those who came before us, and those who will come after us. We are all connected, and the work you do during your terms in this powerful office, should be on the right side of the youth who sit before you and we ask you to stand with us.

That is why I am asking all of you and this entire House to endorse the fundamental rights and the remedy sought in Juliana v. United States on the record, and to sign on to amicus curiae briefs in support of me and my co-plaintiffs, as your other colleagues have, including Senators Ron Wyden, Jeff Merkley, and Sheldon Whitehouse, and Representatives Debra Haaland, Peter DeFazio, Earl Blumenauer, and Rashida Tlaib.

We all have a moral imperative. And you have a constitutional one. If not us, then who? If not now, then when? If not for me, do it for your children, and your children's children, and for all life as we know it. Do it because when you took office, you made an oath "to uphold our Constitution and "secure the blessings of liberty to ourselves and our posterity."

Aji Piper's complete testimony can be found at https://www.govinfo.gov/content/pkg/CHRG-116hhrg36812/pdf/CHRG-116hhrg36812.pdf, pp. 14–36.

Final Thoughts (for Now)

My granddaughter Charlotte was complaining about a math assignment asking students to find the area of an oval shape, asking, what's the point of learning this? Why don't they teach us something that we can actually use? I asked her what that might include, and she had a ready list including items such as learning how credit (and credit cards) works, learning how to do home repairs, how to cook, and other items that were all, to her mind, practical and useful. While I realize that students do not always have a full sense of what will be practical or useful to them when they are in middle school (as she was at the time), I shared with her that I was still trying to figure out why most mere mortals would have any use for a secant or co-secant, which I had to wrestle with several decades ago, in high school. And I agreed with her that much of what I learned in high school was either useless to me or just plain inaccurate and that we need to do better.

I graduated from high school in 1966. I was mis educated about much of U.S. history by Walt Disney and other programs on television. I learned from Disney and other media that U.S. history really began with the "discovery" of America by Christopher Columbus in 1492 and continued as (white) European Americans moved across North America fulfilling their Manifest Destiny to civilize and settle the essentially empty continent. I watched Disney's take on Davy Crockett to learn about what that meant; fighting hostile, savage Indians who stood in the way of that Manifest Destiny, and later, fighting hostile, evil Mexicans who surrounded and murdered heroic Americans at the Alamo. Disney never mentioned the genocide and forced resettlements that were at the heart of Manifest Destiny, or the land grab that was the so-called Mexican War, or its link to perpetuating and maintaining slavery. It was nationalistic myth making that was echoed by virtually everything else that appeared on television, our prime window on the world outside of our neighborhoods.

Disney and other media also (mis) educated me about race relations, gender roles and values, which seemed to center on strong, silent men and pretty, vulnerable and relatively helpless women, and sometimes a clownish or subservient sidekick who might be a person of color. And, of course, all the good guys were white.

What is astounding to me is that, despite the fact that I went through a well-regarded K-12 school system, I did not encounter any real pushback to the Disney version of history until I was in college, and that pushback mostly came from "teachers" and situations outside of the classroom. I was lucky enough to spend my summers living across the street from the Six Nations Museum, in Onchiota, NY (population 62), within a small Mohawk community, and got to know Ray Fadden, the man who built and ran the museum., Uncle Ray and my other neighbors helped me to learn a much more accurate picture of the genocide and forced removal that were the hallmarks of Manifest Destiny, and I learned more about the complex and layered governing and social systems at the heart of the Iroquois Confederacy that challenged virtually everything I'd been taught at school, or by Disney.

This experience awakened me to the need to question, to challenge, and to not automatically accept what I was being told in school, in my neighborhood (which was an essentially middle class, white, quietly racist community of young families), and from media of all sorts, including the news.

When I finally decided on becoming a teacher, more than a decade after graduating from college (and after swearing I would never set foot in a classroom ever again) I thought back on my relentless mis education and realized I had to formulate my own goals, my own purpose as an educator. If I was going to be a teacher, what did I want for my students? Informed as I was by my own education, in school and out, and by the world swirling around us in 1981, I came up with a short list of goals and aspirations for my work as a teacher, which I continued to add to with experience. They included:

The children are more important than any of the subjects.

Every child should feel welcomed and valued.

All children in class should have the opportunity to explore what is most important to them, at least some of the time.

I should avoid using textbooks as much as possible as they are both deadly boring and inaccurate or incomplete.

It is crucial to bring in more points of view and voices than what are featured in textbooks or in mandated curriculum.

I must be a learner, to model what I hope the students will take from their time with me.

I will bring as much joy and excitement to learning as possible.

I want to help students to learn to critically question what they are encountering, including me.

I must do everything I can to tell them the truth, and to help to learn to find the truth for themselves.

I can't say that I have always successful in meeting those goals, but they are always the compass points I try to steer by.

The essays in this book move me to update my list of goals. I would add having an increased awareness of the cultures, histories, and contexts of the students. I want to learn much more about the impact that inequality, white supremacy, racism, and capitalism play in determining, or strongly influencing the lives we lead and on the need for me (as an educator) to be a more active and engaged advocate for social justice outside of the classroom. Being a social justice educator inside the classroom is important, of course, but it is not enough. I would place much greater emphasis on helping students understand the crippling impact of slavery and racism on our society, that continues to this day. I would put a much greater emphasis on students learning to listen and communicate clearly with their peers, and to work with them as allies and cooperators rather than as competitors. I would look to develop alternative ways of organizing education that pattern after the freedom school model so that the focus was on a smaller, more personal educational experience focused on the needs and interests of the young people and not so much the dictates of the state. And finally, I would assess the quality of our work together, in my classroom and in my school by the quality of our lives inside and outside of school. How are we feeling about ourselves and each other, how are we behaving with each other, how much are we engaging in learning that is of interest, and how are we putting what we learn to use in service to what we care about, in school and out. I do believe that the purpose of education is to support our students to learn what they need to so that they are living lives that they value and living in ways that sustains and supports their communities, and if there is no evidence that school is moving them towards becoming engaged, caring, and joyful humans then we are failing them and need to change what we are doing.

I would also add to my list the importance of reaching out to the community to help me to learn about the students, to learn about content I don't know, to help me identify resources and to help me think through how best to make the educational experience as effective and joyful as possible. Many of us enter classrooms thinking we have to do it all ourselves and are reluctant to "blow our cover" by admitting we don't know how to deal with particular content or a particular student or situation. That is evidence of a flaw in how we are trained rather than educated in our K-12 and university systems. The contributors to this book know much that I don't, and I learned so much by asking them to be a part of this project. I hope that readers will keep this learning in mind as you think about how to transform education in your school or district, that you will be well served by inviting others to think and plan and act with you. We are in this together and are wiser and more powerful when we join together.

I want to close with a few words from Myles Horton, the founder of the Highlander Folk School, in Tennessee. He was in dialog with Brazilian educator Paolo Freire and said this.

> If I had to put a finger on what I consider a good education, a good radical education, it wouldn't be about methods or techniques. It would be loving people first.... and that means people everywhere, not just your family or your own countrymen or your own color. And wanting for them what you want for yourself.
> And then next is respect for people's abilities to learn and to act and to shape their own lives. You have to have confidence that people can do that...
>
> The third thing grows out of caring for people and having respect for people's ability to do things, and that is that you value their experiences. You can't say that you respect people and not respect their experiences. (Bell, Gaventa, & Peters, 1990, pp. 177–178)

There is so much that we can do if we trust, respect, and value the people we work with, beginning with our students and their families. When we trust, respect, and value people enough to listen to them when they share who they are, what they care about, and what their goals and dreams are, we have already taken a significant step towards the transformation of their educational experience, and ours.

REFERENCE

Bell, B., Gaventa, J., & Peters, J. (1990). *We make the road by walking: Conversations on education and social change.* Temple University Press.

Contributors

Alyssa Arnell received a M.A. in Legal History from Florida Atlantic University and an M.S. in Legal History from Kaplan University. She is the Chair of History at Greenfield Community College.

Wayne Au, a former public high school teacher, is a Professor in the School of Educational Studies at the University of Washington Bothell, and he is a longtime editor for the social justice teaching magazine, *Rethinking Schools*. An internationally recognized and award-winning scholar, he is author of over 100 publications, and his work focuses on both academic and public scholarship about high-stakes testing, corporate education reform, teaching for social justice, and anti-racist education.

Stephen Bezruchka is Associate Teaching Professor in the Departments of Health Services and Global Health at the School of Public Health, University of Washington. He studied mathematics and physics at the University of Toronto followed by graduate study at Harvard before completing medical school at Stanford. Twenty years later he received a Masters in Public Health from Johns Hopkins. He worked clinically as a doctor for 35 years including three decades as an emergency physician. He transitioned to considering countries as the 'patients.' His focus is on creating greater public understanding of the determinants of health through teaching, talking and writing at various levels from middle school on. Contact him at sabez@uw.edu

Jo Cripps, a veteran of K-12 and alternative schools in the Seattle School District, teaches middle school classes that integrate history, reading, writing, and performance.

Don Fels is a visual artist, writer, and educator. He holds a B.A. from Wesleyan, an M.A.Ed from City University, and has taught Pre-K to Post-Doc. He's been a Fulbright Scholar/Artist in Italy, India, and most recently in Uzbekistan. www.artistthinker.com

Alberto "Beto" Gutierrez was born in Zacatecas, Mexico. Beto's family immigrated to the United States when he was 4 years old and established roots in the San Fernando Valley, a region of Los Angeles. Beto's socio-political conscience has been deeply influenced by his personal experiences. As a kindergartner, he was punished for not knowing English. Throughout k-12, without his consent, Beto was tracked into vocational courses. During the 1980s, Beto experienced the fight that occurred before the white-flight – this manifested by way of racial riots & ongoing micro aggressions in schools. During Beto's final semester at James Monroe High School, the college advisor suggested that he attend a vocational school and learn how to paint cars. Beto rebelled and attended the local community college. This life changing decision led to a B.A. in Social Sciences, M.A. in Urban Planning and a Ph.D. in Education. Beto can be reached at beto911@g.ucla.edu.

Jesse Hagopian is a high school Ethnic Studies teacher in Seattle, an editor for *Rethinking Schools* magazine, and a campaign organizer for the Zinn Education Project's "Teach the Black Freedom Struggle." He is the co-editor of the books, *Black Lives Matter At School: An Uprising for Educational Justice, Teaching for Black Lives, Teacher Unions and Social Justice*, and the editor of *More Than a Score: The New Uprising Against High Stakes Testing.*

Jesse is the recipient of the 2019 "Social Justice Teacher of the Year" award from Seattle Public School's Department of Racial Equity, the Seattle NAACP Youth Coalition's 2019 "Racial Justice Teacher of the Year" award winner, and the 2013 national "Secondary Teacher of the Year" award winner from the Academy of Arts and Sciences.

Leo Hwang received his Ph.D. at the University of Massachusetts in Geosciences, an M.F.A. from the University of Massachusetts at Amherst in fiction writing and his B.A. from the University of the South in English and Fine Arts. Dr. Hwang is the Assistant Academic Dean in the College of Natural Sciences Academic Advising Center at the University of Massachusetts, Amherst.

Jan Maher taught in K-12 public schools and in teacher preparation programs at undergraduate and graduate levels for many years before retiring to write full time. Her books for educators include *Most Dangerous Women: Bring History to Life through Readers' Theater* and *History in the Present Tense: Engaging Students through Inquiry and Action* (co-authored with Douglas Selwyn). She is currently working on a third novel set in the fictional town of Heaven, Indiana, a sequel to her first (*Heaven, Indiana*) and second (*Earth As It Is*). She is a senior scholar at State University of New York Plattsburgh's Institute for Ethics in Public Life, where she can be found leading discussions on empathy in literature, the women's peace movement, and other related issues. Her website is janmaher.com.

Sandra Mathison is Professor of Education at the University of British Columbia in Vancouver Canada, Co-Director of the Institute for Critical Education Studies, and Co-Editor of *Critical Education*. Her research focuses on educational evaluation and especially on the potential and limits of evaluation to support democratic ideals and promote social justice in education. She is editor of the *Encyclopedia of Evaluation* and co-author of *Researching Children's Experiences*. She can be reached at sandra.mathison@ubc.ca

Linda McCarthy teaches Sociology at Greenfield Community College and is actively involved on campus in strengthening diversity and inclusion. She is the advisor for the Social Justice club and sometimes co-chairs her department and chairs the Student Development Standing Committee. Along with teaching Principles of Sociology, she teaches Social Inequality, Sociology of Gender, Sociology of Human Sexuality, and Sociology of the Family. Dr. McCarthy earned her Doctorate in Social Justice Education from the University of Massachusetts Amherst in 2003 and teaches Sociology at GCC from a social justice perspective. Dr. McCarthy's classes each emphasize the connections between current social issues and sociological concepts. She is also an avid outdoors person and crazy cat lady.

Jean Mendoza (European-American) holds a Ph.D. in curriculum and instruction from the University of Illinois, an M.Ed. in early childhood education from the University of Illinois, and an M.A. in counseling psychology from Adler University of Chicago. She worked with children and families for more than 25 years, served on the faculty at Millikin University, and is co-adaptor, with Dr. Debbie Reese, of *An Indigenous Peoples' History of the United States, for Young People*. Jean and her late husband Durango Mendoza (Muscogee/Creek) have four children and six grandchildren. She can be reached at jpmendoza1@gmail.com.

Jerry Price is the social studies coordinator for Washington State. Before that he taught U.S. History and Washington State History and Government at Ridgeline Middle School in Yelm, WA. Jerry has been a member of the Social Studies Cadre since its inception, and also worked on the revision of the Social Studies GLE's. Additionally, Jerry was a middle level writer and presenter for OSPI's "Since Time Immemorial" Tribal sovereignty curriculum.

Debbie Reese, tribally enrolled at Nambé Owingeh, a tribal nation located in what is currently known as the state of New Mexico, Dr. Reese holds a PhD in Curriculum and Instruction from the University of Illinois, and a MLIS from San Jose State University. A former school teacher and assistant professor in American Indian Studies, the emphasis of her research and writing is on depictions of Native peoples in children's books. In 2019, *An Indigenous History of the United States, for Young People* by Mendoza and Reese (adapted from Roxane Dunbar-Ortiz's 2016 book) won an honor book award from the American Indian Library Association.

E. Wayne Ross is Professor in the Department of Curriculum and Pedagogy at the University of British Columbia, Co-Director of the Institute for Critical Education Studies, and Co-Editor of *Critical Education*. His research and teaching focus on the role of curriculum and teaching in building democratic communities that are positioned to challenge the priorities and interests of neoliberal capitalism as manifest in educational and social policies that shape both formal and informal educational experiences. His most recent book is *Rethinking Social Studies: Critical Pedagogy in Pursuit of Dangerous Citizenship* (Information Age Publishing, 2017). wayne.ross@ubc.ca

Yves Salomon-Fernández is the Senior Vice President for Operations Planning and Execution at Southern New Hampshire University. She previously served as President of Greenfield Community College in Massachusetts and Cumberland County College in New Jersey. Dr. Salomon-Fernández is a recognized thought leader, executive, and faculty member who has served at large and medium-sized selective private and public universities, as well as open access colleges in urban, suburban, and rural settings in the United States. Yves has served as a reviewer for the National Science Foundation and Johns Hopkins University Press. In March 2018, Diverse Issues in Higher Education named Yves one of the Top 25 Women in Higher Education.

Outside of academia, Dr. Salomon-Fernández serves as a member of the Federal Reserve Bank of Boston's Community Development Council and a Corporator for Greenfield Cooperative Bank. She sits on the boards of Mass Humanities and Cooley Dickinson Hospital.

Jack Schneider is an Associate Professor of Education at the University of Massachusetts Lowell, where he leads the Beyond Test Scores Project. An award-winning scholar and teacher, his work broadly explores the influence of history, culture, and rhetoric in education policy. The author of four books, Dr. Schneider has explored why particular ideas gain policy traction, how public perception of schools takes shape, why education reform so often fails, and how organizations improve. He writes frequently about education in outlets like the Atlantic, the New York Times and the Washington Post, and (along with Jennifer Berkshire) is co-host of the educational policy podcast "Have You Heard."

Doug Selwyn taught for 14 years in the Seattle Public Schools and then moved to teacher education, in 2000, first at Antioch University in Seattle, and then for 10 years at SUNY Plattsburgh where he was a Professor of Education until he retired in 2017. He has written several books on education, his most recent, All Children Are All Our Children, published in 2019 with Peter Lang. He can be reached at dougselwyn@aol.com.

Peter Suruda teaches sophomore English and Creative Writing at Juanita High School in Kirkland, Washington. Before that, he taught 15 years in Seattle Public Schools, mostly in alternative programs.

Greta Thunberg is a Swedish climate activist who launched the organization #FridaysforFuture after beginning her own activism by striking from school for the climate in 2018. Her action inspired hundreds of thousands of students around the world to participate in their own FridaysforFuture chapters.

Richard Wilkinson is Professor Emeritus of Social Epidemiology at the University of Nottingham Medical School, Honorary Professor at University College London and Visiting Professor at the University of York. His books and research papers have drawn attention to the tendency for societies with bigger income differences between rich and poor to suffer a heavier burden of health and social problems. Two of his books have been the subject of documentary films: *The Great Leveller* (for the Channel 4 TV's Equinox series broadcast in 1996) was based on his *Unhealthy Societies*; *The Divide* (based on *The Spirit Level*) was released in April 2016 (available on Netflix). *The Spirit Level*, written with Kate Pickett is now in 24 languages and has won several awards. His TED talk 'How economic inequality harms societies' has been watched over 4 million times. Richard has received Solidar's Silver Rose Award, the Irish Cancer Society's Charles Cully Memorial medal, was The Australian Society for Medical Research medalist in 2017. He and Kate Pickett published their latest book, *The Inner Level*, in 2018.

Caroline Whitcomb is a teacher educator, writer, and critic of the American South. Her 5-year ethnographic journey with alumni of a former Black, private educational institution cultivated an interest in historic and present-day examples of liberatory education. Caroline has a B.A. in history from Randolph-Macon College, a M.A.T. from Augusta University, and is currently, but not for long, ABD in Curriculum Studies at Georgia Southern University. Recently, she has perfected the art of road tripping with her children, two dogs, and a quirky chicken.

Studies in Criticality

General Editor
Shirley R. Steinberg

Counterpoints publishes the most compelling and imaginative books being written in education today. Grounded on the theoretical advances in criticalism, feminism, and postmodernism in the last two decades of the twentieth century, Counterpoints engages the meaning of these innovations in various forms of educational expression. Committed to the proposition that theoretical literature should be accessible to a variety of audiences, the series insists that its authors avoid esoteric and jargonistic languages that transform educational scholarship into an elite discourse for the initiated. Scholarly work matters only to the degree it affects consciousness and practice at multiple sites. Counterpoints' editorial policy is based on these principles and the ability of scholars to break new ground, to open new conversations, to go where educators have never gone before.

For additional information about this series or for the submission of manuscripts, please contact:

>Shirley R. Steinberg
>c/o Peter Lang Publishing, Inc.
>80 Broad Street, 5th floor
>New York, New York 10004

To order other books in this series, please contact our Customer Service Department:
>peterlang@presswarehouse.com (within the U.S.)
>orders@peterlang.com (outside the U.S.)

Or browse online by series:
>www.peterlang.com

www.ingramcontent.com/pod-product-compliance
Lightning Source LLC
Chambersburg PA
CBHW061713300426
44115CB00014B/2665